CONTEMPORARY REGIONAL DEVELOPMENT IN AFRICA

The International Political Economy of New Regionalisms Series

The International Political Economy of New Regionalisms series presents innovative analyses of a range of novel regional relations and institutions. Going beyond established, formal, interstate economic organizations, this essential series provides informed interdisciplinary and international research and debate about myriad heterogeneous intermediate level interactions.

Reflective of its cosmopolitan and creative orientation, this series is developed by an international editorial team of established and emerging scholars in both the South and North. It reinforces ongoing networks of analysts in both academia and think-tanks as well as international agencies concerned with micro-, meso- and macro-level regionalisms.

Recent titles in the series *(continued at the back of the book)*

The Eastern Mediterranean in Transition:
Multipolarity, Politics and Power
Edited by Spyridon N. Litsas and Aristotle Tziampiris

Eurasian Regionalisms and Russian Foreign Policy
Mikhail A. Molchanov

Africa in the Age of Globalisation:
Perceptions, Misperceptions and Realities
Edited by Edward Shizha and Lamine Diallo

Limits to Regional Integration
Edited by Søren Dosenrode

A New Scramble for Africa?
The Rush for Energy Resources in Sub-Saharan Africa
Edited by Sören Scholvin

Contemporary Regional Development in Africa

Edited by

KOBENA T. HANSON

ASHGATE

Published by
Ashgate Publishing Limited
Wey Court East
Union Road
Farnham
Surrey, GU9 7PT
England

Ashgate Publishing Company
110 Cherry Street
Suite 3-1
Burlington, VT 05401-3818
USA

www.ashgate.com

British Library Cataloguing in Publication Data
A catalogue record for this book is available from the British Library.

The Library of Congress has cataloged the printed edition as follows:
Contemporary regional development in Africa / by Kobena T. Hanson.
pages cm. -- (The international political economy of new regionalisms series)
Includes bibliographical references and index.
ISBN 978-1-4724-5143-9 (hardback: alk. paper) -- ISBN 978-1-4724-5145-3 (epub) -- ISBN 978-1-4724-5144-6 (ebook) 1. Regionalism--Economic aspects--Africa. 2. Africa--Economic integration. 3. Africa--Economic conditions. I. Hanson, Kobena T. (Kobena Tsetse), 1964- editor of compilation. II. Series: International political economy of new regionalisms series.

JQ1873.5.R43C66 2015
337.6--dc23

2014047137

ISBN 9781472451439 (hbk)
ISBN 9781472451446 (ebk – PDF)
ISBN 9781472451453 (ebk – ePUB)

MIX
Paper from responsible sources
FSC® C013985

Printed in the United Kingdom by Henry Ling Limited,
at the Dorset Press, Dorchester, DT1 1HD

Contents

List of Figures and Tables

Figures

Tables

Notes on Contributors

Peter Arthur is Associate Professor of Political Science and International Development Studies at Dalhousie University, Canada. He received his PhD in Political Science in 2001 from Queen's University, Canada. His research interests focuses on sub-Saharan Africa, with emphasis on the contribution of small-scale enterprises, electoral politics, capacity development and post-conflict reconstruction, the governance of oil, and natural resources management. His work has been published in a number of edited volumes and journals, including *Africa Today*, *African Studies Review*, *Commonwealth and Comparative Politics*, and *Journal of Contemporary African Studies*. He may be contacted by email at: pathur@dal.ca.

Kwabena Agyei Boakye is a Monitoring and Evaluation Expert at the African Capacity Building Foundation (ACBF) and responsible for upstream and downstream M&E activities including design, implementation, monitoring and evaluation of the Foundation's support to policy making across the continent. He is the lead person for the evaluation of ACBF's capacity building support to Policy Institutes/Think Tanks in Africa. Prior to working at ACBF, he was International M&E Advisor to the national M&E System, Lesotho and Account Manager, Evidence Based Policy Making Program at the Office of the President of Ghana, funded by UNDP and DFID. He has also served as coordinator of Ghana's M&E forum and as trainer at the Kofi Annan International Peacekeeping Centre.

Barassou Diawara is a Knowledge and Learning Officer at the African Capacity Building Foundation (ACBF). At ACBF, he is a member of the Africa Capacity Indicators Report (ACIR) Team. He is also the focal point of the ACBF's newly created Policy Institutes Committee (PIC) and Strategic Studies Group initiatives. He holds a Master's degree in Economics from Cheikh Anta Diop University in Senegal, and a PhD in Economics from Kyushu University in Japan where he was also a research fellow. His areas of expertise include education and poverty economics where he has published a number of articles.

Kobena T. Hanson is the Chief Executive Officer of Strategic Outlooks, Ghana, and Principal at Causal Links in Washington, D.C. Previously, he was the Head of the Knowledge and Learning Department, ACBF, and lead author of the *Africa Capacity Indicators* (ACI) Report (2010–2014). His research focus includes development policy, capacity building, knowledge management and urban livelihood issues. He has researched on these topics across Africa and authored a number of books, journal articles, book chapters, and reports. His most recent publication, *Managing Africa's Natural Resources: Capacities for Development* (2014) (co-edited with C. D'Alessandro and F. Owusu), is published by Palgrave. He holds a PhD from Queen's University, Kingston, Ontario, Canada.

Olawale Ismail, PhD (Bradford, UK) is Head of Research at International Alert, London, UK. He's also an associated Researcher with the Conflict, Security and Development Group (CSDG), King's College London (KCL), and the Stockholm International Peace Research Institute (SIPRI). Before now, he worked in research capacity at the Stockholm International Peace Research Institute (SIPRI), CSDG, KCL and the New York-based Social Science Research Council. His research interest includes radicalization and counter-terrorism, regional security mechanisms, peace building and post-conflict reconstruction, peace operations, security sector and justice reform, disarmament, demobilization and reintegration, military expenditure and youth, and political violence.

Abbi M. Kedir is an applied development economist and microeconometrician specializing in the design and analysis of large household, firm and cross-country datasets. He did his MSc in Economic and Econometrics with distinction in the School of Economics, University of Nottingham, UK. From the same university he obtained his PhD for his work on microeconometric analysis of household consumption and poverty using the Ethiopian Urban Household Survey (EUHS). He was teaching at the University of Leicester (UK) in the Department of Economics from 2002 to 2013 before returning to Ethiopia. Over the last 18 years, he published widely and conducted numerous growth, welfare, inequality and poverty studies. His work appeared in Journals such as the *Oxford Bulletin of Economics and Statistics; Journal of African Economies; Journal of Development Studies and Journal of International Development.* He has written numerous book chapters including pieces on growth, capital flight, tax evasion, aid, inequality and poverty in the Oxford Companion to the Economics of Africa. He is committed to various capacity building initiatives to various African countries. He is a resource person of African Economic Research Consortium (AERC) and an active participant in the activities of African Capacity Building Foundation (ACBF). He is a consultant to the World Bank, UNDP, DFID-UK and USAID.

William G. Moseley is Professor and Chair of Geography, and Director of African Studies, at Macalester College in St. Paul, MN. He is an environment and development geographer with particular expertise in political ecology, tropical agriculture, food security, land reform and Africa. Before becoming an academic, he worked for 10 years in the field of international development for such organizations as Save the Children (UK), the World Bank and USAID. He has published seven books and over 70 peer reviewed articles and book chapters. He formerly served as a national councilor to the Association of American Geographers, editor of the *African Geographical Review*, and co-authored a National Academy of Science report on strategic directions for geography. His research has been funded by the National Science Foundation and the Fulbright-Hays program.

Joseph R. Oppong is Professor of Geography/Associate Dean for Research and Professional Development at the University of North Texas. He has a BA in Geography from the University of Ghana and MA and PhD from the University of Alberta, Canada. Dr. Oppong's research centers on Medical Geography, particularly the application of spatial analysis to HIV/AIDS and tuberculosis genotypes, computational epidemiology, and racial/ethnic disparities in health. His extensive research publications on Africa includes HIV/AIDS, tuberculosis, maternal health, geographic access to health services, national health insurance systems, and science, technology and innovation for economic development. He is currently the US representative to the International Geographers Union (IGU) Commission on Health and Environment, and served as Chair of the Medical Geography Specialty Group of the Association of American Geographers (AAG) from 2002 to 2005 and Chair of the Africa Specialty Group from 1999 to 2002.

Francis Owusu is a Professor and Chair of the Department of Community and Regional Planning at Iowa State University. He holds a PhD in Geography from the University of Minnesota. He teaches courses on international development, world cities and globalization, economic and urban planning, and planning methods. His research focus includes development policy, public sector reforms and capacity building, and urban development and livelihood issues, and he has published extensively on these topics. He has consulted for several international development agencies, including the World Bank, Partnership for African Social and Governance Research (PASGR), Africa Capacity Building Foundation (ACBF), and National Science Foundation (NSF). He chaired the Africa Specialty Group of the Association of American Geographers from 2005 to 2008.

Korbla P. Puplampu is in the Department of Sociology at Grant MacEwan University, Edmonton, Canada. He has a PhD in Sociology as well as a MEd in International and Global Education. His research interests are in the politics of knowledge production and propagation, global citizenship and identity politics in multicultural societies, as well as the global restructuring of higher education and agriculture. He has recent publications in academic journals such as *Canadian Journal of Learning and Technology, Alberta Journal of Educational Research* and has co-edited or contributed to several books including *The Public Sphere and the Politics of Survival: Voice, Sustainability and Public Policy in Ghana* (with Wisdom Tettey), and *African Education and Globalization* (with Ali Abdi and George Dei).

Timothy M. Shaw is Graduate Program Director of a new PhD program in Global Governance and Human Security at the University of Massachusetts Boston. He is also visiting professor at Aalborg University, Denmark; Carleton University, Canada; Mbarara University, Uganda and Stellenbosch University, South Africa. He has published in *Contemporary Politics, Journal of China and International Relations, Journal of Chinese Political Science*, and *Third World Quarterly*. He is Emeritus Professor at the University of London, UK, and holds an honorary degree from St. Andrew's University, Scotland, UK.

Vanessa T. Tang is a lecturer in international economics at both under and postgraduate level in the School of Accounting, Economics & Finance, University of KwaZulu-Natal (UKZN). As a lecturer, she has taught various courses including Microeconomics, Macroeconomics, Economic Policy, Public Economics and International Economics locally and internationally. Apart from her teaching, she is also a researcher and consultant. As a researcher, her research interests include economics of education, time series analysis, international trade, comparative regional integration, special economic zones and the open-economy policy making in the global South. As a consultant, she has worked for the African Capacity Building Foundation, National Research Foundation, UGU District Council, Ethekwini Municipality Economic Development Unit, Midlands Meander Tourism Association, Umgungundlovu District Council, Institute of Natural Resources and the KwaZulu-Natal Provincial Treasury in areas of trade, investment, welfare and tourism. She is the principal UKZN investigator for NETRIS the Network for Regional Integration Studies and has published on a wide range of topics falling within her research interests. Apart from being a regular reviewer for various journals, she is also a co-editor for the *International Journal of African Integration*.

Rodrigo Tavares is Senior Research Fellow at Harvard University's John F. Kennedy School of Government and member of the World Economic Forum's (WEF) Global Agenda Council on Competitiveness. He served as Head of the Office of Foreign Affairs of the state government of São Paulo (2011–2014) and as UN Secretary General report writer on Africa's development (2008–2010).

Jon Unruh is Professor of Geography, McGill University, Canada. His research, applied, and policy work over the past 20 years has focused on post-war land and property rights in the developing world. His past work has dealt with Islamic, customary, statutory, and war-related approaches to land tenure and how these interact; land restitution, legal pluralism, and agriculture in postwar and peace-building scenarios. His experience includes work with regard to: Darfur, Yemen, Liberia; Somalia; Kenya; Angola; Iraq; Afghanistan; Mozambique; East Timor; Sierra Leone; Zanzibar; Ethiopia; Cambodia; Uganda; and Colombia. He has advised a variety of government ministries and organizations of the international community.

Foreword

Rodrigo Tavares

There is probably no other issue in foreign policy matters that generates more bipolarism than Africa's development. The number of optimistic and compelling texts on the revival of the continent is as copious as other convincing publications on the systematic failures of the region. The development of the African continent can be interpreted in manifold ways, depending on who you are and what your reference point is.

The publication *Contemporary Regional Development in Africa* with a line-up of international experts from scholars to policymakers serves as a good compass in this forest of facts and judgments by providing a critical and encompassing vision on the development of the continent. This is not just another book that aims to provide an unambiguous conclusion over an intricate issue, but, instead, it sparks one's attention over the many layers that compose it.

The publication comes out in an auspicious period. According to the World Bank's *Africa Competitiveness Report 2013*, Africa's growth rates have averaged above 5 percent in the past decade. And, looking ahead, as projected by the Organisation for Economic Co-operation and Development (OECD), African Development Bank (AfDB) and United Nations Development Programme (UNDP), with sustained improvements the economic outlook for Africa is optimistic as growth is expected to accelerate in 2015. Also, foreign direct investment (FDI) is on the rise and many African economies have experienced increased investments in natural resources and infrastructure and with rising incomes a stronger household spending is taking effect. This has leveraged a new wave of attention on Africa internationally and spotting market opportunities has renewed enthusiasm in the private sector. An enthusiastic involvement of the private sector is a powerful driver of growth and development.

The book has much to offer covering an exposition of critical issues that are often neglected, such as the impact of informal cross-border trade on poverty reduction, energy cooperation or regional networks of innovation, science and technology, contributing to a denser analysis of Africa's development.

In the spirit of accelerating Africa's integration, this is a timely and stimulating book that follows onto the latest Ashgate IPENR series of regionalisms collections edited by Fanta, Shaw, and Tang on comparative regionalisms in the South. *Contemporary Regional Development in Africa* is a useful publication for policymakers and scholars alike looking for new dimensions and or directions on the developmental challenges facing the continent.

Acknowledgements

This book could not have been produced without the invaluable contribution of the many dedicated individuals and colleagues who supported the process. I am particularly thankful to colleagues Annet Mulema and Barassou Diawara for the initial thinking and deliberations on topic of regionalism in Africa.

I am equally grateful to Timothy M. Shaw for not only pointing me in the right direction, and introducing me to many great minds in the field of regionalism along the way, but more importantly actively supporting the project from start to finish—including his much nuanced Afterword. I also would like to express my gratitude to Vanessa T. Tang, Francis Owusu, and Korbla P. Puplampu for the invaluable input and support throughout the process.

New ideas need champions. Contributors to the volume are also owed an appreciation. Your intuitive chapters make a compelling argument for why much emphasis needs to be placed on regional development at this particular juncture in Africa's development history.

Indeed I have benefited greatly from comments and suggestions from several quarters. Hence, my heartfelt thanks goes to all the colleagues and friends who not only found time to read the draft manuscript, but also provided insightful commentaries and criticisms that helped polish and crystalize my views and arguments. Recognitions also go to the anonymous Ashgate reviewers whose vital comments helped shape the quality and critical thoughts of the volume. The production of this book would not have been possible without your genuine support and dedication to knowledge generation.

Deep appreciation goes to the Ashgate IPENR editorial team under the leadership of Kirstin Howgate for the very insightful feedback and patient guidance throughout the process. Brenda Sharp, Carolyn Court, and Kathy Bond Borie were extremely efficient and kept me on track throughout the development of this book, for which I am very grateful.

To my daughter Kuukua, thank you for encouraging me to dream. You are a true inspiration and blessing. This wouldn't be possible without you.

The views expressed, however, remain the exclusive responsibility of the individual authors.

List of Abbreviations

ACBF	African Capacity Building Foundation
ACCP	African Centre for Cyber Law and Cybercrime Prevention
ACIR	Africa Capacity Indicators Report
AEC	African Economic Community
AfDB	African Development Bank
AGRA	Alliance for a Green Revolution in Africa
AMU	Arab Maghreb Union
AMV	Africa Mining Vision
AU	African Union
BRICS	Brazil, Russia, India, China, and South Africa
CEN-SAD	Community of Sahel-Saharan States
CET	Clean Energy Technologies
COMESA	Common Market for Eastern and Southern Africa
CPI	Corruption Perception Index
DCs	Development Corridors
DRC	Democratic Republic of Congo
DND	Dakar-Ndjamena-Djibouti Road and Rail Project
EAC	East African Community
EASSy	East African Submarine Cable System
ECA	Economic Commission for Africa
ECCAS	Economic Community of Central African States
ECOWAS	Economic Community of Western African States
EITI	Extractive Industries Transparency Initiative
EPA	Economic Partnership Agreement
EPZs	Export Processing Zones
EU	European Union
FDI	Foreign Direct Investment
FOCAC	Forum on China-Africa Cooperation
FTAs	Free Trade Areas
GDF	Global Development Finance
IBSA	India, Brazil, South Africa
ICBT	Informal cross-border trade
ICGLR	International Conference on the Great Lakes Region
ICTs	Information and Communication Technologies
IGAD	Intergovernmental Authority on Development
IGADD	Intergovernmental Authority on Drought and Development

KPCS	Kimberley Process Certification Scheme
MDC	Maputo Development Corridor
MDGs	Millennium Development Goals
MNCs	Multinational Corporations
NGOs	Non-governmental Organizations
NICs	Newly Industrialized Countries
OAU	Organization of African Unity
OECD	The Organisation for Economic Co-operation and Development
PIDA	AfDB's Program for Infrastructure Development for Africa
PIIGS	Portugal, Italy, Ireland, Greece and Spain
RECs	Regional Economic Communities
SACU	Southern African Customs Union
SADC	Southern Africa Development Community
SAPs	Structural Adjustment Programs
SDIs	Spatial Development Initiatives
SSA	sub-Saharan Africa
STI	Science, Technology and Innovation
TFCA	Trans-frontier conservation area
TICAD	Tokyo International Conferences on African Development
UNCTAD	United Nations Conference on Trade and Development
UNDP	United Nations Development Programme
UNECA	United Nations Economic Commission for Africa
WACD	West African Commission on Drugs
WAGP	West African Gas Pipeline
WTO	World Trade Organization

Chapter 1
Contemporary Regional Development in Africa: Reflections and Implications

Kobena T. Hanson and Vanessa T. Tang

Introduction

There is strong and growing support for regional development and integration in Africa as a strategy for advancing its socioeconomic endeavors. The desire to integrate African economies both at the regional and continental level is shared among African governments and their international development partners such as the European Union (EU), United Nations agencies and the World Bank. The desire for integration dates back to the formation of the Organization of the African Union (OAU) in 1963. However, the objective gained further traction in 1991 with the signing of the Abuja Treaty creating the African Economic Community (AEC), which called for an African common market and monetary integration by 2028.

The celebration of 50 years since the creation of the African Union (AU) and its predecessor the OAU further reaffirmed the desire and intent to integrate in the expressions of solidarity and common purpose from the statements made at the occasion of the celebration in Addis Ababa. The theme of the celebrations entitled "Pan-Africanism and African Renaissance" resulted in a declaration covering a wide range of issues starting with the question of African identity (50th Anniversary Solemn Declaration of the AU 2013). Other issues covered include the commitment to developing human capital; adding value to natural endowments; agricultural production and agro-processing and achieving food security; enhancing democratic governance; continuing in the process of social and economic integration; and determining Africa's place in the world, amongst others.

Regional development facilitates the growth and development of nations which in turn can facilitate the integration of countries, Africa included, into the world economy. Within the trade creation and trade diversion framework, regionalism can lead to net trade creation if it occurs in an environment of least impediments, including increased openness to trade coupled with investments in human and physical capital and institutional resources from each participating country.

Also, the growth and developmental approach of African countries requires a larger role from democratic developmental states the likes of Botswana and Mauritius, as well as from South Africa, the largest competitive African economy and attractive aid-provider, with its link to the recent creation of a US$100 billion BRICS development bank. South Africa's role as a development partner for Africa however, will ultimately as Vickers (2012, p. 553) notes depend on how well it can balance its external expectations with the country's own socioeconomic realities.

Regional development and integration with neighboring large economies and developmental states can enable the less developed nations to learn and address their economic, political and developmental problems and become better positioned to participate in the global value chains, attracting foreign direct investment flows, enhancing private sector activities and increasing economies of scale (World Bank 2009). Also as Clapham (2001) observes, structures at regional level enhance the establishment of good governance, a pre-condition for economic growth. And Hettne further submits, regional development serves to transform micro regions, "as the geopolitical environment becomes transformed and creates new possible alignments and a direct approach to the [global] economy for the subnational regions" (Hettne 1999, p. 15).

Additionally, regional economic agreements have enhanced the bargaining power and expertise of African countries, enabling them to meaningfully contribute to reforming the global economic order and maximizing their commitment to policy reforms (World Bank 2008).

Furthermore, regional development boosts security and lowers the risk of conflict amongst African nations as a result of improved intra-regional confidence and trust, common defense mechanisms and interdependence in key aspects of countries' national development (World Bank 2008), consequently reducing the continent's dependence on foreign assistance (Kedir, this volume). This notwithstanding, Brown et al. (2009) caution that regional development does not necessarily eliminate conflict as some countries continue to opt for armed conflict to settle their differences. There is thus a need for institutional capacity enhancement in conflict management and peace building to foster economic integration (Ismail, this volume).

Proponents of regional development further claim that it enhances food security (in terms of availability of acceptable quality, demand and purchasing power of both rural and urban consumers). Increased intra-regional collaboration promotes economic growth, increases employment opportunities and income generating capacities of the poor thereby enhancing access to food and ultimately improving living standards (FAO 2003; Santi, Saoussen and Shaw 2012). Intra-regional trade can also enhance domestic food supplies to meet consumption needs and reduce food supply variability. Its effectiveness, however, depends on the design of the agreements and the ability to promote more trade creation rather than diversion (FAO 2003).

Although regional development has been strongly supported by different development partners, it has also received vast criticisms (Hass 1970; Lee 2002; Draper 2012). Critics argue that the linear EU model of integration (beginning with a free trade area or preferential trade area and ending with monetary integration) does and will not work for Africa. The model should be redefined to fit the context of Africa's realities (Lee 2002; Draper 2012). Learning from the EU model, a fast-tracking regional enlargement and the existence of major disparities across member states could cause havoc under asymmetric shocks.

In the current era of globalization, regionalism[1] alone is not a solution. Regional and global integration of African economies should be complementary (World Bank 2009; UNDP 2011). Indeed, being more integrated continentally and globally increases Africa's capacity[2] and reduces trading costs which in turn should strengthen and enable African economies to boost trade and investments.

Also, regionalism necessitates regional cooperation, a process by which a group of nations voluntarily and in various degrees have access to each other's markets and establish mechanisms and techniques that minimize conflicts and maximize internal and external economic, political, social and cultural benefits

1 Regionalism refers to the conscious, deliberate and purposive attempts made by national states to create formal mechanisms for dealing with common transnational issues (Breslin and Hook 2002, p. 4). Regionalism seeks to pursue a body of ideas, values and concrete objectives that are aimed at transforming a geographical area into a clearly identified regional social space (Grant and Söderbaum 2003, p. 7). For purposes of this volume, Africa's contemporary regionalism encompasses the efforts by the myriad stakeholders to enhance their economic, geo-political, and socio-cultural interaction. Such efforts at the macro-level include inter-state regional cooperation, market integration, development policy harmonization and regional integration; as well as the micro-level efforts of cross-border interactions; and new or innovative efforts at collaboration (e.g. West African Gas Pipeline, Maputo Development Corridor, Eastern African energy meso-region and trans-frontier peace parks).

2 Capacity refers to "the ability of people, organizations, and society as a whole to manage their affairs successfully; and is the process by which people, organizations and society as a whole unleash, strengthen, create, adapt and maintain capabilities over time. Capacity for individuals, organizations and societies to set goals and achieve them; to budget resources and use them for agreed purposes; and to manage the complex processes and interactions that typify a working political and economic system. Capacity is most tangibly and effectively developed in the context of specific development objectives such as delivering services to poor people; … improving the investment climate … empowering local communities to better participate in public decision-making processes …" (ACBF 2011: 30–31).

of their interaction (Lee 2002, pp. 22–3). And while regional economic cooperation can deliver a number of benefits in the long term, it also produces winners and losers in the short run through trade creation and diversion effects (Venables 2003). The trade creation and diversion effects can arise in any regional grouping that reduces barriers to trade that are not extended to non-members. However, if reductions in barriers to trade are offered on a most favored nation basis, then trade diversion can be avoided. Further, trade creation allows resources to be allocated according to comparative advantage and specialization to higher productivity areas. However, according to Maruping (2005), resources flowing toward existing clusters of economic activity, may leave economically disadvantaged areas to fall further behind. This outcome is more likely to occur if in such areas the infrastructure is insufficient and does not work properly.

Attempts to regionalize Africa have yielded minimal economic benefits due to some of the aforementioned hurdles. Mainstream perspectives even claimed that "if there is any regionalism at all in Africa, it is … characterized mainly by failed or weak regional organizations and a superficial degree of regional economic integration" (Grant and Söderbaum 2003, p. 1). The uneven and unimpressive macroeconomic performance exhibited by many countries is replicated within regional institutions where collective leadership is expected to jolt the continent out of its economic slumber and help promote good governance. While some progress is being made on these fronts within the African Union and sub-regional organizations, the general assessment by most analysts is that substantive movement in support of good governance is still marginal at best (Murithi 2007).

Contemporary African Regionalisms at the Turn of the Second Decade of the Twenty-First Century

The above notwithstanding, there has been strong support for a "new" regionalism in Africa over the last two decades. Africa has witnessed a revival in regionalism since 1990 with the creation of new regional institutions and relationships (Shaw and Fanta 2013; Shaw, Grant and Cornelissen 2012, Söderbaum and Taylor 2008). In the initial, one-party nationalist period, reflective of jealousy surrounding newly realized independence, these were typically "old" inter-governmental arrangements. But in the post-bipolar era, such regionalisms became less exclusively state and more inclusive from economics to emerging issues including shifts in resource flows and supply chains, ecology, energy, security, water and financial innovation (Shaw 2015; Shaw, Grant and Cornelissen 2011).

Reflective of its more than 50 states, Africa has the potential to be the leader in the South to advance regional innovations and institutions. Africa's contemporary regionalisms are characterized by openness as opposed to the more state-centric approach in "old" regionalism. Africa's contemporary regionalism employs a bottom up approach unlike the old system which was top-down, and places emphasis on super national agents in a project as opposed to the dominate state-centric actors of "old" regionalism (FAO 2003; Grant and Söderbaum 2003). It also seeks to include inter-state global and regional institutions and non-state actors such as MNCs, civil societies and national and international nongovernmental organizations (Breslin and Hook, 2002). As Breslin and Hook (2002, p. 221) further note, with the emergence of new spatial patterns that "are less national, and more international in character, these new internationalized economic spaces become dis-embedded from the old national economy." As a result the processes and dynamics of regional development exhibit great "mixes between the formal and informal and, in fact, these two impulses compete for supremacy in quite intriguing ways (Söderbaum and Taylor 2008, p. 17).

The global financial crisis of 2008 has unveiled an emerging Africa and the global South's "new voices" and "new dynamics." According to Shaw and Fanta (2013, p. 5), the new dynamics guiding regionalism in the global South are characterized by entanglements of myriad actors and stakeholders forming heterogeneous coalitions with the aim of regional development. For example, the revived, redefined East African Community (EAC) is emblematic: with five rather than its initial trio of members, with its innovative civil society, parliamentary and security dimensions, qualifying as an instance of African contemporary regional development (Shaw, Grant and Cornelissen 2012; Hanson, Kararach and Shaw 2012). Another example is the Maputo Development Corridor (MDC) which links the Port of Maputo with the industrial heartland of Southern Africa and the city of Johannesburg (Hanson, Puplampu and Owusu, this volume).

The new regional arrangements among Africa's states seek to liberalize markets and increase cross-border trade. While several states have made good progress in developing regional interconnections which cut across national borders, much more is required for Africa to witness a larger boost in trade, growth and human development. Developing intra-African infrastructure is crucial especially for the 15 landlocked countries (UNDP, 2011, p. 17). Similarly, efforts to increase diversification are equally crucial since there are few African economies that are truly diversified and the landlocked countries remain relatively undiversified.

In the new century, regionalisms on the continent cover the spectrum of levels—macro/meso/micro (Söderbaum and Taylor 2008)—and sectoral—civil society, corporate networks, ecology, energy and security. While free trade zones are generally associated with Asia, and gas pipelines with Central Europe, development corridors and peace-parks are largely a function of Southern Africa's distinctive political economy (Shaw and Fanta, 2013). Similarly, Africa has its share of river valley organizations and other cross-border formal micro-regions (Chikozho 2012, 2014; Unruh; Diawara and Boakye, this volume). This notwithstanding, if Africa is to capitalize on its contemporary regionalisms and play a developmental role, efforts need to be made to address past failures (e.g. overlapping membership, over reliance on donor funds, and a lack of political commitment). The pursuit of a developmental state, as Maphunye (2009) suggests, should address issues of capacity development including human resource development and public administration skills.

Africa's efforts toward economic integration have been hindered and undermined by "overlapping regional arrangements and the absence of collective agreements on rationalizing and harmonizing regional initiatives" (Tavares and Tang 2013, p. 229). For consensus building, there is thus a need for capacity development in best practices to regionalism and economic integration at the macro, meso and micro levels.

The volume juxtaposes a set of "dynamic" entanglements—new and micro regionalism, informal cross-border trade, intra-African and African FI/FDI and cross-border investments, infrastructure development, science and technology, regional value-chains, conflict management and regional security—with fluid interpretations of regional development. Clearly, different state and non-state actors have different levels of ability to shape and respond to the myriad entanglements of regional development. Insights concur with the position of Söderbaum and Taylor (2008, p. 52) that regionalism "is not only driven by state elites, who have their own agenda, but also by communities and peoples who utilize [regionalism] for a heterogeneous set of reasons and motives …." To reiterate, the dynamics of regional development and related regionalisms are informed by the strategic considerations of the states and myriad actors in the mix. Bhagwati and Panagariya (1996) highlight the complex entanglements of rules and regulations in what they term the "Spaghetti Bowl." And Söderbaum (2003) also notes the process of contemporary regionalism is "fluid, multi-dimensional, and multi-level" which according to Hettne (2005) evolved in a multi-polar global order.

Africa has generated an innovative range of new regionalisms involving non-state actors: from the Maputo Corridor and Kgalagadi trans-frontier peace-park to the Nile Basin Initiative/Dialogue; and from the International Conference on the Great Lakes Region to corporate supply chains (Hanson, Kararach and Shaw 2012). The Maputo Corridor, for example, has advanced growth in Southern Mozambique as well as the eastern Witwatersrand, reinforcing the cross-border dimensions of the Lesotho Highlands Water Project (http://www.lhwp.org.ls); the latter was informed by the only global commission to be based outside the North—in Cape Town—which also included multinational corporations (MNCs) as well as non-governmental organizations (NGOs) and states in its membership (Khagram 2004). Reflective of growing concern for the environment, Southern Africa is the center of the trans-frontier peace-parks movement which has led to the recognition of several such cross-border parks in the region (www.peaceparks.org).

Again, the continent's pattern of inter-regional relationships is in flux, from classic, inherited North-South dependencies toward a novel South-East axis around China and India but also Japan and Korea (Shaw 2012, p. 11). Symbolically, Africa's regions' reluctance to sign economic partnership agreements (EPAs) with the EU at the turn of the decade despite a mix of pressures and incentives may mark a turning point as global rebalancing continues: the Europe of the Eurozone crisis around the PIIGS (Portugal, Italy, Ireland, Greece, and Spain) and Asia of the BRICS transforms policy options and calculations for the continent as suggested in Cheru and Obi (2010). The tone of annual Forum on China-Africa Cooperation (FOCAC) palavers can be contrasted to that at the third EU-Africa summit in Tunis in November 2010.

Indeed, given its numerous land-locked states, Africa has always experienced informal cross-border migration and trade, some now in illegal goods like drugs and small arms (Shaw 2012). And as MNCs, now from China and India as well as South Africa (hence the transition from IBSA to BRICS), have increased their investments in energy and minerals, franchises and shopping malls, so their logistics and supply chains have come to define their own regional networks (Shaw 2012, p. 12; see also Shaw, Grant and Cornelissen 2012). Exponential infrastructural development will further new regionalisms on the continent in the second decade of the twenty-first century, symbolized by the mobile-phone revolution and the roles of MTN and Celtel/Bharti, including the Mo Ibrahim Foundation (www.moibrahimfoundation.org). Equally important, Nollywood has begun to redefine the continent, as its overwhelming production of DVDs reaches remote villages and myriad diasporas, just as soccer's African Cup now plays on mainstream TV in the global North (Shaw 2012). As the *Economist* (2010, p. 88) indicated at the end of 2010:

> Film is now Africa's dominant medium, replacing music and dance. It links distant societies, fosters the exchange of ideas and drives fashion trends …
>
> Film also profoundly shapes how Africans see their own continent …

There is growing evidence of greater connectivity in time, space and culture. Hence, despite the perceived slow progress at regionalism, Africa endeavors to develop policies that facilitate transnational economic integration but also incorporate the social, cultural, environmental and political strategic concerns to address poverty and inequality (Hanson, Kararach and Shaw 2012). Cross-border regionalism, for instance, is seen as a means by which smaller economies can benefit from the comparative advantage of larger neighboring economies and be able to integrate more fully in the regional and global economy—albeit an uneven and unequal participation (Diawara and Boakye, this volume). Africa is witnessing an array of initiatives at the macro, meso and micro levels to regionalize the continent. Such initiatives and practices support the claim by Cornelissen, Cheru and Shaw (2012, p. 16) that indeed in regionalism "there are not one but multiple Africas" with various forms and levels of regionalisms.

Viewpoints and Reflections

Africa at the turn of the second decade of the twenty-first century is at a crossroads in terms of growth, development, governance, regionalisms and sustainability (Hanson, Kararach and Shaw 2012): can it seize its second chance and transcend its somewhat lacklustre first half-century? Contributing authors to this volume, individually and variously believe so. Evidence put forth suggests Africa is emerging with a more dynamic regional developmental approach.

New regionalisms and regional development should enhance and accelerate Africa's development if existing capacity problems and inefficiencies are addressed. On a positive move forward, recently, the goals and focus of regionalism and regional development in Africa have broadened to include not only economic, political, security, and social issues, but also multi-stakeholders with opportunities for private sector participation. The Program for Infrastructure Development in Africa (PIDA) an initiative implemented by the African Development Bank (AfDB), African Union Commission (AUC) in partnership with the United Nations Commission for Africa (UNECA) and the New Partnership for Africa's Development (NEPAD) which provides a platform for public-private sector involvement is a case in point. Private sector involvement should be encouraged and supported as it can provide much-needed development financing to boost regional integration and performance.

This volume synthesizes viewpoints and reflections premised on an interrogation of the extant literature on contemporary African regionalisms, and incorporates rich empirical materials and case studies from a host of scholars reflecting a nuanced African experience in its complexity and diversity. Contributors to the volume examine and theoretically contextualize key emergent trends related to aspects of geo-political and economic integration, trade, infrastructure, peace and security, and changing socioeconomic dynamics in the African context. The chapters of this book provide snapshots of several emerging and complex regionalisms. Contributing authors focus on salient capacity development strands for the myriad stakeholders engaged in advancing contemporary regionalisms—A set of relevant development issues, trends and analyses drawing on authors' granular understanding of the African landscape.

Chapter 2 (Puplampu) examines the relationship between regionalism and the integration of regional economic institutions in terms of their relevance and performance in the policy environment, specifically capacity development. Placing the relationship in a context of globalization, Puplampu argues that regional economic institutions do not exist in a vacuum and their role has to be situated in a wider global context with a focus on the range of internal and external factors that affect their creation and therefore define their success or failure in African development. The chapter also outlines a theoretical framework to study Africa's regional economic communities (RECs), while analyzing the state of regionalism in economic integration in Africa.

Arthur (Chapter 3), Unruh (Chapter 4), together with Diawara and Boakye (Chapter 5) interrogate the dynamics of emerging regionalisms shaping the continent's development agenda. Chapter 3 assesses the impact of "new" regionalism and the major challenges that have bedeviled African governments in their quest to realize viable regional economic integration. In so doing Arthur argues that deepening new regionalism in Africa requires a range of critical interventions such as increasing intra-regional economic and trade activities, promoting security, building proper infrastructure, fast-tracking the infrastructure to link countries more effectively, and developing the political will to drive regional projects. Unruh (Chapter 4) analyzes the micro-regionalisms taking place, acknowledging their enormous potential to contribute to Africa's development objectives, and offering an array of important opportunities for directing the processes of globalization toward greater economic and political participation. Unruh approaches micro-regionalism in Africa from the perspective of both description and the support needed to encourage its further development—looking at the place of micro-regionalism in the development process, with a focus on how micro-regions emerge and are shaped over time. The chapter also addresses what support in terms of capacity development is most needed; the import of the relationship between the center and the local; and the roles of local actors, governance, and macro-regional organizations.

Diawara and Boakye (Chapter 5) trace the dynamics of informal cross-border trade on Africa's burgeoning regionalism and its impact on poverty alleviation. Aside from the fluidity of dynamics, the chapter highlights the fact that the bulk of such trade and resulting developments goes unrecorded and thus unaccounted for in orthodox international relations data (see also Cornelissen, Cheru and Shaw 2012; Brown 2006; Lemke 2003).

Regional development is a critical variable to the efforts by African countries to increase domestic and foreign investment, boost security, lower the risk of conflicts, and increase global competitiveness (Ariyo 1992; Uzodike 2009). It is also a means to overcome Africa's structural problems such as low per capita incomes, small intra-regional trade, fragmentation of African markets (Soko 2008, p. 56), provide the most appropriate analytical framework to approach the discussion of international security dynamics (El-Affendi 2009, p. 2), as well as a necessary vehicle to accelerate Africa's integration into the new knowledge-driven global economy (Cheru 2002, p. 122).

Acknowledging the centrality of regionalism and regional economic communities in promoting intra-African foreign direct investment, Kedir (Chapter 6), explores the determinants of FDI inflows in Africa highlighting, amongst others, what measures need to be in place to ensure consistent and equitable intra-African FDI. The chapter also maps out the key capacity imperatives for intra-African trade (i.e. infrastructure, technology and skills). Hanson, Owusu and Puplampu (Chapter 7), extend the focus on infrastructure further, to highlight its significance in hastening regional development and economic integration in terms of strengthening value chains and increasing trade. As Hanson, Owusu and Puplampu argue, to effectively compete in global markets, African countries need an efficient infrastructure network, since it is a potent catalyst for wider economic participation, both within and between countries and regional economic communities; and promotes private/individual agency for poverty reduction and rapid growth (ACBF 2009; 2006). The chapter stresses the role of infrastructure as a means of reducing trade costs, as an agent of productivity growth, and as an enabler of regionalism and economic integration.

In Chapter 8, Oppong reviews the potential of science, technology and innovation (STI) for Africa's regional integration efforts, noting the opportunities and possibilities of technological advancements in Africa's economic transformation. Oppong argues, amongst others, that properly harnessed integration promises a bright future in STI-based development for countries that create the right environments, and put in place the appropriate infrastructure.

Indeed, from a monetary perspective, infrastructure development that advances intercontinental/regional trade will prevent capital outflow in the form of payment transactions from the continent. The consequence can benefit the whole region and foster closer economic integration among states. This surplus of foreign exchange reserves under the right economic policies can be used to promote domestic development initiatives (Besada et al. 2013). Under the regionalism model, other states can expect its positive spillover effect. In addition, under the supervision of Africa's regional economic communities (RECs), the money can also be used as loans to other regional low income countries (Besada at al. 2013). Furthermore, this form of regional trade will have the advantage of empowering individual states to collaborate with each other on equal terms.

The discussion on regional value chains and productivity enhancement is at the heart of Moseley's work (Chapter 9) which explores the role of regionalism in value chain development and ways to expand its most valuable aspects. According to Moseley, building more robust value chains is critical for transforming raw materials into finished products, encouraging industrialization, and moving African economies beyond their peripheral position. Key to unlocking this potential is implementation of policies supported by capacity development initiatives that allow African countries and RECs to expand cross-border value chains (at various scales) for economic development and improved livelihoods.

Ismail (Chapter 10) tackles the issue of emerging threats facing Africa, by probing the developing patterns of regional security challenges, and responses using the Boko Haram crisis in the Chad Basin to discern conceptual and policy lessons, and implications for regional security arrangements in Africa. The author argues that Africa's RECs and the AU are hardly able to provide regional security individually or collectively as envisaged in extant policy documents; rather extra regional interests and actors are playing "game-changing" roles as defined by their funding, logistical support, international legitimacy, and robust force projections. Ismail further establishes that insurgencies are rooted in local causes, notably multiple governance failures, in-country horizontal inequalities, subsisting trends in border communities (linked to poor policing and activities of criminal networks), increasing resort to the instrumentality of ethno-religious identities to mobilize for armed violence, and the fusion of local, national, regional and international dynamic to create a "meta narrative" by insurgent groups.

Implications

As we march into 2015, there has been remarkable progress and achievements in human development and economic growth in a number of African countries. Notwithstanding these achievements, sub-Saharan Africa remains the poorest region in the world. And in some parts of West and Central Africa, armed conflict, terrorist incidents and rising epidemics are threatening to reverse human development gains with implications on investments, trade and growth.

A distinct challenge to Africa's integration is its economic disparities. Less than a year to the 2015 deadline, the pace and progress on the Millennium Development Goals (MDGs) remains uneven (see Table 1.1 in this chapter's Appendix). Despite overall improvements in human development, there are areas that have been neglected. For example in education as illustrated in Figure 1.1, although gross enrollment ratio in primary education average 100 percent, however, the primary school dropout rate average 38 percent.

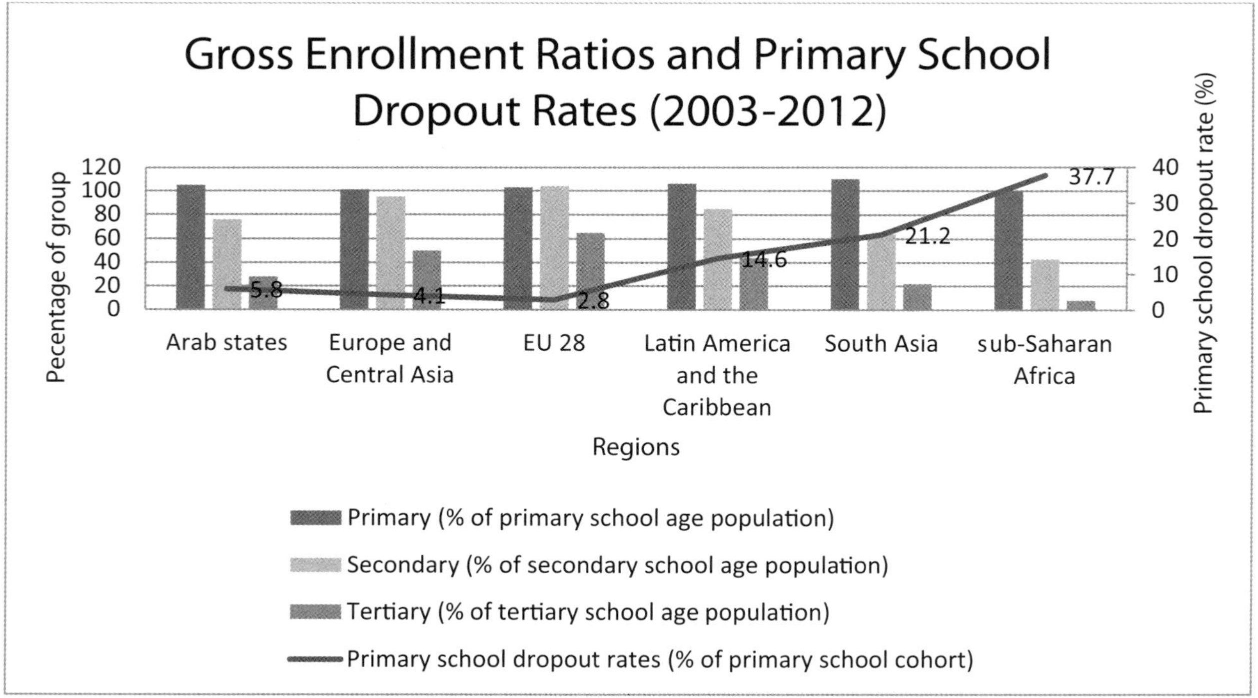

Figure 1.1 Gross enrollment ratios and primary school dropout rates (2003–2012)

Source: Authors' compilation based on the UNDP Human Development Database, 2014

And beyond this level, the gross enrollment ratio in secondary and tertiary education average only 43 percent and 8 percent, respectively. The implication is that the goal for school enrollments has overlooked the need for quality education—one of the basic building blocks for a competitive Africa. Educational reforms and investments are therefore urgently needed to prevent this high dropout rates and low transition from primary to secondary and tertiary education and to close these wide regional differences.

The World Economic Forum (WEF 2014a, p. 8) on Africa under the theme Forging Inclusive Growth, Creating Jobs, has additionally noted that "the existing school and university education model is failing millions of eligible and deserving candidates on various levels, such as cost, limited capacity for enrollment and content misaligned with the jobs market." To empower learners and to build countries' resilience, member states should pool their resources to bolster Africa's educational capacity and target desired skills.

Despite Africa's limitations and challenges, talk of an African "economic renaissance" continues. Given that the outlook for Africa's growth continues to be robust, Africa has the potential to be a leader in the global South and to advance regionalism. In December 2011, the *Economist* noted that "over the past decade six of the world's ten fastest growing countries were African. In eight of the past ten years, Africa has grown faster than East Asia." Also, of added value, as illustrated in Figure 1.2, the continent has the second largest share of world population and its demographic growth rate has remained the highest since 1913. Moreover, it is projected that the demographic growth anticipated for the second half of the twenty-first century will be entirely due to the continent of Africa with an estimated growth of 1 percent relative to the other three continents where growth is projected to stagnate or decrease (Piketty 2014, p. 79).

At the turn of the second decade of the twenty-first century support for South-South trade has indeed grown fueled by the rise of China—in 2010, as a group, the BRICS has surpassed the EU as sub-Saharan Africa's major trading partner. This is an important paradigm shift as African countries become less dependent on their traditional trading partners and continues to intensify relations with non-traditional fast-growing economies. Post-2015, regionalisms may come to balance and even challenge the EU model (Shaw 2015; Vivares 2014; Fanta et al. 2013). The BRICS and especially China have become an important engine of growth for African economies. What is also important to follow in the international trading system, but remains to be seen is the emergence of "mega" regionalism and their potential impact on Africa's trade and investments. "Mega-regional" agreements involving the partnerships between "large" countries or regions, those with a major share of world trade and FDI or can serve as hubs in global value chains (WEF, 2014b) can potentially affect African nations. Contemporary Africa's quest for growth and regional

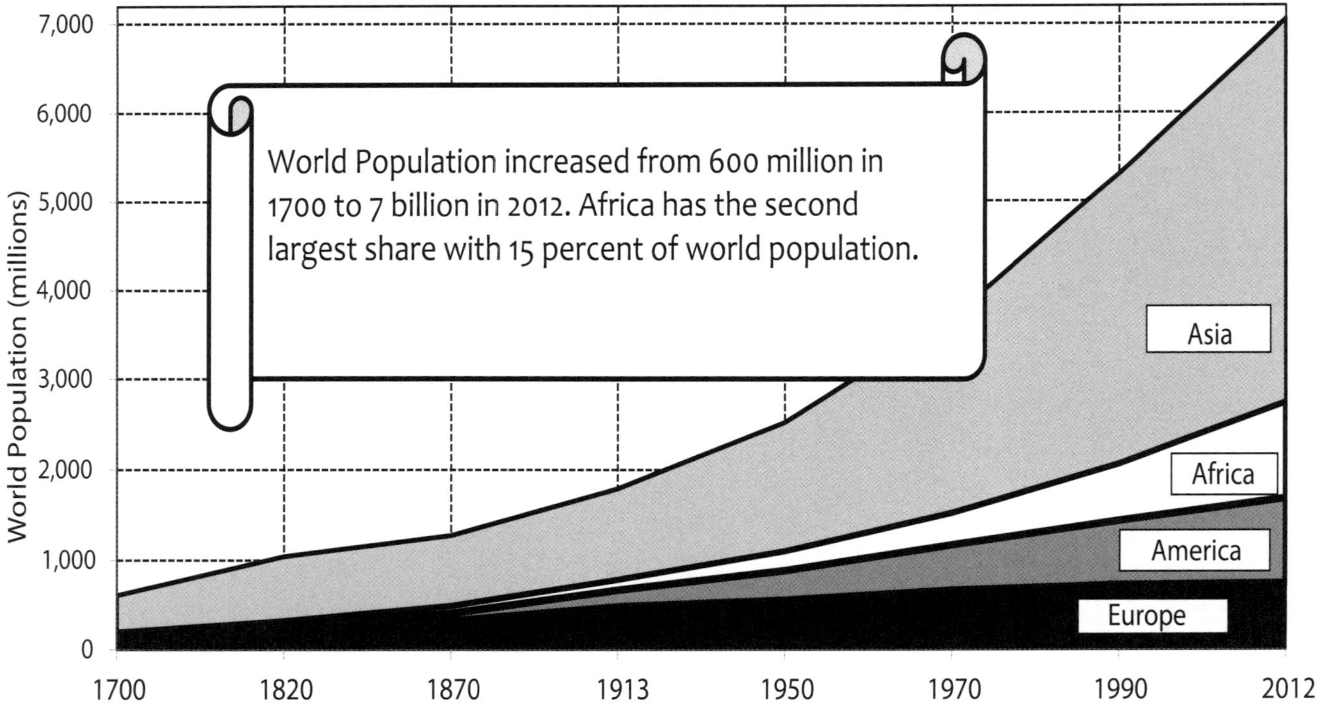

Figure 1.2 The growth of world population (1700–2012)

Source: Authors' compilation based on Piketty Capital in the Twenty-First Century, 2014 database

development hinges on its capacity to forge relations with "large" economies and harness the opportunities and benefits of South-South cooperation.

In spite of the premise of Africa's potential to advance regionalism and lead the way in the global South, Africa's balance score card is however not entirely impressive. As currently exists, various configurations of African countries have constituted negotiating groups; many of which cut across existing neighborhood regional arrangements, adding an additional layer of complexity to Africa's contemporary regional development process (Hartzenberg 2011). Also, the fact that the large number of regional integration arrangements have not rapidly advanced intra-regional trade raises questions about the success of such arrangements (ECA 2010).

That said, given that the various forms of regionalisms developing within Africa are both formal and informal (Söderbaum and Taylor 2007), one will need to view the entanglements and corresponding dynamics holistically. Viewed holistically the forces of regionalism (macro/meso/micro) are without doubt playing crucial roles in shaping the trade regimes and integration efforts that are emerging across Africa—be they informal cross-border arrangements, customs unions, free trade areas, common markets, monetary unions, economic unions, or other types of preferential arrangements. Regionalism on the continent has reached a significant scale and presents unparalleled opportunities that are not present in other domains in Africa (Bach 2008; Boas et al. 2005; Söderbaum 2004).

The volume posits that regionalism promotes opportunities to contribute to the socioeconomic development of the continent. Indeed, there are various examples that demonstrate the value added by regionalism: the East African Community and Maputo Development Corridor are good case in points that demonstrate the possibilities and opportunities for effective regional development cross-continentally. And while it may be argued that the catch phrase of the twenty-first century is "globalization," the case of Africa demonstrates that it is regionalism, rather than globalism, that is serving a more integral role in shaping socioeconomic realities (Besada et al. 2013). This is clearly demonstrated not only by considering the centrality of the major regional blocs, but also by recognizing that the only countries in which regionalism does not play an important role in their make-up are economic outliers, including Equatorial Guinea, Somalia, and Djibouti. Africa can harness many opportunities and possibilities that regionalism presents, especially when viewed holistically to capture its dynamics at all (macro/meso/micro) levels.

Spurring contemporary regional development requires an in-depth understanding of regionalism within the broader political economy of the continent, as well as the overarching global context. Private and public actors have an impact on facilitating or hindering growth of formal and informal sectors through critical factors such as natural capital, the extractive resources and environment. Extractive resources are among the top revenue earner on the continent (ACBF 2013). They have the potential to advance structural transformation and economic development. Ultimately this can serve as the mechanism for greater interdependency among African states with regard to facilitating transportation infrastructure and connecting various communities through informal and formal channels (Besada et al. 2013; Söderbaum 2004). Promoting regional development capacity inevitably harnesses the growth potential of African countries individually and collectively. This, in turn, will effectively strengthen Africa's competitiveness in the global market. In doing so, it commits the continent along a locally defined path of economic integration built on shared social values, common economic interests, and unified political agendas of African stakeholders, including local and national governments, private sector actors, and civil society.

Comprehending the holistic vision of contemporary regional development in Africa requires an understanding of regionalism beyond state systems. In Africa, one can note a variety of regional pockets—from the larger institutions, such as the African Union, or ECOWAS, to smaller projects, such as the Maputo Development Corridor, and informal cross-border regionalisms explored in this volume. Because regionalism on the continent is driven by myriad actors, the individual level of involvement cannot be overlooked. Given the development implications on the continent, it is of paramount importance to recognize how best to meet individuals' and communities' needs and to ensure that sustainable development is practiced. To analyze the interplay between the individual and the regional body, one needs to lose outside biases and simply glance at the evident system of the country (Chabal and Daloz 1999; Besada et al. 2013). Often, this requires not simply glancing at policies and statements of the major regional bodies, but also examining processes and documentation of civil society and public actors (Makhan 2008). Doing do, according to Söderbaum and Taylor (2009, p. 2) is the only way to ensure that regionalism in Africa is "scrutinized at face value." Then again, the viability of Africa's contemporary regional development calls for the necessary and sufficient resources to enable actors and stakeholders to discharge their specific roles and, in the process, shore up the development possibilities of their particular regions and Africa in general. The goal of optimal outcomes of regional development also calls for a better understanding of state–society from the national to the regional and the global level.

Conclusion

In the current international trading system, while bilateral and regional agreements are increasing in relevance, particularly following the stalemate in multilateral trade negotiations (Holden and Tang 2013), post-2015, a number of emerging global developments and restructuring will likely impact "new" regionalisms in Africa. Mega regionalisms are now occupying center stage (WEF 2014b). The co-existence and rise of mega-regional agreements could be a major "game changer" and potentially create a new international trading order. For Africa, the effects of mega-regionalism may be inescapable and potentially impact countries ability to diversify trade, integrate in global value chains and attract investments (Draper and Ismail 2014).

Regionalism whether "minor" or "mega" may be inescapable. But the possible value added of regionalism, makes it a positive shift in global governance (Besada et al. 2013) and better resilience. In addition, as globalization ushers in cross-border issues, regionalism is increasingly viewed as the only appropriate means for securing policy and practices (Cornelissen, Cheru and Shaw 2012; Söderbaum and Taylor 2008; Grant and Söderbaum 2003). Also, from the perspective of commercial transactions a regional approach will ensure a more favorable terms of trade and increase states' bargaining power, which is ultimately mutually beneficial and even egalitarian (Söderbaum 2004).

As contributors to this volume demonstrate, Africa's contemporary regionalism is a multi-dimensional and multi-variable phenomenon which takes into account among others the political, economic, strategic, social, demographic and ecological interactions within regions (Acharya and Johnston 2007, pp. 9–10). In appraising regional integration, there is apprehension on the regionalization phenomenon in Africa and with regard to the peculiarities of the institutional arrangements that have developed on the continent (Fanta 2013, p. 42). Nevertheless, the continent's variety, history, and pervasiveness of regionalisms offer an array of important opportunities and possibilities for directing the processes of globalization toward greater economic and political participation. The emerging levels of regionalisms, whether formal or informal, are expected to serve as the catalyst for the renaissance of both Africa and the global South by advancing their capacity to transcend fragility (Fanta and Shaw 2013, p. 2).

Additionally, for an economic renaissance of Africa, the emergence of "new" development partners in south–south cooperation presents important opportunities to increase trade, investments and aid. As Modi (2011, p. 5) argues, "economic partnerships between countries of Africa and the non-traditional partners from the South have given them more policy space for negotiations than with its traditional partners from the West as they have a wider range of options to choose from." Although Africa is still being referred to as "underdeveloped," the continent has made great strides toward improving its socioeconomic reality. With countries of the South growing at a faster rate than the North, South–South cooperation is growing in its existence and relevance. Regionalism supports this hypothesis in providing connectivity areas where cooperation has facilitated trade. Indeed, with regionalism, policymaking and development of balance sheets can be more reflective of specific geographies and actors (Besada et al. 2013). Africa's contemporary regional development allows for the variances of individual countries and communities to be represented, while the overarching commonalities of the member-states are determined and outlined. This measure of "sameness" helps countries to work together toward common social and economic goals.

This notwithstanding, going forward, the continent's efforts at regional development and economic integration have "to be addressed in a credible manner, with attention paid to the speed and sequencing of its implementation efforts and reforms, which ultimately are [premised on transformative] leadership and capacity of both regional organizations and member states" (Tavares and Tang 2013, p. 230; also see ACBF 2013). In this regard, capacity development efforts require the focus on not only the national, regional, and sub-national levels to allow meaningful regional development to flourish, but should also be tailored to build upon what already exists on the ground. A common commitment and collective action is needed and it is incumbent on Africa's leadership to work cooperatively across silos and rise up when developmental efforts are undermined by natural or human-induced hazards and provide the conduit for all institutions to effectively function and achieve a more integrated and resilient contemporary Africa.

References

ACBF (2006), "Challenges Facing Africa's Regional Economic Communities in Capacity Building." *ACBF Occasional Paper No. 5*. Harare: The Africa Capacity Building Foundation.

ACBF (2009), "Making Regional Integration Work in Africa: A Reflection on Strategies and Institutional Requirements." *ACBF Development Memoirs Series 002/2009*. Harare: The Africa Capacity Building Foundation.

ACBF (2011), *African Capacity Indicators Report: Capacity Development in Fragile States*. Harare: African Capacity Building Foundation.

ACBF (2013), *Africa Capacity Indicators Report 2013: Capacity Development for Natural Resources Management*. Harare: ACBF.

Acharya, A. and Johnston, A. (eds) (2007), *Crafting Cooperation: Regional International Institutions in Comparative Perspective*. Cambridge: Cambridge University Press.

Ariyo, A. (1992), "Tariff harmonization, government revenue and economic integration within ECOWAS: some reflections," *Development Policy Review* 10: 155–74.

Bach, D. (2008), "Beyond Parochialism: Cross Border Regionalism as a Gateway." In F. Söderbaum and I. Taylor (eds), *Afro-Regions: The Dynamics of Cross-Border Micro-Regionalism in Africa*. Stockholm: Nordiska Afrikainstitutet.

Besada, H., McMillan, L. and Sanieipour, A. (2013), "Regionalism, Trade and the Growth of Africa's Economy" (ACIR2014 Background Paper No. 6). Harare: ACBF.

Bhagwati, J. and Panagariya, A. (1996), "Preferential Trading Areas and Multilateralism—Strangers, Friends, or Foes?" In J. Bhagwati and A. Panagariya (eds), *The Economics of Preferential Trade Agreements.* Washington: AEI Press, pp. 1–55.

Boas, M., Marchand, M.H. and Shaw, T.M. (2005), *The Political Economy of Regions and Regionalisms.* Basingstoke: Palgrave Macmillan.

Breslin, S. and Hook, G.D. (eds) (2002), "*Microregionalism and World Order.*" Basingstoke: Palgrave Macmillan.

Brown, W. (2006), "African and International Relations: A comment on IR theory, anarchy and statehood," *Review of International Studies* 32 (1): 119–43.

Brown, O., Kahn, S.R. and Shaheen, F.H. (2009), "Introduction." In S.R. Kahn (ed.), *The Regional Trade Integration and conflict Resolution.* London: Routledge.

Chabal, P. and Daloz, J-P. (1999), *Africa Works: Disorder as Political Instrument.* Woolnough, UK: The International African Institute with Indiana University Press.

Cheru, F. (2002), *African Renaissance: Roadmaps to the Challenges of Globalization.* London: Zed Books.

Cheru, F. and Obi, C. (eds) (2010), *The Rise of China & India in Africa.* London: Zed Books.

Chikozho, C. (2012), "Towards Best-Practice in Transboundary Water Governance in Africa: Exploring the policy and institutional dimensions of conflict and cooperation over water." In K.T. Hanson, G. Kararach and T.M. Shaw (eds), *Rethinking Development Challenges for Public Policy.* Basingstoke: Palgrave Macmillan, pp. 155–200.

Chikozho, C. (2014), "Strategic Capacity-building Imperatives Vital for Transboundary Water Cooperation in Africa." In K.T. Hanson, C. D'Alessandro and F. Owusu (eds), *Managing Africa's Natural Resources: Capacities for Development.* Basingstoke: Palgrave Macmillan, pp. 118–39.

Clapham, C. (2001), "The Changing World of Regional Integration in Africa." In C. Clapham, G. Mills, A. Morner and E. Sidiropoulos (eds), *Regional Integration in Southern Africa: Comparative International Perspectives.* Johannesburg, South African: Institute of International Affairs.

Cornelissen, S., Cheru, F. and Shaw, T.M. (eds) (2012), *Africa and International Relations in the Twenty-first Century.* London: Palgrave Macmillan.

Draper, P. (2012), "Breaking Free From Europe: Why Africa Needs Another Model of Regional Integration," *Italian Journal of International Affairs* 47 (1): 67–82.

Draper, P. and Ismail, S. (2014), "The Potential Impact of Mega-regionals on Sub-Saharan Africa and Least Developed Countries in the Region." In *World*

Economic Forum Global Agenda Council on Trade and Foreign Direct Investment, Mega-regional Trade Agreements: Game-Changers or Costly Distractions for the World Trading System? July 2014, p. 8.

ECA (2010), *Assessing Regional Integration in Africa IV: Enhancing Intra-African Trade.* Available at: http://www.uneca.org/aria4/index.htm (accessed August 20, 2014).

Economist (2010), "Lights, Camera, Africa" 397 (8713), 18 December: 85–7.

Economist (2011), "Africa rising: The hopeful continent," 3 December. Available at: http://www.economist.com/node/21541015 (accessed January 2015).

El-Affendi, A. (2009), "The Perils of Regionalism: Regional Integration as a Source of Instability in the Horn of Africa?" *Journal of Intervention and State-building* 3 (1): 1–19.

Fanta, E. (2013), "Understanding Regional Integration Policies in Africa." In E. Fanta, T.M. Shaw and V.T. Tang (eds), *Comparative Regionalisms for Development in the 21st Century: Insights from the Global South.* Farnham: Ashgate, pp. 41–55.

Fanta, E., Shaw, T.M. and Tang, V.T. (eds) (2013), *Comparative Regionalisms for Development in the 21st Century: Insights from the Global South.* Farnham: Ashgate.

FAO (2003), "*Regional Integration and Food Security in Developing Countries.*" Rome: Food and Agriculture Organization of the United Nations.

Grant, A. and Söderbaum, F. (eds) (2003), *The New Regionalism in Africa.* Aldershot: Ashgate.

Haas, E.B. (1970), "The Study of Regional Integration: Reflections on the Joy and Anguish of Pretheorizing," *International Organization* 24(4): 607–46.

Hanson, K.T., D'Alessandro, C. and Owusu, F. (eds) (2014), *Managing Africa's Natural Resources: Capacities for Development.* Basingstoke: Palgrave Macmillan.

Hanson, K.T., Kararach, G. and Shaw, T. (eds) (2012), *Rethinking Development Challenges for Public Policy: insights from contemporary Africa.* Basingstoke: Palgrave Macmillan.

Hartzenberg, T. (2011), "Regional Integration in Africa" (WTO Staff Working Paper ESRD-2011–14). Geneva: Economic Research and Statistics Division, World Trade Organization.

Hettne, B. (1999), "Globalization and the new Regionalism." In B. Hettne, A. Inotai and O. Sunkel (eds), *Globalism and the New Regionalism.* Basingstoke: Palgrave Macmillan/UNU/WIDER, pp. 1–24.

Hettne, B. (2005), "Beyond the "New" Regionalism: implications for global development and international security," *Research for Action* 14, Helsinki: UNU-WIDER.

Holden, M. and Tang, V. (2013), "Competitive Bilateralism or Regionalism: a South African Perspective." In E. Fanta, T.M. Shaw and V.T. Tang (eds), *Comparative Regionalisms for Development in the 21st Century: Insights from the Global South.* Farnham: Ashgate, pp. 19–39.

Khagram, S. (2004), *Dams and Development: transnational strategies for water & power*. Ithaca: Cornell University Press.

Lee, M. (2002), "Regionalism in Africa: A Part of Problem or a Part of Solution," *Polis/R.C.S.P./C.P.S.R. Vol. 9, Numéro Spécial, 2002.*

Lemke, D. (2003), "African lessons for International Relations research," *World Politics* 56 (1): 114–38.

Makhan, V. (2009), "Making Regional Integration Work in Africa: A Reflection on Strategies and Institutional Requirements." ACBF Development Memoir Series/002/2009. Harare: ACBF.

Maphunye, K.J. (2009), "Public Administration for a Democratic Developmental State in Africa: Prospects and Possibilities," *Center for Policy Studies*, Johannesburg. Available at: http://cps.org.za/cps%20pdf/RR114.pdf (accessed August 14, 2014).

Maruping, M. (2005), "Challenges for Regional Integration in Sub-Saharan Africa: Macroeconomic Convergence and Monetary Coordination." In J.J. Teunissen and A. Akkerman (eds), *Africa in the World Economy: The National, Regional and International challenges*. The Hague: Fondad.

Modi, R. (2011), *South-South Cooperation: Africa on the Centre Stage*. New York: Palgrave Macmillan.

Murithi, T. (2007), *Institutionalising Pan-Africanism Transforming African Union values and principles into policy and practice*. ISS Paper 143 (June). Pretoria: Institute of Security Studies.

Piketty, T. (2014), *Capital in the Twenty-First Century*. London: The Belknap Press of Harvard University Press.

Piketty, T. (2014), *Capital in the Twenty-First Century*. Database available at: piketty.pse.ens.fr/capital21c (accessed September 10, 2014).

Santi, E., Saoussen, B.R., and Shaw, W. (eds) (2012), "Unlocking North Africa's Potential through Regional Integration: Challenges and Opportunities." Tunis-Belvedere, Tunisia: The African Development Bank (AfDB Group).

Shaw, T.M. (2012), "Towards an International Political Economy of Africa's 'Renaissance': for whom?" Available at: http://www.open.ac.uk/socialsciences/bisa-africa/files/bisa-isa-shaw.pdf (accessed August 13, 2014).

Shaw, T.M. (2015), From post-BRICS' decade to post-2015: insights from global governance and comparative regionalisms. Palgrave Communications 1:14004 doi: 10.1057/palcomms.2014.4.

Shaw, T.M., Cheru, F. and Cornelissen, S. (2012), "Conclusion: What Futures for African International Relations?" In S. Cornelissen, F. Cheru and T.M. Shaw (eds), *Africa and International Relations in the Twenty-first Century*. London: Palgrave Macmillan.

Shaw, T.M. and Fanta, E. (2013), "Introduction: Comparative Regionalisms for Development in the 21st Century: Insights from the Global South." In E.

Fanta, T.M. Shaw and V.T. Tang (eds), *Comparative Regionalisms for Development in the 21st Century: Insights from the Global South*. Farnham: Ashgate, pp. 1–17.

Shaw, T.M., Grant, A.J. and Cornelissen, S. (eds) (2012), *The Ashgate Research Companion to Regionalisms*. Farnham: Ashgate.

Söderbaum, F. (2003), "Introduction: Theories of New Regionalism." In F. Söderbaum and T.M. Shaw (eds), *Theories of New Regionalism: A Palgrave Reader*. New York: Palgrave.

Söderbaum, F. (2004), *The Political economy of Regionalism: The Case of Southern Africa*. London: Palgrave Macmillan.

Söderbaum, F. and Taylor, I. (2007), "Micro-Regionalism in West Africa: Evidence from Two Case Studies" (NAI Discussion Paper No. 14), Uppsala: Nordiska Afrikainstitutet.

Söderbaum, F. and Taylor, I. (eds) (2008), *Afro-Regions: The Dynamics of Cross-Border Micro-Regionalism in Africa*. Uppsala: Nordic Africa Institute.

Söderbaum, F. and Taylor, I. (2009), "Afro-regions: The dynamics of region-building In Africa." Paper for 3rd European Conference on African Studies (ECAS)—Panel 83, Regionalizing Africa. Developing Theory and Empiricism on Region-Building.

Soko, M. (2008), "Building Regional integration in Southern Africa: Southern African Customs Union as a driving force," *South African Journal of International Affairs* 15 (1): 55–69.

Tavares, R. and Tang, V.T. (2013), "Regional Economic Integration in Africa: Impediments to Progress?" In E. Fanta, T.M. Shaw and V.T. Tang (eds), *Comparative Regionalisms for Development in the 21st Century: Insights from the Global South*. Farnham: Ashgate, pp. 209–32.

UNDP (2011), *Regional Integration and Human Development: A Pathway for Africa*. New York: United Nations Development Programme.

UNDP (United Nations Development Programme) (2014), *Human Development Report 2014 Sustaining Progress: Reducing Vulnerabilities and Building Resilience*. Database available at: http://hdr.undp.org (accessed September 10, 2014).

Uzodike, U.O. (2009), "The Role of Regional Economic Communities in Africa's Economic Integration: Prospects and Constraints," *Africa Insight* 39, no. 2: 26–42.

Venables, A.J. (2003), "Winners and Losers from Regional Integration Agreements," *Economic Journal, Royal Economic Society* 113 (490): 747–61.

Vickers, B. (2012), "Towards a new aid paradigm: South Africa as African development partner," *Cambridge Review of International Affairs* 25 (4): 535–56.

Vivares, E. (ed.) (2014), Exploring the New South American Regionalism (NSAR). Farnham : Ashgate.

World Bank (2008), *Regional Integration Assistance Strategy for Sub-Saharan Africa*. Washington, D.C.: World Bank.

World Bank (2009), *World Development Report: Reshaping Economic Geography*. Washington, D.C.: World Bank.
WEF (World Economic Forum) (2014), *World Economic Forum on Africa Forging Inclusive Growth, Creating Jobs, Abuja, Nigeria 7–9 May 2014*.
WEF (World Economic Forum) (2014), *World Economic Forum Global Agenda Council on Trade and Foreign Direct Investment, Mega-regional Trade Agreements: Game-Changers or Costly Distractions for the World Trading System? July 2014*.

Websites

50th Anniversary Solemn Declaration of the AU of May 25, 2013. Available at: http://summits.au.int/en/21stsummit/events/50th-anniversary-solemn-declaration (accessed August 13, 2014).
Lesotho Highlands Water Project. Available at: http://www.lhwp.org.ls (accessed August 13, 2014).
Peace Parks Foundation. Available at: http://www.peaceparks.org (accessed August 13, 2014).

Appendix

Table 1.1 African human development index (HDI) and its components

HDI rank in Africa 2013	HDI rank in world 2013	Country	HDI value 2013	Life expectancy 2012	Mean years of schooling 2012	Expected years of schooling 2012	Gross national income per capita (PPP$) 2013	HDI value 2012
High human development								
1	55	Libya	0.784	75.3	7.5	16.1	21,666 h	0.789
2	63	Mauritius	0.771	73.6	8.5	15.6	16,777	0.769
3	71	Seychelles	0.756	73.2	9.4 o	11.6	24,632	0.755
4	90	Tunisia	0.721	75.9	6.5	14.6	10,440	0.719
5	93	Algeria	0.717	71.0	7.6	14.0	12,555	0.715
Medium human development								
6	109	Botswana	0.683	64.4 v	8.8	11.7	14,792	0.681
7	110	Egypt	0.682	71.2	6.4	13.0	10,400	0.681
8	112	Gabon	0.674	63.5	7.4	12.3	16,977	0.670
9	118	South Africa	0.658	56.9	9.9	13.1 p	11,788	0.654
10	123	Cape Verde	0.636	75.1	3.5 p	13.2	6,365	0.635

11	127	Namibia	0.624	64.5	6.2	11.3	9,185	0.620
12	129	Morocco	0.617	70.9	4.4	11.6	6,905	0.614
13	138	Ghana	0.573	61.1	7.0	11.5	3,532	0.571
14	140	Congo	0.564	58.8	6.1	11.1	4,909	0.561
15	141	Zambia	0.561	58.1	6.5	13.5	2,898	0.554
16	142	Sao Tome and Principe	0.558	66.3	4.7 w	11.3	3,111	0.556
17	144	Equatorial Guinea	0.556	53.1	5.4 p	8.5	21,972	0.556
Low human development								
18	147	Kenya	0.535	61.7	6.3	11.0	2,158	0.531
19	148	Swaziland	0.530	49.0	7.1	11.3	5,536	0.529
20	149	Angola	0.526	51.9	4.7 w	11.4	6,323	0.524
21	151	Rwanda	0.506	64.1	3.3	13.2	1,403	0.502
22	152	Cameroon	0.504	55.1	5.9	10.4	2,557	0.501
23	152	Nigeria	0.504	52.5	5.2 w	9.0	5,353	0.500
24	155	Madagascar	0.498	64.7	5.2 p	10.3	1,333	0.496
25	156	Zimbabwe	0.492	59.9	7.2	9.3	1,307	0.484
26	159	Comoros	0.488	60.9	2.8	12.8	1,505	0.486
27	159	Tanzania (United Republic of)	0.488	61.5	5.1	9.2	1,702	0.484
28	161	Mauritania	0.487	61.6	3.7	8.2	2,988	0.485
29	162	Lesotho	0.486	49.4	5.9 b	11.1	2,798	0.481
30	163	Senegal	0.485	63.5	4.5	7.9	2,169	0.484
31	164	Uganda	0.484	59.2	5.4	10.8	1,335	0.480
32	165	Benin	0.476	59.3	3.2	11.0	1,726	0.473
33	166	Sudan	0.473	62.1	3.1	7.3 p	3,428	0.472
34	166	Togo	0.473	56.5	5.3	12.2	1,129	0.470
35	170	Djibouti	0.467	61.8	3.8 r	6.4	3,109 h	0.465
36	171	Côte d'Ivoire	0.452	50.7	4.3	8.9 p	2,774	0.448
37	172	Gambia	0.441	58.8	2.8	9.1	1,557	0.438
38	173	Ethiopia	0.435	63.6	2.4 w	8.5	1,303	0.429
39	174	Malawi	0.414	55.3	4.2	10.8	715	0.411
40	175	Liberia	0.412	60.6	3.9	8.5 p	752	0.407
41	176	Mali	0.407	55.0	2.0 b	8.6	1,499	0.406
42	177	Guinea-Bissau	0.396	54.3	2.3 r	9.0	1,090	0.396
43	178	Mozambique	0.393	50.3	3.2 w	9.5	1,011	0.389
44	179	Guinea	0.392	56.1	1.6 w	8.7	1,142	0.391
45	180	Burundi	0.389	54.1	2.7	10.1	749	0.386
46	181	Burkina Faso	0.388	56.3	1.3 r	7.5	1,602	0.385
47	182	Eritrea	0.381	62.9	3.4 p	4.1	1,147	0.380

48	183	Sierra Leone	0.374	45.6	2.9	7.5 p	1,815	0.368
49	184	Chad	0.372	51.2	1.5 s	7.4	1,622	0.370
50	185	Central African Republic	0.341	50.2	3.5	7.2	588	0.365
51	186	Congo (Democratic Republic of the)	0.338	50.0	3.1	9.7	444	0.333
52	187	Niger	0.337	58.4	1.4	5.4	873	0.335
Human development index-regions								
		Arab States	0.682	70.2	6.3	11.8	15,817	0.681
		East Asia and the Pacific	0.703	74.0	7.4	12.5	10,499	0.699
		Europe and Central Asia	0.738	71.3	9.6	13.6	12,415	0.735
		Latin America and the Caribbean	0.740	74.9	7.9	13.7	13,767	0.739
		South Asia	0.588	67.2	4.7	11.2	5,195	0.586
		sub-Saharan Africa	0.502	56.8	4.8	9.7	3,152	0.499

Table Definitions:

- Human Development Index (HDI): A composite index measuring average achievement in three basic dimensions of human development—a long and healthy life, knowledge and a decent standard of living. See Technical note 1 (http://hdr.undp.org/en) for details on how the HDI is calculated.
- Life expectancy at birth: Number of years a newborn infant could expect to live if prevailing patterns of age-specific mortality rates at the time of birth stay the same throughout the infant's life.
- Mean years of schooling: Average number of years of education received by people ages 25 and older, converted from education attainment levels using official durations of each level.
- Expected years of schooling: Number of years of schooling that a child of school entrance age can expect to receive if prevailing patterns of age-specific enrollment rates persist throughout the child's life.
- Gross national income (GNI) per capita: Aggregate income of an economy generated by its production and its ownership of factors of production, less the incomes paid for the use of factors of production owned by the rest of the world, converted to international dollars using PPP rates, relative to population.

Main Data Sources:

- HDI calculations based on data from UNDESA (2013a), Barro and Lee (2013), UNESCO Institute for Statistics (2013), UN Statistics Division (2014), World Bank (2014) and IMF (2014).

- Life Expectancy based on UNDESA (2013).
- Mean years of Schooling based on Barro and Lee (2013), UNESCO Institute for Statistics (2013) and HDRO estimates based on data on educational attainment from UNESCO Institute for Statistics (2013) and on methodology from Barro and Lee (2013).
- Expected years of Schooling based on UNESCO Institute for Statistics (2013).
- Gross National Income and HDI calculations based on data from World Bank (2014), IMF (2014) and UN Statistics Division (2014).

Chapter 2
Regionalism, Globalization and Economic Integration in Africa

Korbla P. Puplampu

Introduction

Africa has, in the recent past, recorded impressive gains on specific economic indicators (World Bank 2013, 2012; Africa Progress Panel 2013; ACBF 2013, 2012). The World Bank (2013), for example, argues that economic growth in sub-Saharan Africa remains strong with a growth forecast of 4.9 percent in 2013, attributing the growth to increasing levels of investment. Even though growth might be improving, the challenge is how to translate it into reducing the incidence of poverty in the region. This is because growth does not seem to have a parallel impact on reducing poverty and other forms of social inequality (World Bank 2013). In order to address the relationship between growth and poverty rates, analysts are beginning to focus their attention on regional organizations or regional economic communities (Bowles et al. 2007; Mbaku and Saxena 2004; Söderbaum and Taylor 2003; Grant and Söderbaum 2003).

The focus on regional entities is consistent with broader changes in society, particularly in the economic sphere. These changes are a product or response to current manifestations of globalization, leading to an interest in how the relationship between globalization and regionalism would impact African development (Bischoff 2004; Nnadozie 2004; Söderbaum and Taylor 2003). In its contemporary incarnation, globalization calls for a minimal role of the state in the economic and social spheres, the privileging of non-government or non-state activities, especially for-profit entities, in the economy under the aegis of free market arrangements (Bøås, Marchand and Shaw 2005; Söderbaum and Shaw 2003; Grant and Söderbaum 2003). The assumed de-territorialization of the state "does negate the continuing political relevance of territory. Instead, it implies that territory is no longer *as* relevant, and certainly not the main source of political and economic power as it once was" (MacLean 2003, p. 111; italics in original).

Regionalism has two essential features, sponsored by both state and non-state actors on the basis of "economic, commercial, military, political and societal interactions" (Bischoff 2004, p. 124). Regionalism requires states to give up control of some economic activities by integrating with others under one umbrella for the ultimate benefit of citizens within the region. Regional economic integration is therefore the getting together of various states within a particular region, sometimes at different states of socioeconomic development and institutional capacities for the purpose of enlarging economic opportunities and better responding to globalization in a process of dialogue, cooperation, integration and ownership (Kitipov 2012; Ginkel, Court and Langenhove 2003; Mistry 2003).

Regional Economic Institutions in Africa: A Survey

There are macro and micro regional economic communities in Africa. At the macro level, there are two major institutions: the UN-sponsored Economic Commission for Africa and the Organization of African Unity and its subsequent incarnation as the African Union (AU). The Economic Commission for Africa (ECA), established in 1958, was "the first-ever inter-governmental organization in Africa whose geographical scope covered the whole continent … [and also] paved the way for the founding of the OAU [Organization of African Unity] five years later" (Adedeji 1979, p. 6). The Organization of African Unity (OAU) was established in 1963 and brought together the then newly independent African countries. The OAU spearheaded various resolutions, for example, the 1963 Algiers, 1970 and 1973 Addis Ababa Declarations, but the most significant resolution for this study was the 1980 Lagos Plan of Action and the Final Act of Lagos which formed the basis for the 1991 Abuja Treaty. The Treaty actualized the establishment of the African Economic Community (AEC) and "clearly envisaged that the Community must be established mainly through the coordination, harmonization and progressive integration of the activities of the RECs [regional economic communities]" (Tavares 2009, p. 62).

Of the seventeen major regional economic organizations in Africa, eight are officially acknowledged as integral to the eventual establishment of the African Economic Community (AEC). These eight are: the Economic Community of West African States (ECOWAS); East African Community (EAC); Common Market for Eastern and Southern Africa (COMESA); Southern African Development Community (SADC); *Union de Maghreb Arabe* (Arab Maghreb Union, AMU); Economic Community for Central African States (ECCAS); Intergovernmental Authority on Development (IGAD) and finally the Community of Sahel-Saharan States (CEN-SAD) (Thonke and Spliid 2012; Tavares 2009; Bischoff 2004; Mistry 2003).

The Economic Community of West African States (ECOWAS) was established in 1975. Its main aim is to promote economic integration in areas ranging from agriculture, industry, energy and natural resources, telecommunications to financial and monetary affairs. Apart from the exit of Mauritania in 1999, the community is made of the same 15 member states since its inception. However, over time, the community has added security and conflict resolution to its mandate, largely in response to the various conflicts (for example in Liberia, Sierra Leone, Côte d'Ivoire and Mali) that have gripped the region.

The East African Community (EAC) has gone through two distinct phases in its development. In its first phase, from 1967 to 1977, it was made up of Tanzania, Uganda and Kenya. The relationship among these three countries can be traced to their common colonial status under the British and also part of the 1910 Southern Africa Customs Union. The demise of the first phase was due to the worsening relationship between Uganda and Tanzania as well as the perception that a disproportionate share of benefits of the community went to Kenya (Bischoff 2004). The second phase of the organization dates from 2000 and includes the subsequent membership of Burundi and Rwanda in 2007. EAC, like ECOWAS, aims at deepening and broadening cooperation among member countries in political, economic and social spheres. The community is currently pursing regional integration through the East African Customs Union with ongoing negotiations on a common market and future political federation of the East African States.

The history of the Common Market for Eastern and Southern Africa (COMESA) dates back to the mid-1960s. Beginning with the Lusaka Declaration on a Preferential Trade Area (PTA), the treaty establishing the commission was signed in 1982. The PTA was subsequently transformed into a common market for Eastern and Southern Africa in 1994 and has a current membership of 19 countries. The group envisages the creation of a common framework to improve or present greater economic (free trade and customs union) and social development. Its membership, including states like Madagascar, the Democratic Republic of Congo and Egypt, reflects significant historical differences compared to other regional communities in Africa (Thonke and Spliid 2002).

Southern African Development Community (SADC) has been in existence since 1980. The history of the organization, previously called South African Development Coordinating Conference (SADCC), was mostly to coordinate development activities in order to lessen dependence on the then apartheid regime in South Africa and the Southern African Customs Union (SACU) which it also controlled. The organization became a development community in 1992, transforming itself at the end of South Africa's apartheid system in 1994 and the eventual admission of the country in 1995. SADC currently has a membership of fifteen countries.

SADC has economic, and political and security objectives. The former include the creation of a free trade area, and a customs union. The issue of customs union has become a nightmare, since five SADC countries, South

Africa, Botswana, Namibia, Swaziland, and Lesotho—are members of SACU which is negotiating on how to share revenues of the oldest customs union of the world (Thonke and Spliid 2002). Political and security related objectives ranged from the prolonged conflict in the Democratic Republic of Congo to the political uncertainties associated with Robert Mugabe's long rein in Zimbabwe.

The *Union de Maghreb Arabe* (Arab Maghreb Union, AMU) dates back to 1964 when economic ministers from Algeria, Libya, Morocco and Tunisia met to coordinate and harmonize their development plans. Its current status can be traced to 1989 with the Marrakech Treaty and has a membership of five countries (Mauritania, Algeria, Libya, Morocco and Tunisia). The revived union ratified multilateral agreements on issues that included "tariffs and trade in relation to industrial products and trade in agricultural products, investment guarantees, double taxation, and sanitary standards" (Bischoff 2004, p. 134). Beyond the economic imperatives, the union also has a focus on political and security issues, specifically a common regional defense policy. The Arab region and the Union has been the site of political unrest in the last few years, raising questions about the direction of the region and the extent to which the economic objectives can be realized (Thonke and Spliid 2012; Pinfari 2012).

The Economic Community for Central African States (ECCAS) was established in 1983. The group comprises countries previously attached to the Central African Customs and Economic Union and the Economic Community of the Great Lakes States (Burundi, Rwanda and the then Zaire). With a current membership of ten countries, the fundamental objective is sustained, balanced and integrated development in economic and social activities.

The Community of Sahel-Saharan States (CEN-SAD) was created in 1998 and includes countries like the six founding members—Burkina Faso, Chad, Libya, Mali, Niger and Sudan. However, the group has become the largest regional economic community in Africa with 28 member countries. The main objective of the group is the free movement of people, capital, free trade and movement of goods and services and finally the right of establishment, ownership and exercise of economic activity. In sum, the general improvement of economic activities including concerted efforts to improve communications among member states.

The other set of regional economic institutions in Africa or micro organizations specialize in one particular aspect of the development process and could also align with the broader regional economic institutions. One example of such an institution is the Maputo Development Corridor, which is integrated or aligned with the Southern Africa Development Commission (SADC) (Söderbaum and Taylor 2003; Rogerson 2000; Shaw 2012, 2000). Another institution is the Intergovernmental Authority on Development (IGAD). The Maputo Development Corridor (MDC) straddles between South Africa and Mozambique, specifically the northern Mpumalanga Province in South Africa and parts of the Gaza and Maputo provinces in southern Mozambique. MDC is a special development initiative based on an agreement to improve the economic conditions of the affected regions in both Mozambique and South (Söderbaum and Taylor 2003; Rogerson 2000). In addition to improving the infrastructure (roads, water, electricity and telecommunications) and the rehabilitation and promotion of new investment opportunities, the MDC also aims to showcase the tourism potential of the area through biodiversity initiatives (Ngwenya and Taylor 2003). The MDC is "an excellent example of regional cooperation among countries and between the private and public sectors" (World Bank 1999, p. 11).

The Intergovernmental Authority on Development (IGAD), created in 1996, succeeded the Intergovernmental Authority on Drought and Development (IGADD) which was established in 1986. The original focus on examining the relationship between drought and development underscores the complexities of development, especially in the context of climate change (ACBF 2013). With a current membership of seven countries, the revitalized organization seeks to expand regional cooperation against the backdrop of the continued effort to address the drought conditions in the region.

Regionalism and Economic Integration in Africa: A Theoretical Framework

A useful point of departure for discussing regionalism and economic integration in Africa is the aftermath of the Second World War. A central initiative was the Colonial Development Corporation (CDC). Established in 1947 under the 1940 Colonial Development Welfare Act, the Corporation was to spotlight schemes for the production of primary produce in partnership with colonial and other Commonwealth governments (Havinden and Meredith 1993). CDC reflected a regional approach in colonial development theory and practice and was a major shift in colonial thinking to the extent that it was interested in providing the machinery for "the promotion of industrial capitalism within the colonies" (Phillips 1989, p. 151). Meanwhile, the underlying economic perspective was that the colonies would be developed through revenue generated through trade in the export of agricultural raw materials and that tied the historical and contemporary dimensions of African development to the export of agricultural raw materials (Puplampu 2014; Boone 1994; Berry 1993).

Two main theoretical frameworks underpin regionalism and economic development: classical economic and regional trading relations argument; and developmental regionalism. The traditional economic argument is about markets, specifically the notion of free market (Smith 1776/1976). Likened to an "invisible hand," a free market is supposed to allocate resources and offer rewards in the most efficient and impersonal manner. It is assumed that competitive forces of demand and supply are better able to reward goods and services and should remain free from all forms of intervention, the context for a minimal presence of the state. The argument is about perfect competition in the market and the implications for the allocation of resources, trade creation and trade diversion (Schiff and Winters 2003; Asante 2000; Baldwin 1997).

The case for regional trade includes accumulation or growth and investment effects and overall credibility from successful integration (Matthews 2003). While the traditional economic approach on regional integration has welfare consequences, it is not without critique. Proponents tend to minimize the role of the state in society at large and the market in particular. However, as Heilbroner (1992) correctly argues, Adam Smith provides important duties for the state, one of which is to erect and maintain certain public institutions. It has also become increasingly clear that markets are not apolitical institutions because the state structures the conditions of their operations (Mackintosh 1990). A related difficulty with the market model is that many African countries have participated in export agriculture since the dawn of colonial rule and have suffered the consequences of doing so (Puplampu 2003; Jamal 1993). These difficulties, among others, account for the emergence of developmental regionalism or what is widely referred to as the new regionalism

The new regionalism framework draws from diverse sources, but, in the main, includes perspectives in international relations and the political economy of development (Grant and Söderbaum 2003; Söderbaum and Shaw 2003). There are two related central issues in this perspective. The first is an emphasis on the role of both state and non-state actors in African development and the second factor is recognition of the importance of both formal and informal institutions and networks. While the formal trappings of the state and non-state actors constitute a legitimate site of inquiry, so also are, for example, informal or sometimes illicit or illegal trade networks (MacLean 2003). The focus on formal, informal or illicit institutions and activities is because "the forces of state-making and state-destruction are at the core of understanding regionalism" (Grant and Söderbaum 2003, p. 5). In the case of formal or state institutions vis-à-vis informal and sometimes illegal networks, the emergence of parallel markets is an appropriate illustration which are replacements for failed public or formal state marketing institutions and a demonstration of civil society to operate beyond the apparatus of the public sphere (Fatton 1992; Ninsin 1988).

By pursing regionalism from a broader context, the new approach acknowledges the significance of forces like globalization (Grant and Söderbaum 2003). In exploring the relationship between globalization and regionalization, developmental regionalism focuses on the state, but it acknowledges that the state is not an autonomous entity. The focus on state–society relations makes it possible to explore regionalism from both an internal and external dimension (Buzdagan 2013).

A key aspect of state–society relations is governance and its impact on regional economic communities. The governance structure involves all processes and related laws on decision making and the analysis of policy outcomes. The governance structure of regionalism and economic integration has been complicated by the changing role of the state in globalization and the emergence of various non-state actors, within and beyond the nation state. Söderbaum (2004) introduces the notion of "nuanced governance" to analyze regionalism and governance in contemporary Africa. Nuanced governance bears in mind the role of different actors in the governance structure.

Regionalism and Economic Development in Africa

The theoretical review underscores the complex interaction of state and non-state actors at different levels of intensity and, consequently, outcomes. The ensuing analysis shows the impact of formal and informal process, legal and illegal networks on stated and unstated policy outcomes. The four major factors at the center of the analysis of regional economic communities and economic integration in Africa are: motivation and underlying reasons; structure; impact; sustainability (Matthews 2003). Motivation is about the underlying reason for the creation of the regional economic community. However, motivation should not be construed as a static concept. There are dynamic aspects to motivation, traits that are essential in terms of organizational renewal or revival, in order to better respond to social change and attain short and long term benefits.

Political or economic factors were the major impetus in the historical formation of all the regional economic entities in Africa. The political rationale was how to harness state-to-state relations for regional cooperation and development while the economic reason was based on market-driven principles and the removal of barriers to the free mobility of goods, services, capital and investment within and beyond the region (Söderbaum 2004). Few macro regional communities (SADC and Arab Maghreb) acknowledged the significance of both political and economic factors from the onset of the organization. For SADC, the political objective was to create an organization that would serve as a bulwark against the then apartheid regime in South Africa.

Political and economic motivations, specifically the cross-border dynamics of development, the role of the state in development were central in the origins of the Maputo Development Corridor (MDC) (Roodt 2008; Söderbaum and Taylor 2003, 2001; Rogerson 2000; Mitchell 1998). Although MDC is situated within the Southern Africa Development Community (SADC), the two are separate. Mitchell (1998, p 758) notes that the "MDC was the first regional integration effort between the democratic South African government and Mozambique." The MDC project was consistent with "changes in the global political economy, but also ... a political opening in both countries that has meant a retreat by each state within the political realm ... [and] outside forces that ... equally encompasses the economic, [specifically] the role of the state in development strategies ..." (Söderbaum and Taylor 2001, p. 677).

Regional communities have to focus on political and economic factors in a serious and direct manner, since barriers in one would have negative consequences for the other. Indeed, that understanding finds tangible expression in the contemporary activities of several regional economic communities in Africa. ECOWAS, in the face of protracted conflicts in Liberia, Sierra Leone and Côte d'Ivoire, added security and conflict resolution to its activities and decided to intervene in the Liberian conflict in the early 1990s (Mortimer 1996; Kieh 1992). In redefining its mandate in the face of social change, ECOWAS signaled a firm understanding of the close interaction between economic and political forces in the development process. The festering conflict in Liberia threatened not only human life in Liberia, but also created a huge migration and humanitarian crisis that affected several countries in the sub-region.

The second relevant factor is the structure of the economic communities, specifically the relationship between state and non-state actors as well as internal and external forces. No economic community is an island unto itself. All the economic communities have multiple lines of relationship, beginning with the relationship with each other in the region and then with external actors like the European Union and the World Trade Organization. With the AU coordinating the work of the eight recognized major regional economic communities, states have attained membership in several economic communities beyond those recognized by the AU. The result is that twenty-six African countries are members of two regional organization, nineteen are members of three, with two countries (DRC and Swaziland) belonging to four and only six countries have membership in one regional community (Kitipov 2012; Thonke and Spliid 2012; Tavares, 2009; Franke 2007).

Membership in different RECs suggests multiple responsibilities in administrative, financial and technical matters. Countries will have to stretch available resources to cover similar issues in respective economic communities. The cost associated with multiple memberships will prevent the emergence of a critical mass of competence. With different memberships, a related outcome is different pace towards the larger objective of the economic integration of the continent, since "RECs are not progressing towards the AEC [African Economic Community] at the same pace, nor are they following similar procedures and processes to reach that aim" (Tavares 2009, p. 64).

A further aspect of the structure of regional communities in Africa is their relationship with external communities or institutions, particularly the

European Union (EU) and the World Trade Organization (WTO). The EU, in terms of regional economic communities, has a long history in Africa and other parts of the world, symbolized by the Caribbean and Pacific, hence the EU-ACP (African, Caribbean and Pacific) framework. However, the EU, in 2002, began negotiating Economic Partnership Agreements (EPAs) with the African, Caribbean and Pacific group of states, an agreement which also includes bilateral free trade agreements, and a situation Faber and Orbie (2003) characterize as a watershed in Europe-Africa relations. A useful reference point is the EU-SADC negotiations.

The EU-SADC negotiations on an EPA which began in early 2005 quickly brought to the fore asymmetrical power relations. The EU included items of self-interest (under the broad banner of trade and development), for instance, provisions on industrial policy that "would prevent host countries from making certain demands with respect to levels of local employment … [since] their inclusion would make it very difficult for governments in southern Africa to adopt an industrial policy that sought to protect and develop its own local firms. Similarly, liberalization of government procurement would also prevent any preferences for domestic providers over European ones" (Hurt 2012, p. 505). It is not surprising that the EU-SADC EPA negotiations deeply affected the "coherence of regional integration within the SADC region" since most of the SADC members were also "involved in other regional EPA negotiations" (Hurt 2012, p. 505).

The EU presents EPAs as an attempt to synchronize its policies with that of the WTO (Wade 2003). While there is some credibility and justification in the EU argument, the position conceals more than it reveals. The EU has supported WTO efforts in the multilateral system, the difficulties and prolonged deadlock on the Doha Development Round of negotiations which are vital to Africa and other developing societies. In effect, the EU is offering the EPA as a way out, rather than lending its support to addressing the basis of the deadlock. The EU has opted for EPAs, because developing countries have a weaker bargaining position in EPAs, relative to their bargaining power in the WTO and whatever gains African states attain in the multilateral system are likely to be compromised by emerging bilateral agreements with the EU (Hurt 2012). The structure of relations is also about power relations. These power differences affect outcomes in the access to the human and physical resources required for regional development. In a world of systematic and systemic inequality, these global trade agreements are likely to reinforce rather than address the structural nature of global trade relations (Nwoke 2009; Gibb 2003).

One significant aspect of the new regionalism framework is the emphasis on both state and non-state actors, hence a focus on "emerging networks of individuals and groups that extend beyond the state. Such networks support various activities ranging from information gathering and dissemination to analysis, capacity building in indigenous institutions and advocacy on environment, health, gender and human rights" (MacLean 2003, p. 113). These networks are "deeply entrenched in informal market activities with the purpose of promoting patronage networks and (hidden) private self-interests" (Söderbaum 2004, p. 428). MacLean (2003) identifies two types of networks, networks of plunder and networks for peace. Networks of plunder are essential parts in the creation and promotion of conflict, war and the destruction of society, for example, in Angola, the Democratic Republic of Congo (DRC) and Zimbabwe during the closing decade of the last millennium (MacLean 2003). MacLean (2003, p. 115) cites a UN Report which details the key actors in the DRC crisis. The report shows a close relationship between political and military officers from Zimbabwe, Namibia, Uganda and Rwanda associated with some of the leading business from these countries doing business in the DRC. While many of the companies are "legally constituted and their direct involvement in illegal operations has not been proved" in a court of law, "the individuals named are profiting from the conflict and questions of probity have been raised because of their close personal connections with political leaders" (MacLean, 2003, pp. 115–16).

There are also regional dimensions to the networks for peace. These networks work towards the promotion of peace related activities (making, keeping and building), social justice initiatives and single human insecurity issues like the trade in guns and drugs (MacLean 2003). The case of "blood diamonds" eventually led to the establishment of the Kimberley Process Certification Scheme on diamonds which came into being with the South African government working with several governments and non-state actors to establish a mechanism to reduce the illegal trade in diamonds (Wright 2012). The networks of plunder and networks for peace, connected at multiple levels, from the national, to the regional and transnational, make a compelling case to focus on state–society relations in order to offer a more sophisticated analysis of the structure of regional communities and the implications for economic outcomes.

The third organizing factor for analysis is the impact of regional economic communities in Africa. Kirkpatrick and Watanabe (2005) note significant variations in the volume of trade among the three countries in the East African Community between 1970 and 2001. However, the study also documented that "Kenya accounts for the largest share of intra-EAC trade, reflecting the economy's relatively more advanced level of development" (Kirkpatrick and Watanabe 2005, p. 145). There are unequal benefits in the economies of member countries within the EAC and other regional economic communities (Thonke and Spliid 2012).

Furthermore, the volume of intra-African trade is very low, although the potential for intra-regional is promising, if a renewed emphasis can be placed on creating common markets (Thonke and Spliid 2012). Underlying this state of affairs is the fact that "although important progress has been made in removing tariff barriers through regional trade agreements, much less attention has been devoted to the numerous non-tariff and non-border measures that most countries impose on one another preventing any substantial increases in intra-regional trade flows" (Olarreaga and Rocha 2003, p. 104).

In the case of ECOWAS, the volume of trade flows between ECOWAS member states and industrial countries in the global North was "proportionately much higher than intraregional trade flows" (Deme 1995, p. 117). However, annual "rate of growth of trade among ECOWAS partner countries has been higher than that between ECOWAS member countries and industrial countries" (Deme 1995, p. 118). The latter outcome demonstrates the potential that can be attained with significant improvements in infrastructure-led development and relevant economic policies. A valuable example of a relevant economic policy is the regional bulk purchase of specific imported goods, specifically rice (Seck et al. 2010). Using the 2007 to 2008 global food crisis as a backdrop, Fiamohe et al. (2012, p. 86) argued that if all member states of ECOWAS coordinated their purchase of rice from the world market, that will have significant "bargaining power in the rice import market." This calls for synergies in regional economic activities. The Maputo Development Corridor (MDC) offers a worthy illustration of how to utilize synergies in regional development.

The Maputo Development Corridor (MDC) has delivered in the sense of "infrastructure-led development" and the empowerment of citizens and emerging industries in South Africa and Mozambique (Peberdy and Crush 2001; Rogerson 2000). Infrastructural development, for instance, provided a critical pathway for tourism within the Corridor (Rogerson 2000). The boom in ecotourism (fresh produce, curios, taxidermy, provision of local cultural displays) as part of the broader agenda on tourism is significant, because it demonstrates an attention to the needs of and an attempt to involve local communities in regional development (Rogerson 2000). There has also been a sizeable emergence of what Peberdy and Crush (2001) called "invisible trade [and] invisible travelers" within the Corridor. These invisible trade and invisible travelers complement broader economic activities, such as the manufacturing sectors in the two countries.

Perhaps, the outcomes of the Maputo Development Corridor and other projects like the Trans-Kalahari Corridor, linking Lobatse in Botswana and Windhoek in Namibia and, by extension, connecting Gauteng (a dominant province in South Africa) with the Atlantic coast in Walvis Bay demonstrate the renaissance at the heart of developmental states in Africa in the twenty-first century (Shaw 2012; 2000). These projects bring in private capital, create public-private partnership and have a transformative potential beyond the narrow economic focus that seem to characterize the work of regional economic communities. To be sure, the MDC paradigm is not without critique

(Söderbaum and Taylor 2001). One key area of critique is the nature of the public-private partnership at play in the program. Specifically, the differential costs and benefits for public and private institutions.

The final analytical variable is sustainability. This is about how political leadership and institutional capacity can lead to desirable outcomes for regional economic communities. Political leadership works around bureaucratic and managerial leadership, focusing on the ability of state officials to outline and implement the development agenda (Wanasika et al. 2011). Political leadership needs to be examined relative to the question of governance, because leadership and governance are essential to Africa's development agenda (Obi 2001). The state's cardinal responsibility, even if theoretically speaking, is the economic development of its citizens. The notion of minimal state under globalization does not align with the "'developmental state approach' in which burgeoning growth would be advanced through sustained infrastructural, institutional and social development based on lessons from East Asia, including Malaysia and Singapore, but also Brazil and Chile" (Shaw 2012, p. 838).

Therefore, the question is not whether the state should play a role in regional economic communities in particular or development in general. It is what kind of state and how it can actualize its role in development, since the state continues to play a role in development, even if not in the same dominant historical pattern. The state of Zambia was able to make a decision in terms of membership in SADC and COMESA in terms of the relative benefits and costs attached to each (Thonke and Spliid 2012). Kenya, in another context, has membership in both IGAD and EAC, since it leans on IGAD to address security concerns in Somalia and the EAC for economic interests (Thonke and Spliid 2012; El-Affendi 2009).

In terms of institutional capacity, in view of the overlapping membership of several African states in regional economic communities, one can reasonably argue that African states are eager to join forces with others to bring about the economic development of their people. While membership is the easy part, institutional capacity requires resources and political will. Many political leaders do not "put in any more effort than was absolutely necessary in order to maintain influence and credibility on the African stage" (Franke 2007, pp. 43–4). This is the context for what Söderbaum (2004) calls "sovereignty-boosting governance." The key here is that many African states exist only in the formal recognition they receive or are accorded in regional and international meeting and not because of their ability to perform functions that improve the lives of their citizenry. By putting in only the minimum effort to formalize their legitimacy in regional institutions, African leaders are able to use "regional governance to promote rather than to reduce absolute state sovereignty and its legitimacy" (Söderbaum 2004, p. 426).

In signing up for membership in several economic communities, there is also an unprecedented stretching of institutional capacity in the face of varying levels of state-building capacity (Thonke and Spliid 2012). Because RECs are, by definition, a conglomeration of states, they also suffer from any deficits of the state in the broader regional economic community. The different levels of state capacity are reflected in the overall capacity of each regional economic community hence the argument that RECs in Africa vary significantly in "levels of state-building, implementing capacity and political governance" (Thonke and Spliid 2012, p. 56).

There are legitimate questions about the relationship between regional economic communities in Africa and their international or global partners (Buzdugan 2013; Carmody 2012). On one hand, the EU-South Africa or EU-SADC can be celebrated in terms of any valuable lessons that it can offer other African countries or regional communities. On the other hand, such a partnership can also undermine the coherence of the regional entity. The EU-SADC Economic Partnership Agreement made it possible for the EU to insert and wield influence in the region, especially when the negotiations on the Partnership Agreement excluded Zambia and Zimbabwe, which were principal players in the early beginnings of the regional group (Buzdugan 2013). The EU-ECOWAS EPA also brings to the fore the issue of regional coherence, especially when the EPA did not provide the necessary framework for development oriented initiatives like economic diversification, market access and technology transfer (Nwoke 2009).

Conclusion and Recommendations

The debate continues on the state and the ability of regional economic communities to advance the development prospects of Africa. The dearth of political leadership that can be leveraged for regional economic development remains a perennial issue. Regional economic communities, without effective political leadership, cannot play a major role in African development. Neo-liberal globalization calls on the state to play a minimal role in the political and economic spheres of the society. At the same time, regional economic communities, which have become the preferred sites for development, are made up of states. Will the broader character of regional economic communities affect how they respond to issues at the national or local context? How will the restructured or minimal state be able to address local development issues, when the source of such issues are, sometimes, located in a regional context and vice versa? While some degree of strategic balancing is called for, the mechanics of that balancing should first begin with a concerted effort at building the capacity of existing state institutions. Capable national state institutions will be able to bring valuable human and cultural capital to the activities of regional economic communities. After all, it is the former institutions that come together to create the latter.

Second, since economic considerations, even at the national level, do not take place in a vacuum, it is important and necessary to situate the work of regional economic communities in a broader political economy framework. The critical issue here is the nature of the state, especially in terms of governance. In effect, the focus should be on the governance implications of regional economic communities both on the African continent and beyond. The fact is that several, if not all, "African governments have at various times claimed that they should be judged on their ability to bring about development. Therefore, development serves as a legitimating norm for many African leaders, but it is the type of governance in play that, in large part, determines the content and direction of development" (Makinda 2012, p. 67).

Regional economic communities show the complexities of inter-state relations. Such relations further depend on internal domestic policies. Since domestic and regional politics might not necessarily coincide or reinforce each other, it is imperative to keep an eye on the dynamics of the relationship in order to better understand the direction of regional economic communities. The external dimensions of politics will also affect the activities of regional economic organizations. Pinfari's (2012) insightful analysis of the role of multiple regional organizations in the North Africa in 2011 (the so-called Arab Spring) political upheaval in Tunisia, Egypt and Libya highlight the significance and shortcomings of external actors in regional issues. While the sudden and intense interest can be touted as a triumph of multilateral governance, the flurry of activities were not coherent because the various entities lacked the legal basis to intervene and their interests were not mutually consistent. The viability of regional economic communities, like other institutions in the development process calls for the necessary and sufficient resources that will enable them to discharge their specific role in the development possibilities of their particular regions and Africa in general. This calls for a better understanding of state–society relations from the national to the regional and the global levels.

References

African Union (AU) and New Partnership for African Development (NEPAD) (2010), *Africa's Capacity Development Strategic Framework*. Midrand: NEPAD Planning and Coordinating Agency.

African Capacity Building Foundation (ACBF) (2013), *Africa Capacity Indicators 2013—Capacity Development of Natural Resources Management.* Harare: Africa Capacity Building Foundation.

——— (2012), *Africa Capacity Indicators 2012—Capacity Development for Agricultural Transformation and Food Security*. Harare: Africa Capacity Building Foundation.

——— (2011), *Africa Capacity Indicators 2011—Capacity Development in Fragile States*. Harare: Africa Capacity Building Foundation.

Adedeji, A. (1979), *The Economic Commission for Africa—Its Origin, Development, Problems and Prospects*. Addis Ababa: UNECA.

Africa Progress Panel Report (2013), *Africa Progress Panel Report, 2012*. Geneva: Africa Progress Panel.

Asante, S. (2000), "Overcoming the Development Problem of the Nation-State in Africa through Regionalism," *South African Journal of Economic Management Studies*, vol. 3, no. 1, pp. 1–18.

Baldwin, R. (1997), "Review of Theoretical Developments on Regional Integration." In A. Oyejide, I. Elbadawi and P. Collier (eds), *Regional Integration and Trade Liberalization in Sub-Saharan Africa, Vol. 1, Framework, Issues and Methodological Perspectives*. Basingstoke: Macmillan, pp. 24–88.

Berry, S.S. (1993), *No Condition is Permanent: The Social Dynamics of Agrarian Change in Sub-Saharan Africa*. Madison, WI: University of Madison Press.

Bischoff, P-H. (2004), "Regionalism and Regional Cooperation in Africa: New Century Challenges and Prospects." In J.M. Mbaku and S.C. Saxena (eds), *Africa at the Crossroads: Between Regionalism and Globalization*. London and Westport, CT: Praeger, pp. 121–46.

Boone, C. (1994), "States and Ruling Classes in Post-Colonial Africa: The Enduring Contradictions of Power." In J.S. Migdal, A. Kohli and V. Shue (eds), *State Power and Social Forces: Domination and Transformation in the Third World*. Cambridge: Cambridge University Press, pp. 108–40.

Bøås, M., Marchand, M.H. and Shaw, T.M. (eds) (2005), *The Political Economy of Regions and Regionalisms*. New York: Palgrave Macmillan.

Bowles, P., Veltmeyer, H., Cornelissen, S., Invernizzi, N. and Tang, K. (eds) (2007), *Regional Perspectives on Globaliation*. New York: Palgrave Macmillan.

Buzdugan, S.R. (2013), "Regionalism from without: External involvement of the EU in regionalism in southern Africa," *Review of International Political Economy*, vol. 20, no. 4, pp. 917–46.

Carmody, P. (2012), "Another BRIC on the Wall? South Africa's Developmental Impact and Contradictory Rise in Africa and Beyond," *European Journal of Development Research*, vol. 24, no. 2, pp. 223–41.

De Melo, J. and Tsikata, Y. (2014), *Regional Integration in Africa: Challenges and Prospects*. WIDER Working Paper, No. 2014/037.

Deme, M. (1995), "The Impact of ECOWAS on Intraregional Trade Flows: An Empirical Investigation," *Review of Black Political Economy*, vol. 23, no. 3, pp. 113–29.

El-Affendi, A. (2009), "The Perils of Regionalism: Regional Integration as a Source of Instability in the Horn of Africa?" *Journal of Intervention and Statebuilding*, vol. 3, no. 1, pp. 1–9.

Faber, G. and Orbie, J. (2003), "EPAs between the EU and Africa: Beyond Free Trade?" In G. Faber and J. Orbie (eds), *Beyond Market Access for Economic Development: EU-Africa Relations in Transition*. London: Routledge, pp. 3–20.

Fatton, R.J., Jr. (1992), *Predatory Rule, State and Society in Africa*. Boulder, CO and London: Lynne Rienner Publishers.

Fiamohe, R., Bamba, I., Seck, P.A. and Diagne, A. (2012), "Regional Bulk Purchase of Imported Rice Initiative by ECOWAS," *OIDA International Journal of Sustainable Development*, vol. 5, no. 11, pp. 79–89.

Franke, B.F. (2007), "Competing Regionalisms in Africa and the Continent's Emerging Security Architecture," *African Studies Quarterly*, vol. 9, no. 3, pp. 31–64.

Gibb, R. (2003), "Globalisation and Africa's Economic Recovery: a Case Study of the European Union-South Africa Post-Apartheid Trading Regime," *Journal of Southern African Studies*, vol. 29, no. 4, pp. 885–901.

Ginkel, H., Court, J.C. and Langenhove, L. (eds) (2003), *Integrating Africa: Perspectives on Regional Integration and Development*. Tokyo: United Nations University Press.

Grant, J.A. and Söderbaum, F. (eds) (2003), *The New Regionalism in Africa*. Aldershot: Ashgate.

Havinden, M. and Meredith, D. (1993), *Colonialism and development: Britain and its tropical colonies, 1850–1960*. New York: Routledge.

Hentz, J.J. (2008), "South Africa and the 'Three Level Game': Globalisation, Regionalism and Domestic Politics," *Commonwealth and Comparative Politics*, vol. 46, no. 4, pp. 490–515.

Heilbroner, R. (1992), *Twenty-First Century Capitalism*. Concord, Ontario: Anansi Press.

Hurt, S.R. (2012), "The EU-SADC Economic Partnership Agreement Negotiations: 'Locking in' the Neoliberal Development model Southern African?" *Third World Quarterly*, vol. 33, no. 3, pp. 495–510.

Jamal, V. (1993), "Surplus extraction and the African agrarian crisis in a historical perspective." In A. Singh, and H. Tabatabai (eds), *Economic Crisis and Third World Agriculture*. Cambridge: Cambridge University Press, pp. 65–90.

Kieh, G.K., Jr. (1992), "Combatants, Patrons, Peacemakers, and the Liberian Civil Conflict," *Studies in Conflict and Terrorism*, vol. 15, no. 2, pp. 125–43.

Kirkpatrick, C. and Watanabe, M. (2005), "Regional Trade in Sub-Saharan Africa: An Analysis of East African Trade Cooperation, 1970–2001," *The Manchester School*, vol. 73, no. 2, pp. 141–64.

Kitipov, J. (2012), "African Integration and Inter-Regionalism: The Regional Economic Communities and their Relationship with the European Union," *Strategic Review for Southern Africa*, vol. 34, no. 1, pp. 21–44.

Mackintosh, M. (1990), "Abstract Markets and Real Needs." In H. Bernstein, B. Crow, M. Mackintosh and C. Martin (eds), *The Food Question: Profit versus People*. London: Earthscan Publications, pp. 43–53.

MacLean, S.J. (2003), "New Regionalism and Conflict in the Democratic Republic of Congo: Networks of Plunder and Networks for Peace." In Grant and Söderbaum (eds), pp. 110–24.

Makinda, S.M. (2012), "Africa's Leadership Malaise and the Crisis of Governance." In K.T. Hanson, G. Kararach and T.M. Shaw (eds), *Rethinking Development Challenges for Public Policy: Insights from Contemporary Africa*. New York: Palgrave Macmillan, pp. 54–82.

Matthews, A. (2003), *Regional Integration and Food Security in Developing Countries*. Rome: Food and Agriculture Organization (Training Materials for Agricultural Planning, No. 45).

Mawuko-Yevugah, L. (2010), "From Exclusion to Inclusion? Examining Participation in the PRSP Process in Ghana." In K.P. Puplampu and W.J. Tettey (eds), *The Public Sphere and the Politics of Survival: Voice, Sustainability and Public Policy in Ghana*. Accra: Woeli Publishing, pp. 67–89.

Mbaku, J.M. and Saxena, S.C. (eds) (2004), *Africa at the Crossroads: Between Regionalism and Globalization*. London: Praeger.

Mitchell, J. (1998), "The Maputo Development Corridor: A Case Study of the SDI Process in Mpumalanga," *Development Southern Africa*, vol. 15, no. 5, pp. 757–69.

Mistry, P.S. (2003), "New Regionalism and Economic Development." In Söderbaum and Shaw (eds), pp. 117–39.

Mortimer, R.A. (1996), "Senegal's Role in Ecomog: The Francophone Dimension in the Liberian Crisis," *Journal of Modern African Studies*, vol. 34, no. 2, pp. 293–306.

Ngwenya, X. and Taylor, I. (2003), "Public-Private Partnership and African Development: The Case of the N4 Toll Road." In Söderbaum and Taylor (eds), pp. 70–82.

Ninsin, K. (1988), "Three Levels of State Reordering: The Structural Aspects." In D. Rothchild and N. Chazan (eds), *The Precarious Balance: State and Society in Africa*. Boulder, CO and London: Westview Press, pp. 265–81.

Nnadozie, E. (2004), "Africa at the Crossroads." In Mbaku and Saxena (eds), pp. 21–47.

Nunn, A. and Price, S. (2004), "Managing Development: EU and African Relations through the Evolution of the Lomė and Cotonou," *Historical Materialism*, vol. 12, no. 4, pp. 203–30.

Nwoke, C.N. (2009), "Towards a Development-Oriented Economic Partnership Agreement between West Africa and the European Union," *African Journal of International Affairs and Development*, vol. 14, nos. 1 and 2, pp. 40–68.

Obi, C.I. (2001), "Reconstructing Africa's Development in the New Millennium Through NEPAD: Can African Leaders Deliver the Goods?" *African Journal of International Affairs*, vol. 4, nos. 1 and 2, pp. 142–75.

Olarreaga, M. and Rocha, M. (2003), "Multilateralism and Regionalism Trade Opportunities for Sub-Saharan Africa," *Africa Spectrum*, vol. 38, no. 1, pp. 99–109.

Peberdy, S. and Crush, J. (2001), "Invisible Trade, Invisible Travellers: The Maputo Corridor Spatial Development Initiative and Informal Cross-Border Trading," *South African Geographical Journal*, vol. 83, no. 2, pp. 115–23.

Phillips, A. (1989), *The Enigma of Colonialism: British Policy in West Africa*. London: James Currey.

Pinfari, M. (2012), "A Changing Mediterranean: Regional Organizations and North Africa during the Arab Spring," *The International Spectator: Italian Journal of International Affairs*, vol. 47, no. 1, pp. 134–50.

Puplampu, K.P. (2014), "The Shifting Boundaries of the African State in Agricultural Institutions and Policies in an Era of Globalization." In E. Shizha and A.A. Abdi (eds), *Indigenous Discourses on Knowledge and Development in Africa*. New York: Routledge, pp. 215–27.

——— (2003), "Globalization of Agriculture: Lessons from Ghana." In M.S. Smith (ed.), *Globalizing Africa*. Trenton, NJ: Africa World Press, pp. 385–96.

Rogerson, C.M. (2000), "Spatial Development Initiatives in Southern Africa: The Maputo Development Corridor," *Journal of Economic and Social Geography*, vol. 92, no. 3, pp. 324–46.

Roodt, M.J. (2008), "The Impact of Regional Integration Initiatives and Investment in a Southern Africa Cross Border Region: The Maputo Development Corridor," *African Sociological Review*, vol. 12, no. 1, pp. 90–104.

Schiff, M. and Winters, A. (2003), *Regional Integration and Development*. Washington, D.C.: Oxford University Press.

Seck, P.A., Tollens, E., Opereis, M.C.S., Diagne, A. and Bamba, I. (2010), "Rising Trends and Variability of Rice Prices: Threats and Opportunities for Sub-Saharan Africa," *Food Policy*, vol. 35, no. 5, pp. 403–11.

Shaw, T.M. (2012), "Africa's Quest for Developmental States: 'renaissance' for whom?" *Third World Quarterly*, vol. 33, no. 5, pp. 837–51.

——— (2000), "New Regionalisms in Africa in the New Millennium: Comparative Perspectives on Renaissance, Realisms and/or Regressions," *New Political Economy*, vol. 5, no. 3, pp. 399–414.

Smith, A. (1976), *An Inquiry into the Nature and Causes of the Wealth of Nations*. 2 volumes. Chicago: University of Chicago Press (first published 1776).

Söderbaum, F. (2004), "Modes of Regional Governance in Africa: Neoliberalism, Sovereignty Boosting, and Shadow Networks," *Global Governance*, vol. 10, no. 4, pp. 419–36.

Söderbaum, F. and Shaw, T.M. (eds) (2003), *Theories of New Regionalism—A Palgrave Reader*. New York: Palgrave Macmillan.

Söderbaum, F. and Taylor, I. (eds) (2003), *Regionalism and Uneven Development in Southern Africa: The Case of the Maputo Development Corridor*. Aldershot: Ashgate.

——— (2001), "Transmission belt for transnational capital or facilitator for development? Problematising the role of the State in the Maputo Development Corridor," *Journal of Modern African Studies*, vol. 39, no. 4, pp. 675–95.

Tavares, R. (2009), "Unloving Brothers: The African Union and the Regional Economic Communities," *Studia Diplomatica*, vol. 62, no. 3, pp. 61–7.

Taylor, I. (2011), "South African 'Imperialism' in a Region Lacking Regionalism: A Critique," *Third World Quarterly*, vol. 32, no. 7, pp. 1233–53.

Thompson, L. (2005), "The Contradictions between Globalization and Development? A Perspective from Southern Africa." In Bowles et al. (eds), pp. 118–34.

Thonke, O. and Spliid, A. (2012), "What to expect from regional integration in Africa," *African Security Review*, vol. 21, no. 1, pp. 42–66.

Wade, R.H. (2003), "What Strategies are viable for Developing Countries Today: The World Trade Organization and the Shrinking of 'Development Space,'" *Review of International Political Economy*, vol. 10, no. 4, pp. 621–44.

Wanasika, I.H, Littrell, J.P. and Dorfman, P. (2011), "Managerial Leadership and Culture in Sub-Saharan Africa," *Journal of World Business*, vol. 46, no. 2, pp. 234–41.

World Bank (2013), *Africa's Pulse: An Analysis of Issues Shaping Africa's Economic Future*. Washington, D.C.: The World Bank (Office of the Chief Economist for the Africa Region), October, vol. 8.

——— (2012), *Africa's Pulse: An Analysis of Issues Shaping Africa's Economic Future*. Washington, D.C.: The World Bank (Office of the Chief Economist for the Africa Region), October, vol. 6.

——— (1999), *Southern Africa—A Regional Strategy*. Washington, D.C.: World Bank Africa Region.

Wright, C. (2012), "The Kimberley Process Certification Scheme: A Model Negotiation." In P. Lujala and S.A. Rustad (eds), *High-Value Natural Resources and Peacebuilding*. London: Earthscan, pp. 181–7.

York, R. (1993), *Regional Integration and Developing Countries*. Paris: OECD.

Chapter 3
"New" Regionalisms in Africa: Approaches, Challenges, Opportunities and Implications

Peter Arthur

Introduction

Throughout the world, governments' policy choices have the ability to improve healthcare, education, and citizens' overall well-being. Among the various approaches to achieving these goals, one model has recently taken center stage: promotion of regional integration, which is an outgrowth of free trade areas, customs unions, common markets and economic unions (Ravenhill 2011). In Africa, regional integration has remained an integral part of development strategy and has underpinned most pan-African development policies for the past 50 years. The appeal of regionalism was, for many policy makers in Africa, geographically intuitive. Colonialism created an extremely fragmented state system that, combined with economic and political marginality, encouraged the formation of a large number of inter-state organizations and institutions (Gibbs 2009). The elite consensus, at least rhetorically, was that most national markets were too narrow and inadequate to sustain sizeable economic operations. Integration would make it possible to promote intra-regional trade with neighbors and to pool resources for investment and efficient industrialization by taking advantage of the economies of scale that large markets provide. Cooperation and integration were therefore seen as important catalysts for utilizing Africa's industrial potential and for accelerating economic growth and the development process (Iheduru 2011).

The growing belief is that regional integration is a critical variable in African countries' efforts to increase domestic and foreign investment, boost security, lower the risk of conflicts, and increase global competitiveness (Ariyo 1992; Uzodike 2009). In addition, it is viewed as a means to overcome Africa's structural problems such as low per capita incomes, small intra-regional trade (Soko 2008); and to serve as a necessary vehicle to accelerate Africa's integration into the new knowledge-driven global economy (Cheru 2002). An increase in the levels of intra-regional trade is expected to lead to the "defragmentation" of African markets, an increase trade in goods and services, stimulation of economic development, and a reduction in poverty in the region (Mulaudzi 2009). The increase on the continent in the creation and strengthening of regional economic communities (RECs) aims to help realize the objective of the 1991 Abuja Treaty, which called for the integration of African economies through the establishment of an African Economic Community (AEC) by 2025 (United Nations Economic Commission for Africa (UNECA)/African Union Commission (AUC)/African Development Bank (AfDB) (UNECA/AUC/AfDB 2012).

The proliferation of regional integration agreements in Africa is therefore unsurprising (Gibbs 2009). Meanwhile, during the last decade, regionalism in sub-Saharan Africa (SSA) has increasingly lost its peculiar pan-African and solidarity motives. Regional integration organizations have broadened their focus to include economic, political, security, and social issues and have sought to involve the private sector and non-state actors in their activities (Hettne 1999; Soko 2008; El-Affendi 2009; Warleigh-Lack and Rosamond 2010; Iheduru 2011; Lorenz and Cornelissen 2011; Kitipov 2012; Perrin 2012; Fanta 2013). According to Shaw, Grant, and Cornelissen (2011), this approach to regionalism, referred to in the literature as "new regionalism" and discussed in detail below, emphasizes the overtly formal as well as informal nature of regions; it also pays attention to state and non-state constituents and processes and covers both established and emerging regional entities. Indeed, new regionalism is a multi-dimensional and comprehensive phenomenon that takes into account a whole range of political, economic, strategic, social, demographic, and ecological interactions within regions (Acharya and Johnston 2007).

Notwithstanding the gains and benefits associated with the existence of multiple RECs on the African continent, the consensus is that regional groupings' performance has been unsatisfactory and has in most instances failed to realize their stated socioeconomic and political goals and objectives (Iheduru 2011; Stephan and Hervey 2008). In this vein, this chapter examines the nature of new regionalism and its impact on African countries.

Specific questions and issues examined are as follows:

- What has been the nature of regionalism and how different is new regionalism from old regionalism?
- What has been the impact and influence of new regionalism on African countries?
- What are the major challenges and barriers that have bedeviled African governments and hindered the efforts to realize viable regional and economic integration?

Finally, what are the necessary conditions and approaches that should be adopted to not only make the underlying principles and values of various RECs and new regionalism a reality but also to bring about socioeconomic and geo-political change to ensure the integration of Africa? While there are a high number of regional integration groupings in Africa, and reference is made to their aims, objectives, and activities, this research draws on a number of more established and formal regionalisms—Economic Community of West African States (ECOWAS),[1] Southern African Development Community (SADC),[2] Southern Africa Customs Union (SACU),[3] and Common Market for Eastern and Southern Africa (COMESA),[4]—to determine the successes and failures of regional integration.

---

1 ECOWAS is a regional group of fifteen West African countries (Benin, Burkina Faso, Cape Verde, Côte d'Ivoire, The Gambia, Ghana, Guinea, Guinea-Bissau, Liberia, Mali, Niger, Nigeria, Senegal, Sierra Leone, and Togo). Founded in 1975, its mission is to promote economic integration in "all fields of economic activity, particularly industry, transport, telecommunications, energy, agriculture, natural resources, commerce, monetary and financial questions, social and cultural matters."

2 The Southern African Development Coordination Conference (SADCC), the predecessor to the Southern African Development Community (SADC), was established in 1980 with the primary objective of reducing the economic dependence of the region on South Africa. The demise of apartheid in South Africa created conditions more conducive to regional political and economic cooperation and culminated in the formation of SADC (Soko 2008). Member states of SADC are Angola, Botswana, the Democratic Republic of the Congo (DRC), Lesotho, Madagascar, Malawi, Mauritius, Mozambique, Namibia, the Seychelles, South Africa, Swaziland, Tanzania, Zambia, and Zimbabwe.

3 The SACU, the world's longest-standing Customs union, was originally set up in 1910 and made up of South Africa and the BLNS states (Botswana, Lesotho, Namibia and Swaziland). However, in October 2002, the five member states of SACU concluded a comprehensive, revised SACU Agreement, which came into force in July 2004. Central to the new SACU is investment liberalization, which has been spurred on by the SACU countries' commitments in the World Trade Organization (WTO) and their participation in bilateral and regional trade agreements. The reforms are designed to strengthen coherence in policy formulation, expand regional trade, and fulfill SACU's desire for deeper integration into the global economy (Soko 2008).

4 COMESA, previously known as the Preferential Trade Area for Eastern and Southern Africa (PTA), was established in 1981 and transformed into a common market in 1992 to promote the development of its member states by creating a single internal market, undertaking regional development projects and programs, and encouraging cooperation in all fields of economic activity. The original members include Burundi, Comoros, Djibouti, Ethiopia, Kenya, Lesotho, Malawi, Mauritius, Mozambique, Rwanda, Somalia, Swaziland, Tanzania, Uganda, Zambia and Zimbabwe (Cheru 2002).

Understanding Regionalism: Theoretical Discussions and Literature Review

Old and New Regionalism

While there is no single explanation that encompasses the origins and development of the regional idea (Fawcett 1995), regionalism became the focus of attention by scholars in the 1950s and 1960s as a result of the emergence of European regional organizations. Farrell (2005) points out that the first wave of studies emerged in the 1950s, coinciding with the appearance of the European Coal and Steel Community (ECSC) and the European Community. Influenced by the increasing globalization of the world, the desire to be able to compete in today's globalized world, and the perceived successes of integration elsewhere, notably in the European Union, countries throughout the world have sought to promote their integration at various levels (Tavares and Tang 2011). From the 1990s, however, the Eurocentricism of the theoretical apparatus of the field being seriously questioned; at the same time, regionalism evolved within a renewed political and economic context (Acharya 2012). In the new regionalism approach, Farrell (2005) notes that regions are regarded not simply as formal organizations (as was the case in studies of the EU), nor as a "given," but rather are understood as constructed and re-constructed in the process of global transformation.

Thus, while historically and traditionally, the focus of research in the field of regionalism was on formal regional organizations, defined as institutionalized cooperation among three or more countries within a geographic space (Jetschke and Lenz 2013), the period from the late 1980s saw a shift toward new regionalism (El-Affendi 2009; Bachinger and Hough 2009; Söderbaum 2004; Mittelman 2000). While the early theoretical debate on regional integration was influenced by the European integration experience (Gómez-Mera 2008), new regionalism as an approach has captured the intellectual interests and imagination of scholars interested in regionalism outside of the perspective and understandings of integration based on studying the European Union (Warleigh-Lack and Rosamond 2010; Acharya 2012). Moreover, older versions of regional integration were deficient inasmuch as they understated power relations, dealt inadequately or not all with production, and failed to offer explanations of structural transformation (Mittelman 2000). According to Perrin (2012, p. 461), factors such as economic globalization, the improvement of information and communication technologies, the growth of individualism, the reduction of the welfare state, and "the demystification of the State with the end of the Cold War," changed the deal by "breaking the territorial frame for both society and politics."

While the meaning of new regionalism may refer to a variety of approaches and theories (Söderbaum and Sbragia 2010), for Lorenz and Cornelissen (2011), underpinning this shift to new regionalism are several interrelated forces: a stronger construction among geographically contiguous states of their collective identity as cohesive regions; greater political intent by leaders to foster consolidation; and the perceived need to strengthen regional blocs as a means to integrate more effectively into the globalizing world economy. Thus, the new regionalism is characterized by two features: it exceeds the framework of the nation-state and projects the regions in a competitive mode (Perrin 2012). Moreover, new regionalism is characterized by increased cross-border trade at a regional level (Kitipov 2012), as well as cross-border coalitions of states, intergovernmental organizations, civil society, business coalitions and multinational firms engaged in the co-construction of an emerging regional governance framework (Iheduru 2011). Thus, in the new century, regional development may be advanced more by corporate strategies than by state directives. These now include branding, franchising, and logistics as well as old-fashioned foreign direct investment (FDI) (Shaw et al. 2011). Furthermore, compared with the old regionalism of the 1960s, today's new regionalism is not only emerging more or less all over the world, but often takes different shapes in different parts of the world. Moreover, whereas the old regionalism was generally specific with regard to objectives and content, and it (often) had a narrow focus on preferential trade arrangements and security alliances, the number, scope and diversity of the new regionalism has grown significantly during the last decade. It has become more inclusive around emerging issues like ecology, energy, land, security and water (Fanta and Shaw 2013; Shaw 2012; Acharya and Johnston 2007). Another characteristic of "new" regionalism is the relevance of bottom-up phenomena (albeit at a nascent stage) as opposed to the primarily top-down approach of the past. It offers a regionally centered model of institutions in which governments, interest groups and individuals from different backgrounds can engage in common institutions, present proposals and liaise directly with policy makers (Kitipov 2012). In short, compared with the old regionalism, which was Eurocentric and narrow, the new regionalism is both global and pluralistic (Söderbaum 2003); has developed in a multipolar context; is multifaceted and more comprehensive; and has worldwide reach that extends to more regions with greater external linkages (Mittelman 2000). Finally, new regionalism at several levels, whether formal or informal, is expected to serve as the catalyst for the renaissance of both Africa and the global South by advancing their capacity to transcend fragility (Fanta and Shaw 2013).

New Regionalisms in Africa: Accomplishments and Achievements

The Role and Contribution of Non-state Actors, Private Investment and Multinational Corporations (MNCs)

Whatever the goals and objectives, it is reasonable to argue that a number of positives could be gleaned from the efforts to promote new regionalism in Africa. First, in Southern Africa for example, new regionalism has contributed to more openness and interdependence both within the region and between the region and the outside world (Shaw 2000). It has generated an innovative range of new regionalisms involving non-state actors such as the Maputo Corridor, the Kgalagadi Transfrontier Peace Park, the Nile Basin Initiative/Dialogue, the International Conference on the Great Lakes Region (ICGLR), and standards for corporate supply chains from conflict areas, especially in the automotive, electronics, and jewelry sectors (Shaw 2012). The Maputo Corridor between Gauteng and Maputo port, a regional project aimed at advancing development in the relatively impoverished Mpumalanga Province of South Africa as well as in southern Mozambique, saw the private sector in the driver's seat but also had city and provincial authorities and the two national regimes positively engaged (Shaw 2000). The corridor has advanced growth in Southern Mozambique as well as the eastern Witwatersrand, reinforcing the cross-border dimensions of the Lesotho highlands water project for electricity and water; the latter was informed by the only global commission (the World Commission on Dams) to be based outside the North—in Cape Town—that also included multinational corporations (MNCs) as well as NGOs and states in its membership (Shaw 2012). These spatial development initiatives (SDIs) show that micro-regions such as the Maputo Development Corridor (MDC) are linked to the larger regional project and thus an important aspect of the promotion of development and new regionalism in the larger SADC region. In particular, it demonstrates that regionalism is not only driven by state elites, who have their own agenda, but also by communities and peoples who utilize the micro-region for a heterogeneous set of reasons and motives (Söderbaum and Taylor 2007).

Another benefit of new regionalism is evident in the fact that South African capital, with its substantial interests in the region, is producing a greater penetration throughout the subcontinent. As a result of economic regionalism, SADC has not only provided an export market for internationally uncompetitive products made in South Africa, but also a huge opportunity for investment by South African-based capital across a whole portfolio of interests, including mining, transport, energy and consumer and financial services (Taylor 2011). Mulaudzi (2009) adds that South African multinational companies, with the support of the South African government, have played an increasingly significant role in promoting foreign direct investment in the region and elsewhere in Africa.

Notable investments made in energy projects include US$1.1 billion in Pande and Temane gas fields in Mozambique by South Africa's fuel corporation (SASOL); US$860 million in the expansion of the Mozal aluminum smelter project by BHP Billiton, the Independent Development Corporation (IDC), and Mitsubishi; and millions spent by mobile communications company Vodacom in Tanzania. In the energy sector, integration was expressed through the Southern African Power Pool, which sought to integrate the power grids of Southern African states and distribute electricity to rural and underserved communities. A major component of the Power Pool is the rehabilitation of Mozambique's Cahora Bassa hydroelectric dam on the Zambezi River, which links power lines between Mozambique, South Africa, and Zimbabwe. The project involved the governments of Mozambique and South Africa and the electricity utility companies of the two countries (South Africa's ESKOM and Mozambique's electricity producer, Hidroelectrica de Cahora Bassa). Moreover, as a result of new regionalism, sub-Saharan Africa in general (and Southern Africa in particular) is now characterized by its own emerging pattern of "hubs-and-spokes" that encompasses airlines (notably Kenya Airways and South African Airways, but also Ethiopian Airlines), cable TV and Internet servers plus websites (MNet and iAfrica), distribution or logistics companies (DHL and Lonrho), financial centers (Johannesburg Stock Exchange), 39 franchises (Spur, Nandos), think tanks, and universities, especially business and economics programs, both private and state-funded (Shaw 2000).

Similarly, ECOWAS is now palpably characterized by a vast network of informal flows, which may yet be augmented by large-scale official schemes, such as the proposed $500 million West African Gas Pipeline agreed in mid-1999 with Chevron and Shell to transport natural gas from their Nigerian wells to Ghana through Benin and Togo (Shaw 2000). Moreover, as a result of recent financial liberalization and foreign exchange regime reforms, as well as private action, many West African peoples can now access their funds anywhere in the sub-region because of the availability of automated teller machines (ATMs) in all the major commercial centers issued by regional banks with government approval. In addition to a variety of multiple-currency card schemes, Ecobank[5] and other regional bank ATM and debit card-holders in particular are now able to travel across the region with only one card and still access local currencies in 14 countries. In addition, public-private partnerships in transport and telecommunications links have transformed West Africa into the world's fastest growth market for cellular telephony. From a colonial legacy of stronger economic ties to the developed world than to the region, there has been a

5 ECOBANK, which was established by ECOWAS in 1985, is now a full-service regional banking institution with 57 branches and offices in 12 countries across West Africa (Bensah 2012).

conscious attempt by ECOWAS and its member states to deploy information technology and telecommunications infrastructure as a critical component of other regional development strategies (Iheduru 2011, p. 226).

Delivering Regional Security

In view of the scale and resilience of regional conflict, regional bodies have made several attempts to promote security and peacebuilding on the African continent. These security and peacebuilding efforts increasingly involve a range of actors in a heterogeneous coalition, from international non-governmental organizations (INGOs) to multinational corporations (MNCs) (Shaw 2012). Since 2002, the African Union (AU), for example, has developed the African Peace and Security Architecture (APSA) for the prevention, management, and resolution of conflicts in the Africa region. The APSA includes the AU Peace and Security Council, African Peace Fund, Panel of the Wise, Continental Early Warning System (CEWS), and African Standby Force (ASF), which will be fully operational by 2015 (Akuffo 2013). The AU has played significant roles in resorting to the use of force to protect civilians in various conflict zones on the continent. Since 2003, when the AU entered into its operational phase, it has deployed missions to Burundi (AMIB), Sudan/Darfur (AMIS), Somalia (AMISOM), and Comoros (AMISEC) (Vines 2013). The AU has taken a significant step by shifting away from the Organization of African Unity's sacrosanct respect for sovereignty, which prevented it from effectively intervening in times of internal crises in member states. By the principle of non-indifference, the AU has arrogated the authority to intervene and not cower behind the cloak of sovereignty (Aning and Salihu 2011). ECOWAS also adopted the Protocol on the Mechanism for Conflict Prevention, Management, Resolution, Peacekeeping, and Security in 1999. The protocol called for the establishment of an ECOWAS Mediation and Security Council (MSC) to authorize all forms of intervention, including military in the sub-region. It provided a clear vision, mandate, and guidance for the conduct of peace support operations including complex and multidimensional missions. Paragraph 46, specifically, provided for military intervention by ECOWAS in the event of crises in a member state that threatened to trigger a humanitarian disaster and posed a serious threat to peace and security in the sub-region (Aning and Salihu 2011). In addition, ECOWAS has established the ECOWAS Conflict Prevention Framework (ECPF), which it believes can contribute to creating an environment that would ensure a more peaceful way of settling political and economic disputes (Bah and Aning 2009).

New Regionalisms in Africa: Challenges and Problems

Poor Infrastructure and Low Intra-regional Trade

Despite the establishment of various free trade areas (FTAs) in Africa, intra-regional trade is low. As UNCTAD (2013) points out, by most accounts, African countries have not made significant progress in boosting regional trade. Over the period from 2007 to 2011, the average share of intra-African exports in total merchandise exports in Africa was 11 percent compared with 50 percent in developing Asia, 21 percent in Latin America and the Caribbean, and 70 percent in Europe. Indeed, the direction of trade in sub-Saharan Africa has changed very little since independence, oriented largely to markets of former colonial powers (Cheru 2002). Colonial structural arrangements such as the transport and communications infrastructure and modes of resource extraction were fashioned to serve the direct interests of the colonial metropoles as well as facilitate trade with Europe rather than intra-regional trade (Uzodike 2009). For example, in the SADC area, intraregional trade was 13–15 percent of total exports and 15–21 percent of total imports in the time period between 2000 and 2007 (Krapohl and Muntschick 2009). Meanwhile, more recently, the BRICS countries (Brazil, Russia, India, China, and South Africa) have become Africa's largest trading partners, with trade expected to reach more than US$500 billion by 2015, with 60 percent from China. Trade between the BRICS and Africa rose to as much as US$340 billion in 2012—10 times higher than the value recorded in 2002. For example, trade volume between China and Africa increased from US$10 billion in 2000 to US$190 billion in 2012. In addition, the BRICS are becoming significant investors in Africa, especially in the manufacturing and service sectors. In 2010, for example, the BRICS' share in FDI inward stock and FDI inflows to Africa reached 14 percent and 25 percent, respectively (Ncube 2013).

According to the UNCTAD (2013), one of the reasons for the weak regional trade performance in Africa is that the approach to regional integration on the continent has so far focused more on the elimination of trade barriers than on the development of the productive capacities necessary for trade. While the elimination of trade barriers is certainly important, it will not have the desired effect if it is not complemented by policy measures to boost supply capacities. Similarly, for Mutambara (2009), the lack of an adequate and reliable road and rail network and other constraints in the transport and communications systems within the SADC region, which generally explains the low intra-regional trade, poses significant non-tariff barriers. This is because road and rail transport are the main means of handling the bulk of imports and exports in the various countries, thus providing a vital transport link for the countries' diverse import and export commodities. Equally significant is the fact that most of the SADC countries are landlocked, making road and rail networks very important in linking countries to principal ports in South Africa, Mozambique, Angola, and Namibia. The national road and rail systems also provide links to all major centers in each country as well as access to remote districts, thus serving as strategic links to these areas, some of which have valuable resources that need to be harnessed. Similarly, there are serious deficits in both the supply and distribution of energy in the West African sub-region and in power supply, which is inadequate, expensive, and unreliable (Chambers, Foresti, and Harris 2012). It is therefore unsurprising that over the past two or three decades, successive Organization of African Union (OAU) and AU summits have identified poor transport and communications infrastructure; deficient maintenance of road networks; and the inflexibility, unreliability, and inefficiency of rail transport, power supply, and water as key factors holding back inter-REC and intra-African trade (UNECA/AUC/AfDB 2012).

The problem of poor and infrastructure deficit in Africa is compounded by the lack of tradable goods of international quality within regional groups. Thus, although there has been some increase in intra-regional trade in SADC, a reflection of the reintegration of post-apartheid South Africa into the regional economy, simple statistics of this type do not tell us whether the regional trade agreement itself has been a significant influence on trade among the member economies (Ravenhill 2011). Out of the 19 member states, only 12 treat COMESA as their main regional trading bloc. Zambia, Zimbabwe, Mauritius, Malawi, and Swaziland, even though members of COMESA, trade mainly with SADC member states (Dirar 2010). In SADC, the region's stagnant trade pattern is explained by three challenges: an underdeveloped and non-diversified industrial manufacturing base in most SADC countries; inadequate infrastructure to support trade in goods; and non-tariff barriers (NTBs) that inhibit market access (Vickers 2011). Moreover, from an economic perspective, negotiations for the liberalization of regional trade have helped to unmask the analytical limits of abstract concepts like "free trade" and "trade liberalization" in the Southern African context. Far from being "free," the trade regime among the SADC countries is tightly planned politically. Moreover, the focus on trade liberalization is proving unequal to the task of promoting equitable and sustainable development in the region; on the contrary, it seems conducive to a further polarization of political and economic relations among SADC member states (Pallotti 2004). Finally, the success of regional economic integration often depends on the emergence of strong and diversified economies and presupposes economic complementarity and a strong political commitment that would make it possible to overcome the inevitable problems of uneven distribution of the benefits and costs. However, the weakness, slow growth and competitive nature of underdeveloped economies, as found in many African countries, militates against economic cooperation, as the benefits are meager, slow to materialize and unevenly distributed, while the costs have to be paid up front (El-Affendi 2009).

Regional Hegemons

The effort to strengthen intra-African trade is further complicated by the existence of regional hegemons in the various communities and organizations. With SADC, South Africa is the de facto, if reluctant, hegemon: the country accounts for approximately 60 percent of all intra-SADC trade and approximately 70 percent of its GDP, while South African firms dominate the region's services sectors (Vickers 2011). In addition, South Africa's economic predominance is underscored by the fact that the country produces approximately 80 percent of Southern Africa's gross domestic product (Soko 2008). South Africa's overwhelming economic dominance of the SADC region was a key reason why Zimbabwe opted to negotiate economic partnership agreements (EPAs) under the Eastern and Southern Africa configuration created by COMESA. COMESA's attraction to Zimbabwe derived partly from Harare's calculation that it had a competitive advantage over its COMESA regional partners that it did not have within the SADC (Soko 2008). Finally, according to Lorenz and Cornelissen (2012), as a first step toward economic integration, a trade protocol was signed by the Heads of State in 1996, by which it was agreed to establish a free trade area. Many member states have, however, been slow to ratify the protocol and even slower to reduce import tariffs. By 2008, the self-imposed deadline for the attainment of the FTA, only the richer states in the region (South Africa, Botswana, Namibia and Mauritius) had been able to comply (more or less) with the required tariff reduction targets. It is in this vein that Mulaudzi (2009) argues that the rhetoric of new regionalism and development through cooperation needs to be treated with caution. Perceived national self-interest is still the driving force and determinant of state behavior. For example, South Africa facilitated the relocation of the two motor assembly plants through a combination of tariff barriers that made it almost impossible for the smaller operations to export their cars to South Africa.

Furthermore, although the economic reforms undertaken by SACU countries since 1998 are commendable, some concerns about the SACU trade regime persist. The lack of harmonization within SACU of non-tariff barriers (such as quantitative restrictions, Customs procedures, standards and technical regulations, sanitary and phytosanitary measures, competition policy, and internal taxes) distorts trade flows and undermines the efficacy of the common external tariff (CET). It remains unclear how SACU intends to compensate for a possible decrease of its common revenue pool as a consequence of a decline in Customs and excise revenue. In addition, within SACU, concerns exist about South Africa's commitment to the principle of collective decision-making. This follows the country's decision late in 2006 to impose quotas on certain categories of Chinese clothing imports entering the South African market (Soko 2008). Also, the SACU Agreement exhorts SACU countries to conduct future trade relations and negotiations with third parties as a single entity. It states that no SACU member state is authorized to undertake negotiations with or enter into new preferential trade agreements with third parties or alter existing agreements without the approval of other member states (Soko 2008). Despite the existence of this agreement, South Africa concluded a bilateral free trade arrangement with the EU in 1999 that provided for a reciprocal process of removing tariffs on bilateral trade, governed by the rules of the WTO on free trade agreements. The South Africa-EU agreement did not sit well with many SADC/COMESA governments, who are suspicious of South Africa's hegemonic impulse (Cheru 2002). More importantly, this agreement means that it is binding on other members of COMESA/SADC and thus clearly demonstrates that governments' loyalties are to themselves, so they therefore are often unable to put the interest of the entire region above that of individual national interest (Cheru 2002).

Within ECOWAS, similar concerns are evident in the efforts to promote regional integration. First, there is the overwhelming Nigerian identity of cross-border banks whose acquisition of national banks in neighboring countries elicits xenophobic reactions against a Nigerian "invasion" despite unprecedented innovations in banking and other businesses (Iheduru 2012). In addition, ECOWAS' military dependency on Nigeria means that it will be unlikely to be able to address the insurgencies and unrest in Nigeria itself, which represent a significant share of the region's conflicts (Chambers et al. 2012). Furthermore, although Nigeria is a signatory to the ECOWAS Trade Liberalization Scheme (TLS), which stipulates that member countries are free to export and import items into each other's country devoid of quotas or any forms of restriction, Nigeria is developing a penchant for banning goods such as rice, poultry, and textiles from entering its markets. This policy by Nigeria creates unnecessary tension and contravenes the very aims of the TLS: to promote and facilitate intra-ECOWAS trade. Moreover, it contributes to an atmosphere conducive to retaliatory measures instead of cooperation (Bensah 2012).

Lack of Political Will

The foregoing challenges to regional integration are exacerbated by the fact that many African leaders are unwilling or reluctant to surrender some element of sovereignty to common institutions in shaping the direction of regionalism (Mulaudzi 2009). For example, Uzodike (2009) regards the creation of a monetary union as implying that member states' ability to initiate and implement independent monetary policy would be curtailed. However, the record of regional integration in Africa shows that most countries are reluctant to cede control over fiscal and monetary issues to RECs. Long-term regional goals have remained paper objectives because African governments have been unwilling to subordinate their national decision-making to the dictates of RECs, as often demonstrated by little or no national support for RECs. Also, many protocols have been signed but remain unimplemented, due to the absence of effective sanctions against defaulting member states and weak enforcement and implementation capacity. In addition, lack of political will and commitment has been reflected in the failure to meet target dates set for attaining objectives (Sako 2006). Ambitious agendas are also severely constrained by the uneven ability or willingness of member states and their rulers to dissociate "public" policies from private interests (Bach 2012). As Acharya and Johnston (2007, p. 262) argue, the new regionalism literature may have underestimated the resilience of the state, as "regional institutions in the developing world are more likely to possess design features that preserve state sovereignty than to challenge it." Also, the multidimensional connections between globalization and regionalism often increase the complexity of regional dynamics and hence the involvement of non-state actors, including business groups, labor movements, and other civil society movements (Gómez-Mera 2008).

Promoting New Regionalism in Africa: Recommendations and the Way Forward

Increasing Intra-regional Economic Activities

The foregoing has demonstrated not only the efforts to promote regionalism and regional integration on the African continent but also some of the constraints and challenges that have bedeviled these efforts. Indeed, Fanta (2013) notes that analysts tend to point out that regional organizations in Africa have failed most notably because of their inability to establish themselves as strong institutions that ensure the application of their regional policies. Regional organizations have thus been criticized for structural weakness that hinders their capacity to contribute to the socioeconomic development of the African continent. It is in this regard that the subsequent discussions look at some of the measures and policies that should be adopted to ensure that the goals and objectives of regional integration in Africa become a reality.

First, to overcome the various challenges and justify the optimism surrounding new regionalism in Africa, there is a need to ensure that member states make some policy choices with regard to increasing intra-regional economic activities. Undoubtedly, the rise of the BRICS countries' interest in Africa adds many positive dimensions to African countries' economies. The BRICS powers, as Carmody (2012) points out, provide alternative sources of trade, investment, infrastructure financing, loans, aid, and arms from traditional western "partners." Chinese and Indian demand for natural resources has dramatically increased their prices to the benefit of many African economies, as these are often their primary exports. Chinese infrastructure for resource swaps, where new roads and railways are paid for in copper, for example, is less susceptible to corruption. Also, the fact that the BRICS are less prescriptive about economic policy has opened up space for policy experimentation and learning based on African rather than western conditions (Carmody 2012). Despite their contributions, the spectacular increase of private investment flows and the entry of new capital from China, India, South Africa, and other emerging economies could undermine the pan-African ideals of state-centric and private-sector-led regional integration (Iheduru 2011). Critics contend that BRICS countries are "neo-colonizers" and "neo-imperialists" who are exploiting the natural resources of African countries without adequately contributing to job creation and badly needed industrialization on the continent. The increasing land grab through lease and purchase of African lands by BRICS companies, the lack of labor and human rights, the blatant disregard for the environment, as well as investors' rhetoric of "South–South cooperation" and "win-win" globalization disguises huge and deepening power inequalities between African countries and BRICS (Carmody 2012), and in particular China.

Since trade is central to a successful regional cooperation and integration process, a means by which the goals of new regionalism could be realized in Africa is for member countries of regional organizations to take more initiatives to trade among themselves rather than with more advanced economies (Sako 2006). Defragmenting African markets by means of improving cross-border trade, removing a range of non-tariff barriers to trade, boosting local entrepreneurship and supply capacity, reforming regulations and immigration rules, and creating unified economic specification through harmonization of Customs, trade and commercial documents and operational procedures within regional groups would thus be a step in the right direction. Similarly, as UNCTAD (2013) notes, to reap developmental gains from intra-African trade and regional integration, African countries will need to place building productive capacities and domestic entrepreneurship at the heart of the policy agenda for boosting international trade. In addition, priorities include liberalization of trade among member states, introduction of a simplified trade regime, and harmonization of African countries' regional protocols with national laws. Furthermore, because of the glaring disparities in economic weight among members of some groupings have the potential to increase economic polarization, it is important that new policy arrangements are put in place to address these concerns. These new policies could take the form of making compensation arrangements, devising guaranteed payments systems, and allowing economically vulnerable and weaker members more time to liberalize their economies.

Moreover, as Dent (2008) argues, governments and other actors involved in new regionalism should demonstrate an increasingly strong interest in promoting regionally integrated markets that enable all countries to benefit by generating opportunities for region-wide capture of economies of scale. The creation of more coherent regional economic spaces would be conducive to the operation of more efficient internationalized and transnationalized business activities. As a real political commitment on the part of national governments is essential if greater regional integration is to be achieved (Chambers et al. 2012), it is a welcome development that Article 54 of the ECOWAS Revised Treaty of 1993, for instance, requires member states and Community institutions to facilitate the emergence of a regional policy network in which the private sector is guaranteed wider participation. In 2007, the ECOWAS Commission created a Private Sector Department charged with developing strategies to mobilize the private sector to promote greater efficiency of business operations through consultation and coordination. These policy networks, drawn from exporters and local industrialists, along with domestic financial capital would help steer the region away from an ECOWAS of states to an ECOWAS of people (Iheduru 2011). Moreover, in SACU, a dedicated formula pools and allocates tariff income among the member states, and a proportionate share goes to South Africa's neighbors. Indeed, the SACU has proven to be a vital source of revenue for states such as Lesotho and Swaziland, which receive between two-thirds and three-quarters of their annual revenue from the SACU (Lorenz and Cornelissen 2011). All these measures have the potential to promote regionalism, improve the socioeconomic situations of many African countries, and, in turn, address issues pertaining to poverty and inequality both within and among participating countries.

Building and Deepening Infrastructure Linkage

Deepening regional integration in Africa requires building proper and integrated infrastructure; fast-tracking the infrastructure to link countries more effectively; and developing the political will to drive regional infrastructural projects. Access to good roads, bridges, railways, airline service, public transit and other infrastructure would boost tourism and foster job creation; it is also vital to the economic success and quality of life for people in Africa. Therefore, it is important that RECs have comprehensive policy and frameworks on the development of regional inter-REC cross-border transport, information communication technology (ICT) connections, water and transport development, and power supply coordination (UNECA/AUC/AfDB 2012). Thus, there has been improved connection of traffic and passenger corridors in cities such as Mopti, Mail and Ouahigouya, Burkina Faso. African states have also made strides in promoting regional electricity integration and cooperation through grid interconnections and power pooling in order to deal with the unevenly distributed energy resources, to lower electricity prices, and scale out access by encouraging trade and investment in electricity (ACBF 2013).

It is also a welcome development that through the NEPAD-Infrastructure Project Preparation Facility (IPFF), the Dakar–N'djamena–Djibouti Corridor (Trans-Sahelian Highways) as well as Djibouti–Libreville transport corridors, which would boost economic integration in the region, is taking place. In a similar vein, SADC has a very ambitious infrastructure program: its target is to raise US$100 billion to finance its projects by 2015. Investment in energy generation alone is estimated to require US$47 billion over the next five years, as well as up to US$26 billion in surface transport, US$ 18 billion in ports and inland waterways, and US$9 billion in ICT, postal systems, meteorology, and water (UNECA/AUC/AfDB 2012). Finally, Chambers et al. (2012) argue that functioning railway networks would do much to rectify the under-provision of transport infrastructure and improve the ground transport network within ECOWAS. The existence of rail connections from seaports would enable the use of dry ports that could operate as centers for trans-shipment of cargo to inland destinations and could be used to reduce irregular Customs activity. Thus, it is a positive development that the West African region not only has adopted a comprehensive, coordinated strategy for transport and infrastructure, but also has undertaken several initiatives aimed at improving transport for landlocked countries and conforming to the sub-Saharan Africa Transport Program (UNECA/AUC/AfDB 2012).

Promoting Regional Security

Because the success of regional integration often depends on the existence of peace and security, the continued wars, violence, and other forms of insecurity that have characterized a number of African regions do not augur well for new regionalism. In particular, emerging global threats such as international terrorism, human trafficking, trafficking of small-arms and light weapons, trans-border crime and trade in narcotics, cross-border diseases, and piracy, pose serious challenges to stability and economic prosperity. These threats hinder integration and development by curtailing economic activities, destroying infrastructure, and constituting a serious barrier to the flow of trade and investment (Sako 2006). For example, the rise of militant Islamist groups such as Boka Haram in Nigeria and Al-Shabbab in Somalia pose significant threats to new regionalism. It is therefore a healthy sign that various regional groups have made security in their geographical areas a core aspect of their regional integration efforts. For instance, the SADC Standby Force (SADCBRIG) was launched in 2007 by SADC to unite in the efforts toward collective self-defense and security and the preservation of peace and stability. The SADC Standby Force was expected to perform observations and monitoring missions, peace support missions, and interventions for peace and security restoration in grave circumstances at the request of a member state. The force will also be used for preventive deployment in order to prevent a conflict from escalating; an ongoing violent conflict from spreading to neighboring areas or states; and the resurgence of violence after parties to a conflict have reached an agreement (Madakufamba 2007).

Similarly, West African states have responded to various trans-sovereign security threats by adopting national legislation along with regional and international protocols and conventions. Specifically, ECOWAS Foreign Affairs Ministers adopted a Political Declaration and Action Plan Against Human Trafficking in December 2001 in Senegal, by which they committed their respective governments to ratifying and fully implementing relevant international instruments that strengthen laws against human trafficking and protect trafficked victims, especially women and children. Early in 2002 in Libreville, officials from West and Central African countries agreed to a common Platform of Action to enact laws designed to protect child workers, improve the system of custody for child victims of trafficking, strengthen cooperation among governments, and establish transit and reception centers for repatriated children (Iheduru 2011, p. 219). The new regionalism in West Africa has also seen the building of a network of national human rights and economic empowerment committees and initiatives with international partners (for example, the US$15 million UN Peace Building Fund set aside for a broad range of livelihood-boosting projects) to address respect for human rights and post-conflict reconstruction rehabilitation. Important principles, such as zero tolerance for illegal changes of governance, strengthening the capacity of parliaments, civil control over armed forces, autonomy for political parties, and promotion and protection of human rights are some of the norms of the new "democratic clause" on which ECOWAS election monitoring activities are based (Iheduru 2011).

Conclusion

The study of regionalism has become an increasingly significant aspect not only of political science and development-related courses and disciplines, but also of broader efforts to promote socioeconomic development. In Africa, aside from the substantive progress made by the various established and formal regionalisms, in the last two decades, various state and non-state actors have played dominant roles in promoting the various aspects involved in new regionalism. In addition to promoting informal flows, more openness and interdependence both within regions and between regions, new regionalism in Africa has led to increased economic growth, the establishment of regional partnership projects with the private sector, and peacebuilding initiatives (Shaw 2000, 2012).

Notwithstanding these successes and benefits, African countries face a number of challenges and constraints in their quest to effectively promote the tenets of new regionalism. How can one explain these constraints and challenges? While several answers are self-evident, a number of explanations stand out. The first relates to the hegemonic position of some member states in various regional blocs. There is, for example, the overwhelming political and economic dominance and advantages enjoyed by South Africa and Nigeria in SADC and ECOWAS respectively, relative to other countries. Beyond the issues surrounding the power and hegemony of some countries, one can also argue that new regionalism in Africa suffers from problems relating to reluctance to cede some sovereignty, low intra-African trade, and poor infrastructure. In addition, regional integration has yielded limited results due to inward-looking and protectionist macroeconomic environments, budgetary constraints and non-payment of dues by members, competition among member countries for investment opportunities, and weak institutional capacity (Iheduru 2011). These are compounded by the lack of political will to implement policies, and other security-related challenges.

It is in this regard that adopting the right measures and policies would be crucial to ensuring that the goals of "new regionalisms" in Africa become a reality. In particular, deepening regional integration in Africa requires a range of critical interventions such as promoting regional security, harmonizing RECs membership and policies, increasing intra-regional trade and other economic activities, building proper infrastructure to link countries more effectively, and developing the political will to drive and implement regional projects and policies. In sum, as Taylor (2011) argues, successful regionalism is most likely if and when the demand from non-state economic actors seeking the commercial gains that a regional market may offer is matched by the supply of institutional support from political elites who anticipate benefits for themselves and their constituencies from consequent regional cooperation.

References

African Capacity Building Foundation (ACBF). Call for Papers: African Capacity Indicators Report (ACIR 2014). Available at: http://www.acbfpact.org/images/docs/procurement/FINALACIR2014CallforPapers_En.pdf (accessed August 5, 2013).

Acharya, A. (2012), "Comparative regionalism: A field whose time has come?" *The International Spectator: Italian Journal of International Affairs* 47, no. 1: 3–15.

Acharya, A. and Johnston, A. (ed) (2007), *Crafting Cooperation: Regional International Institutions in Comparative Perspective*. Cambridge: Cambridge University Press.

Akuffo, E.A. (2013), "Canada's Engagement with African Regional Peace and Security Architecture." In *Canada Among Nations 2013: Canada-Africa Relations, Looking Back, Looking Ahead*, edited by R. Medhora and Y. Samy. London: The Centre for International Governance Innovation and the Norman Paterson School of International Affairs at Carleton University.

Aning, K. and Salihu, N. (2011), "Accountability for Intervention: Negotiating Civilian Protection Dilemmas with Respect to Economic Community of West African States and African Union Interventions." *African Security* 4: 81–99.

Ariyo, A. (1992), "Tariff harmonization, government revenue and economic integration within ECOWAS: Some reflections." *Development Policy Review* 10: 155–174.

Bachinger, K. and Hough, J. (2009), "New regionalism in Africa: Waves of Integration." *Africa Insight* 39, no. 2: 43–59.

Bach, D. (2012). "From new regionalism to new regions: The pitfalls of thick regionalism in Africa." Available at: http://www.tralac.org/2012/02/22/from-new-regionalism-to-new-regions-the-pitfalls-of-thick-regionalism-in-africa/ (accessed October 6, 2013).

Bah, S.A. and Aning, K. (2009), *ECOWAS and Conflict Prevention in West Africa: Confronting the Triple Threats*. New York: Centre on International Cooperation.

Bensah, E. (2012), "Thirty Years of ECOWAS: An Appraisal." Available at: http://www.modernghana.com/news/391065/1/from-the-archives-thirty-years-of-ecowas-an-apprai.html (accessed September 22, 2013).

Carmody, P. (2013), "Brics in Africa: prizes and pitfalls of building a new global order: Brics' rhetoric of 'win-win' globalization masks huge and deepening power inequalities in new scramble for Africa." *The Guardian* (September 12). Available at: http://www.theguardian.com/global-development/2013/sep/12/brics-africa-global-order (accessed November 9, 2013).

Chambers, V., Foresti, M. and Harris, D. (2012), *Final Report: Political Economy of Regionalism in West Africa: Scoping study and prioritisation*. London: Overseas Development Institute. Available at: http://www.odi.org.uk/sites/odi.org.uk/files/odi-assets/publications-opinion-files/7720.pdf (accessed September 24, 2013).

Cheru, F. (2002), *African Renaissance: Roadmaps to the Challenges of Globalization*. London: Zed Books.

Dent, C.M. (2008), "The Asian Development Bank and Developmental Regionalism in East Asia," *Third World Quarterly* 29, no. 4: 767–86.

Dirar, L. (2010), "Common Market for Eastern and Southern African Countries: Multiplicity of Membership Issue and Choices," *African Journal of Comparative and International Law* 18, no. 2: 217–32.

El-Affendi, A. (2009), "The Perils of Regionalism: Regional Integration as a Source of Instability in the Horn of Africa?" *Journal of Intervention and Statebuilding* 3, no. 1: 1–19.

Fanta, E. (2013), "Understanding Regional Integration Policies in Africa." In E. Fanta, T. Shaw and V. Tang (eds), *Comparative Regionalisms for Development in the 21st Century: Insights from the Global South*, 41–55. Farnham: Ashgate.

Fanta, E. and Shaw, T. (2013), "Introduction: Comparative Regionalisms for Development in the 21st Century: Insights from the Global South." In E. Fanta, T. Shaw and V. Tang (eds), *Comparative Regionalisms for Development in the 21st Century: Insights from the Global South*, 1–17. Farnham: Ashgate.

Farrell, M. (2005), "The Global Politics of Regionalism: An Introduction." In M. Farrell, B. Hettne and L. van Langenhove (eds), *Global Politics of Regionalism: Theory and Practice*, 1–20. London and Ann Arbor: Pluto Press.

Fawcett, L. (1995), "Regionalism in Historical Perspective." In Louise Fawcett and Andrew Hurrell (eds), *Regionalism in World Politics*, 9–36. Oxford: Oxford University Press.

Fawn, R. (2009), "Regions' and their study: wherefrom, what for and where to?" *Review of International Studies* 35, Special Issue 1: 5–34.

Gibb, R. (2009), "Regional integration and Africa's Development and Africa's Development Trajectory: meta-theories, expectations and reality," *Third World Quarterly* 30, no. 4: 701–21.

Gómez-Mera, L. (2008), "How 'new' is the 'New Regionalism' in the Americas? The case of MERCOSUR," *Journal of international relations and development* 11, no. 3: 279–308.

Hettne, B. (2005), "Beyond the new regionalism," *New Political Economy* 10, no. 4: 543–71.

Iheduru, O.C. (2011), "The 'new' ECOWAS: implications for the study of regional integration." In T. Shaw, J.A. Grant, and S. Cornelissen (eds), *Ashgate Research Companion to Regionalisms*, 213–39. Farnham: Ashgate.

Jetschke, A. and Lenz, T. (2013), "Does Regionalism Diffuse? A New Research Agenda for the Study of Regional Organizations," *Journal of European Public Policy* 20, no. 4: 626–37.

Kitipov, J. (2012), "African Integration and Inter-Regionalism: The Regional Economic Communities and Their Relationship with the European Union," *Strategic Review for Southern Africa* 34, no. 1: 21–44.

Krapohl, S. and Muntschick, J. (2009), "Two Logics of Regionalism: The Importance of Interdependence and External Support for Regional Integration in Southern Africa." In J.M. Kaunda and F. Zizhou (eds), *Furthering Southern African Integration*, 3–17. Proceedings of the 2008 Foprisa Annual Conference. Gaborone: Botswana Institute for Development Policy Analysis.

Lorenz, U. and Cornelissen, S. (2011), "Regional organization, regional arena: The SADC in Southern Africa." In T. Shaw, J.A. Grant, and S. Cornelissen (eds), *Ashgate Research Companion to Regionalisms*, 241–54. Farnham: Ashgate.

Madakufamba, M. (2007), "SADC Brigade anchors regional peace support operations," *The Southern African Development Community Today* 10, no. 3, October. Available at: http://www.sardc.net/editorial/sadctoday/view.asp?vol=564&pubno=v10n3 (accessed September 27, 2013).

Mittelman, J. (2000), *The Globalization Syndrome: Transformation and Resistance.* Princeton: Princeton University Press.

Mulaudzi, C. (2009). "New regionalism in Southern Africa: Between South African hegemony and globalization," *Lusotopie* 16, no. 1: 47–66.

Mutambara, T.E. (2009), "Transport challenges within the Southern African Development Community and their implications for economic integration and development," *Journal of Contemporary African Studies* 27, no. 4: 501–25.

Ncube, M. (2013), "Africa and the BRICS: a Win-Win Partnership?" African Development Bank Group website. Available at: http://www.afdb.org/en/blogs/afdb-championing-inclusive-growth-across-africa/post/africa-and-the-brics-a-win-win-partnership-12098/ (accessed November 9, 2013).

Pallotti, A. (2004), "SADC: A Development Community without a Development Policy?" *Review of African Political Economy* 101, no. 31: 513–31.

Perrin, T. (2012), "New Regionalism and Cultural Policies: Distinctive and Distinguishing Strategies, from Local to Global," *Journal of Contemporary European Studies* 20, no. 4: 459–75.

Ravenhill, J. (2011), "Regionalism." In John Ravenhill (ed.), *Global Political Economy*, third edition, 173–212. New York: Oxford University Press.

Sako, S. (2006), "Challenges Facing Africa's Regional Economic Communities in Capacity Building." ACBF Occasional Paper No. 5. Available at: http://www.sarpn.org/documents/d0002737/RECs_Occasional_Paper5_ACBF_2006.pdf (accessed August 3, 2013).

Shaw, T. (2012), "Africa's quest for Developmental state: renaissance for whom?" *Third World Quarterly* 33, no. 5: 837–51.

——— (2000), "New Regionalisms in Africa in the New Millennium: Comparative Perspectives on Renaissance, Realisms and/or Regressions," *New Political Economy* 5, no. 3: 399–414.

Shaw, T., Grant, J.A. and Cornelissen, S. (2011), "Introduction and Overview: the Study of New Regionalisms at the Start of the Second Decade in the Twenty-First Century." In T. Shaw, J.A. Grant, and S. Cornelissen (eds), *Ashgate Research Companion to Regionalisms*, 3–30. Farnham: Ashgate.

Söderbaum, F. (2005), "The International Political Economy of Regionalism." In N. Phillips (ed.), *Globalizing International Political Economy*, 221–45. London: Palgrave Macmillan.

——— (2004), *The Political Economy of Regionalism: The Case of Southern Africa.* London: Palgrave Macmillan.

——— (2003), "Introduction: Theories of New Regionalism." In F. Söderbaum and T. Shaw (eds), *Theories of New Regionalism: A Palgrave Reader.* Basingstoke: Palgrave.

Söderbaum, F. and Taylor, I. (2007), "Micro-regionalism in Africa: Competing Region-building in the Maputo Development Corridor." UNU-CRIS Working Paper W-2007/6. Brugge: United Nations University Institute-Comparative Regional integration Studies. Available at: http://www.cris.unu.edu/fileadmin/workingpapers/20070504105447.W-2007–6.pdf (accessed November 11, 2013).

Söderbaum, F. and Sbragia, A. (2010), "EU Studies and the 'New Regionalism:' What can be Gained from Dialogue?" *Journal of European Integration* 32, no. 6: 563–82.

Soko, M. (2008), "Building regional integration in Southern Africa: Southern African Customs Union as a driving force," *South African Journal of International Affairs* 15, no. 1: 55–69.

Stephan, H. and Hervey, A.F. (2008), "New regionalism in Southern Africa: Functional Developmentalism and the Southern African Power Pool," *Politeia* 27, no. 3: 54–76.

Tavares, R. and Tang, V. (2011), "Regional economic integration in Africa: impediments to progress," *South African Journal of International Affairs* 18, no. 2: 217–33.

Taylor, I. (2011), "South Africa 'imperialism' in a region lacking regionalism: A critique," *Third World Quarterly* 32, no. 7: 1233–53.

United Nations Conference on Trade and Development (UNCTAD) (2013). *Economic Development Report in Africa 2013: Intra-African Trade: Unlocking Private Sector Dynamism.* Available at: http://unctad.org/en/PublicationsLibrary/aldcafrica2013_en.pdf (accessed November 12, 2013).

United Nations Economic Commission for Africa /African Union/African Development Bank (2012). *Assessing Regional Integration in Africa: Towards an African Continental Free Trade Area.* Addis Ababa: United Nations Economic Commission for Africa. Available at: http://uneca.africa-devnet.org/files/uneca_aria_v_june_2012.pdf (accessed July 30, 2013).

Uzodike, U.O. (2009), "The Role of Regional Economic Communities in Africa's Economic Integration: Prospects and Constraints," *Africa Insight* 39, no. 2: 26–42.

Vickers, B. (2011), "Between a rock and Hard Place: Small states in the EU-SADC EPA Negotiations," *Round Table* 100, no. 413: 183–97.

Vines, A. (2013), "A decade of African peace and security architecture," *International Affairs* 89, no. 1: 89–109.

Warleigh-Lack, A. (2006), "Towards a conceptual framework for regionalization: Bridging 'new regionalism' and 'integration theory,'" *Review of international political economy* 13, no. 5: 750–71.

Warleigh-Lack, A. and Rosamond, B. (2010), "Across the EU Studies-New Regionalism Frontier: Invitation to a Dialogue," *Journal of Common Market Studies* 48, no. 4: 993–1013.

Chapter 4
Micro-regionalisms in Africa: Dynamics, Opportunities and Challenges

Jon Unruh

Introduction

Development and Micro-regionalism

A great deal of attention is currently placed on the examination of globalization and the costs and benefits of this process to nations, states, peoples, communities, villages and individuals. One important component of globalization, thought to provide significant developmental potential, is regionalization at various scales. This document examines the potential of micro-regionalism to contribute to development in Africa. A number of researchers note that micro-regionalism on the continent has reached a significant scale and presents unparalleled opportunities that are not present in other domains in Africa (Torre and Kelly 1992; Trémolières 2007; Tache 2000; Söderbaum 2004). Bach (2008) argues that an important part of this potential lies in the fact that micro-regionalism in Africa often involves a powerful cognitive component wherein boundaries defined through geo-ethnic or religious bonds have greater meaning than state boundaries. Highlighting the potential of micro-regions on the continent, Torre and Kelly (1992) state that Africa has the highest number of such regional groupings in the world, together with the largest number of dormant and ineffective arrangements that could contribute to development. Such a mix of ingredients provides a potential that very likely does not exist elsewhere in the world. Thus, the value of providing capacity building assistance to micro-regional development in order to take advantage of what already exists on the ground would seem to be quite large. Examples of approaches for the successful development of micro-regions can be instructive. In Europe there exist very specific technical approaches for the realization of micro-regional goals and objectives (Schmidt-Kallert 2005).

Paradoxically, some of the more problematic aspects of Africa's history have contributed to the large number of existing and latent micro-regions and the great potential for their development. Colonialism and the drawing of state boundaries through ethnic, cultural, religious and language groups has not in reality meant in most cases that such groups became completely divided. Instead, such groups have continued to function and thrive as cross-border micro-regions throughout the colonial and independence periods. Such cross-border micro-regionalism can often center on local actors' capacity to escape the state's control over territory (Bach 2008). Similarly, the way personal rule has occurred in Africa has resulted in an erosion of a sense of broad public accountability. Such a problematic aspect of governance has favored narrower networks of influence and informal politics; in other words, effectively governed micro-regions (Hyden 2000). In addition, micro-regions of trade, migration and resistance have emerged as an alternative to neglect or persecution by the state or as a way to get around or avoid the state. Micro-regions also have emerged as a product of natural and human-made disasters that result in dislocation, migration, residence in new areas and return or partial return to areas of origin. The resulting livelihoods can encompass new rural-urban, rural-rural and urban-urban linkages.

This chapter reviews the primary definitions of micro-regionalism; a brief typology of micro-regions and micro-regionalism in Africa; the theoretical foundations of micro-regionalism as they pertain to the continent; and patterns of micro-regionalism (with a focus on patterns of opportunity and constraint). It further examines development and capacity building with regard to micro-regionalism in Africa and then, connecting micro-regions to macro-regions, looks at the local, the center and areas that require capacity building.

Definitions of Micro-regionalism

The variations in the definition of micro-regionalism in the African context depend primarily on whether the definition refers to internal sub-national forms or cross-border forms (Söderbaum and Taylor 2008). Generally, a micro-region is defined as a bounded area possessing some kind of organizing principle(s) that distinguish it from other regions (Johnston et al. 2002). However, because of the variation in types of micro-regionalism, this document will adopt the more general definition of "flows or potential flows of goods, people, and services within cohesive sub-national and cross-national areas," along the lines of what Söderbaum and Taylor (2008) describe. This definition allows for the inclusion of a variety of forms of micro-regions that have emerged due to diverse historical circumstances—economy, ethnicity, culture, administration and geography, among others—and encompasses "potential" micro-regions. These areas are cohesive with regard to specific characteristics but are at present constrained from operating as effective micro-regions due to policy, political, economic, legal or corruption constraints. The definition also includes micro-regions started or supported by governments, NGOs, and the international community and those that contain flows of goods and people regarded as illegal (smuggled goods and illegal movement of non-citizens). With regard to the latter, the laws defining what is legal and illegal can have a variety of purposes, including attempts to stem the flow of harmful goods (weapons, narcotics) or goods that fuel harmful processes (such as movement of certain natural resources that spark wars) but also laws that unduly constrain robust prosperity by prohibiting legitimate goods and people that could exist as a matter of accepted commerce.

Theoretical Foundations

Emergence of Micro-regionalism

There are several theories regarding how micro-regions emerge. Shaw et al. (2012) relate the emergence of micro-regions to the development of civil society in parallel to decolonization and globalization, such that micro-regions emerge "in response" to a process or "state of being." Such processes can include alienation, migration, and economic aspiration and ambition; "states of being" can include ethnicities, diasporas, genders, and religions. In this regard, the authors note that micro-regions can emerge as a function of diasporas, ethnicities, alienation, migration, religions, genders and economic opportunities and ambitions (Shaw et al. 2012).

Neumann (2003) postulates that the emergence of micro-regions is preceded by the presence and activities of specific "region builders." In other words, micro-regions do not come about naturally; rather, the geographical space is perceived, thought about and treated as an entity via the repetitive and iterative activities of such actors who then generate the idea of the space as a "natural" micro-region. Certainly among the more important actors are those involved in the private sector, be they individual or commercial interests. The activities of such interests can lead to cross-border employment, migrations and various shadow economies, and draw in the involvement of the state, NGOs, and macro-regional actors. At the same time, the ongoing development of civil society—formal and informal—is thought to serve as a significant catalyst for the emergence of micro-regions (Yeates 2007). This occurs as civil society associations emerge, become organized, and engage in dispute resolution, the provision of health and educational services, cooperation in agriculture and herding, and economic opportunities such as markets (Abdoul and Trémolières 2007).

Shaw et al. (2012) discuss the rise of transnational gangs operating both within and as their own micro-region. Such gangs emerge in the interstices of the formal processes of state regulation and policing on one hand, and on the other by the informal economic spaces that are created by the low capacity of the state. These gangs then traverse sub-national regions and can therefore influence larger regional dynamics in a number of ways.

How Micro-regions are Shaped over Time

Micro-regions are perhaps much more easily influenced than are regions at other scales by a variety of variables that can shape how they function over time. This is perhaps one of their greatest assets, for it allows them to adapt to new circumstances, possibly more quickly and more adeptly than can regions at other scales. Slocum-Bradley (2008) even postulates that micro-regions should not be seen as "natural" entities, but rather are more subjective phenomena that are constantly being shaped through discourses by a number of actors across regions.

There are a number of processes by which micro-regions are shaped. Jessop (2003) describes the processes of "re-localization" and "re-regionalization," along with the "re-valorization" of local and regional economies in response to: 1) the emergence of new industrial districts, corridors, and triangles; 2) innovations that can advantage some micro-regions and disadvantage others; 3) the emergence of or change in "gateway cities"; 4) as the formation of "bridges" between regions (for example between Europe and northern Africa); and 5) the variable effects (positive and negative) on micro-regions due to a national economy in decline or recession, economic crisis, civil war, state failure or other disruptive events and processes.

In addition, the processes of "inter-localization" and "inter-regionalization" are thought to shape how micro-regions function and change over time. These processes focus on the emergence of horizontal linkages between neighboring localities that exist on the same scale but in different countries (cross-border micro-regions, trans-local alliances), and the reorientation of sub-national regions on different sides of an international border that come to have shared or complementary political or economic interests (Joess 2003). Such linkages can bypass the national scale but can be supported or sponsored by one or more local or sub-national authorities and interests due to the development or prospective development of binational production zones, or cross-border metropoles (Albert and Brock 1996). Such shaping can follow international development corridors along transportation arteries. Such micro-regions can be regarded as "glocal" (globalized locations) (Joess 2003).

While this variety of theories beyond the new regionalism theory do resonate with different micro-regional processes, they do not offer a cohesive explanation of the unofficial reality of what is perhaps the majority of micro-regions, why they have emerged, and the economic role they play. This chapter argues that what is still needed theoretically is a way to explain the fundamental issue of the fact that Africa has the highest number of such micro-regions and potential micro-regions in the world, together with the most lacking institutional, legal and other state support arrangements that would facilitate their contribution to development.

Typology of Drivers of Micro-regionalism in Africa

This section attempts a broad and brief typology of micro-regions that focuses on their drivers, dynamics, origin, and particular characteristics of movement of goods, services and people. Due to the fluid and informal nature of many African micro-regions and how they came about, what they do and what they comprise, a good deal of overlap between categories is unavoidable; thus, categories are not mutually exclusive. Typologies already exist for micro-regions in Europe along the lines of "mapping space" consisting of proximity, likeness, and linkage, but also along historical lines, resilience, historical characteristics, and by their place in networks (Jonsson et al. 2000). However, attempting to apply these to the African context has proved difficult; thus the present typology attempts to reflect the African reality.

Economic Micro-regions

There exists a broad spectrum of economic micro-regions, and in one sense almost all micro-regions are economic or have an economic aspect. For our purposes this category will cover those micro-regions that are explicitly economic as their central originating purpose.

Söderbaum and Taylor (2008) describe the development of "spatial development initiatives" (SDIs) along corridors and "triangles" in southern Africa and how they are derived (Figure 4.1).

Such corridors are the most distinctive forms of policy-driven micro-regionalism in Eastern and Southern Africa. In this case, existing networks developed by migration and trade have become purposefully economically formalized and supported with national and supra-national policies and incentives. What has appeared to play a large role in the development of such corridors is the regional domination by South Africa, such that its comparative institutional strength related to region-building has an ongoing legacy (Söderbaum and Taylor 2008). The greater strength of Southern Africa's formal institutions and policy-driven processes lends a comparative advantage to the type of economic micro-region (corridors, development triangles) that sees formal and informal processes working together. This type of micro-region would appear to hold significant potential. The approach uses existing informal micro-regions and then engages in "formalizing the informal" or

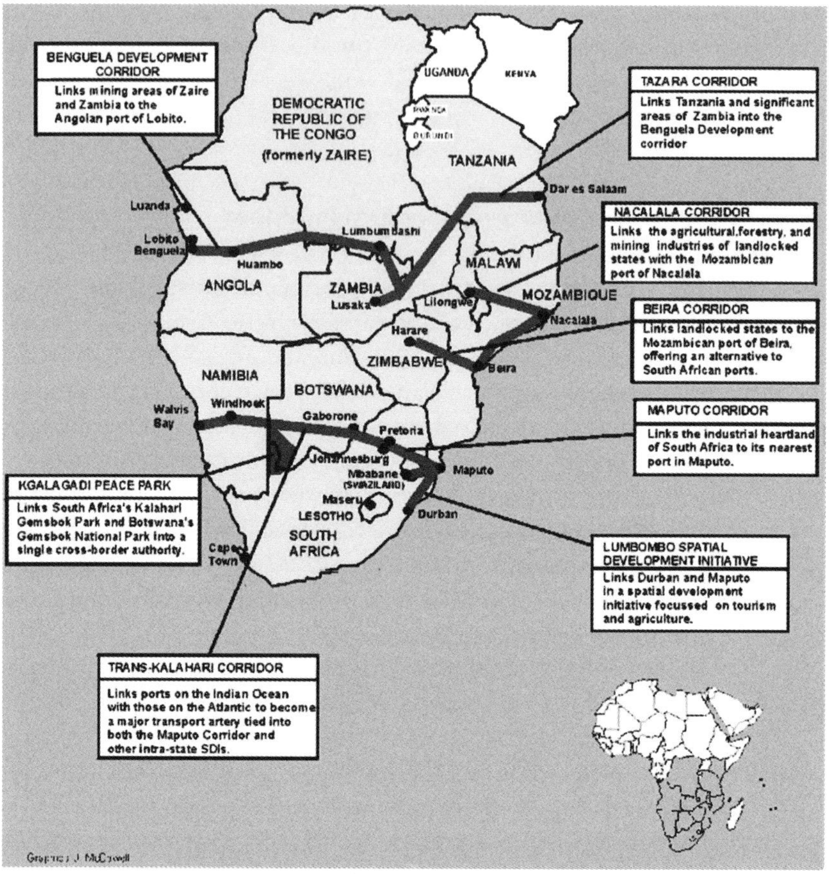

Figure 4.1 Spatial development corridors in Southern Africa

Source: Richard A Griggs, International Boundaries Research Unit Durham, NC, USA

taking advantage of what already exists. Söderbaum and Taylor (2008) describe examples in Mozambique (Maputo Development Corridor and the Zambezi Valley), Namibia (Walvis Bay-Swakopmund Corridor), and the Zambia-Malawi-Mozambique growth triangle.

The Maputo Development Corridor merits particular attention. In this case, a combination of the formal and informal, operating in specific ways, has benefited a set of actors in the micro-region. Thus, while the state plays active roles in the corridor, it does so only in certain directions and by attending to specific agendas. This occurs by business and state elites constructing a specific model for growth promotion based on neoliberalism and state-private partnerships. What occurs then is an entrenchment of certain forms of patronage and corruption, while privatizing certain aspects of state power.

In this variant of micro-regionalism, the well-placed business and state elites benefit considerably, with the common citizen much less so (Söderbaum and Taylor 2008).

Apart from corridors and triangles, there exists a variety of spatial configurations of economic micro-regions. Often, they reflect the economic aspects (primarily infrastructure) of the landscape they are situated in: along transportation routes; around and between markets, towns, cities or ports; and aligned along commodity sources and commodity market destinations. Such economic micro-regions can be cross-border or reside entirely within specific countries.

While migration for economic reasons is not new, it does appear to be occurring at increased rates as labor markets in Africa and beyond respond to new opportunities. The microeconomics of such markets and the migrations that influence them extend well beyond urban centers, back to areas of origin as people and goods move back and forth (Sabot 1979). The determinants of such economic migration are varied, from colonial era wage labor market functioning, to structural change and its effects on migration and labor markets, to the economic background and regional origin of migrants, along with the age of migrants. As an example, Manger and Ahmed (2000) describe the micro-regions of eastern Africa as they pertain to livestock marketing. In this context, they consider specific aspects of marketing and how these contribute to micro-regional functioning—livestock price, the cost or attraction of crossing borders, market organization, the linkages between pastoralists and exporters and the resulting marketing chain, and the policies of cross-border livestock trade, along with pastoralist coping strategies in emergencies.

Natural Resource-based Micro-regions

A number of micro-regions are derived along the lines of natural-resource locations and their movement. The numerous cross-border conservation examples and "peace parks" in Africa are a variant of natural resource based micro-regions that might best be termed "resource pooling." Notable examples are the Kenyan-Tanzanian borderlands (Massai-Mara–Serengeti) for wildlife, and the South Africa–Mozambique (Kruger–Limpopo) conservation areas and parks micro-region. Natural resource conservation-based micro-regions appear to need considerable state and international support (Peace Parks Foundation 2013), but their cross-border character and sub-national interaction acknowledges the specific location of such resources (Linde et al. 2001). In addition, conservation efforts initiated by the international community along with host country governments can focus on specific cross-border areas due to their biodiversity content. Such efforts can seek to work with local communities, including those that span international borders, in terms of development, marketing of agricultural products, communication, education and health, in order to engage in conservation and preservation objectives. Such attention can support and even create micro-regional development in a wide variety of situations (Linde et al. 2001).

For example, the existence of elephant herds and their migration patterns have focused international development attention on the areas included in and along these migration routes as well as subsequent forms of interaction between elephants and local communities (Linde et al. 2001). Such development support is often aligned with the objectives of conservation as they pertain to local communities—land tenure, micro-enterprise formation, capacity building, and income.

Other types of natural resources can create a separate kind of micro-region. Tache (2000) describes how micro-regions are shaped by changing patterns of resource control in the Southern Ethiopia–northern Kenya micro-region. And, in an overlap with the economic category, several authors highlight the importance of how informal linkages operate across borders in Côte d'Ivoire's cocoa sector, Sierra Leone's diamond sector, and Ghana's gold sector, and the relationship of these sectors to migration and violent conflict (Shaw et al. 2012). And as mentioned above, river systems that cross or comprise international borders can have a significant influence on micro-regions.

Smuggling

Certain micro-regions are able to take advantage of porous borders to engage in forms of smuggling. These micro-regions often contain both the locations of the resource and the cross-border corridors and characteristics that facilitate the movement of the resource as a commodity. An example of this is the "Parrot's Beak" micro-region in the area of southern Guinea and the border regions of Liberia and Sierra Leone (Grant 2008). While the Parrot's Beak has been active in trading since pre-colonial times, a significant reason for its current functioning as a micro-region is the largely illicit extraction and movement of diamonds, gold, timber, rubber and palm oil (Grant 2008).

Migration and Displacement-based Micro-regions

A number of micro-regions have emerged as a result of forced population displacement and then a subsequent return or partial return to areas of origin. Subsequent to forced dislocation, the presence of refugees and IDPs (internally dislocated persons) in new locations can continue for years. In the meantime, dislocated persons keep their connections to home areas and often travel back and forth. But they also pursue economic opportunities, connections and alternative livelihood arrangements in their new locations. These can persist long after the initial reasons for dislocation have subsided and they have returned to areas of origin—but often with ongoing interests in and obligations to maintaining ties to areas in which they sought refuge.

Darfur is such an example, with the hundreds of thousands of IDPs in and around towns now having been there long enough to have established considerable connections of economy, education, and livelihood, to the extent that many are unlikely to return to the exclusively rural lifestyle they pursued prior to dislocation. Instead, they will operate a mixed-livelihood approach that makes use of the new micro-region created by the combination of opportunities in areas of origin, and areas of displacement, and the connecting corridors. In Darfur, for most IDPs and refugees, postwar livelihoods will be a mix of options. As in other conflicts (and natural disasters) among populations with extended kin networks and tribal and lineage affiliations, dislocation leads to a diversification of livelihood strategies not experienced prior to conflict and dislocation (Unruh and Abdul-Jalil 2012). As a result, dislocated persons' return to lands and properties frequently occur only with some family members who pursue some rural activities while other family members remain in camps or move to urban or peri-urban areas to engage in a variety of income generating activities and educational opportunities. Family members who do return to rural lands will often come and go (creating micro-regional corridors), given the timing of the agricultural calendar, the degree of tenure security and personal security, and the presence of other economic opportunities. In part, this is due to the lack of and damage to livelihood assets in areas of origin—including houses, food, water sources and water facilities, seeds, plows and other tools, livestock, economic trees, fuel wood, and field condition—with such damage in Darfur being quite pronounced (Vanrooyen et al. 2008). Many dislocated persons intend to regain control and use of rural lands incrementally over time, while they concurrently seek to gain tenure security for urban or peri-urban residences that would allow the pursuit of a variety of economic, health and educational opportunities. Such a mixed livelihood approach engages the reality in rural areas of origin—security that will improve over time and the need to rebuild and reacquire over years the household, economic and agricultural assets necessary for rural livelihoods (Unruh and Abdul-Jalil 2012).

In West Africa, the societal disruption associated with the Liberia, Sierra Leone, and Ivory Coast civil wars resulted in large-scale displacement for a significant period of time. The resulting populations of IDPs and refugees and their connections to home areas have lent considerable economic and human activity to the Parrot's Beak micro-region (Grant 2008). Similarly, chronically refugee producing regions, such as the Horn of Africa, can see a great deal of migration across landscapes over time, followed by the pursuit of a wide variety of livelihood options in a micro-regionalism context. Thiollet (2007) describes such an example of how dislocation in Eritrea has led to micro-regional development based on refugee movements that continue today, as diaspora communities and migrants move to and from Sudan, Yemen, and Saudi Arabia. Until, 2002, the UNHCR provided Eritreans refugee status in these countries, but this has since been withdrawn. However, as a consequence of the connections, opportunities, and obligations gained during their period as refugees, Eritreans have continued to cross borders in the ongoing exploitation and establishment of significant networks of mutual assistance, employment and movement of goods.

Self-determination in Micro-regions

A number of micro-regions contain movements that push for self-determination. As such, they can be largely political while having economic aspects. The Cabinda enclave in Angola is such an example, having agitated for independence for some 40 years (Grant 2003). Zanzibar and Somaliland are other examples of a micro-region with a secessionist aspect; the Somaliland case is perhaps best described as a successful self-determination example. In addition, there are self-determination movements that seek greater autonomy, whether that means wanting to replace the government or wanting greater autonomy within the present state construct. Examples of self-determination movements that participate fully in micro-regional functioning are the Oromo of Ethiopia and the Tuaregs in Mali and Western Sahara, but the cases are numerous. Thus, the dynamics of self-determination can operate in a range of types, all of which can have significant influence on the development and operation of different micro-regions.

Conflict-related Micro-regions

Armed conflicts can have a significant effect on the emergence of micro-regions. And in reality, considerable micro-regionalization comes about through the "exploitation of the dividends of violence within and among states" (Bach 2008, p. 171). The movements of people, the networks of supply, revenue-generating activities, and areas of control, can leave a lasting form of micro-region in place subsequent to armed conflict. In West Africa, the exploitation of conflict diamonds by the Revolutionary United Front (RUF) depended on the informal patterns of cross-border and international commercial linkages to move and market diamonds and exchange these for weapons, which then require logistical networks to get them into the field where they can be used (Söderbaum and Taylor 2008). The networks of small arms flows in and around a number of current and past conflicts are well known (UNOCHA 2004).

There is a significant overlap between conflict and natural resources in a micro-regional context. Indeed, the politics relating to the management and exploitation of Africa's natural resources have drawn out the extremes in the complexities of African security and conflict (Alao 2007). It is important to acknowledge that the negative aspects of the natural resource–conflict mix can have a significant micro-region building effect. Processes of interaction take place between certain natural resources and ethno-nationalism, intergroup relations in alliance making and breaking, small arms trafficking, corruption, money laundering, cross-border mercenary activities and even alleged links with global terrorism (Alao 2007). As an example, the Great Lakes area comprises several "micro-regions of conflict" that have at various times included Uganda, Rwanda, Angola and Zimbabwe (Boas and Jennings 2008).

Ethnically-based Micro-regions

Long regarded as a constraint to trade and development, ethnic groups in Africa can also facilitate trade within micro-regions, largely among members and their confidants. When such groups span international boundaries, ethnic micro-regions can facilitate movement of goods and people between states. Such micro-regions hold considerable potential if capacity can be built among both local inhabitants and state authorities so as to align these with relevant local to international institutions. As an example, Abdoul and Trémolières (2007) describe the robust functioning of the Hausa trading network in the Benin–Niger–Nigeria border-zone micro-region and highlight the long history of this network and how this history has served as a foundation for the micro-region today. And certainly the Somali occupied areas of Kenya, Ethiopia, and Djibouti, in addition to Somalia itself, constitute an ethno-trading zone in which livestock movement, cell phone service, and currency strength and circulation constitute a micro-region that in many regards is able to function quite well in the absence of state institutions for governance.

Opportunities and Constraints

An Enabling Environment

One of the more pervasive patterns of opportunity in the development of micro-regions in Africa is that of the socioeconomic, sociopolitical and cultural elements joining an existing micro-region or potential micro-region where one or more elements already exist (Albert and Brock 1996; Bach 2008). An example perhaps best describes this phenomenon. The micro-region that occupies the borderlands of Mali and Burkina Faso connecting the cities of Mopti and Ouahigouya (Figure 4.2) currently comprises a significantly wide number of functional cross-border elements that interact (Trémolières 2007).

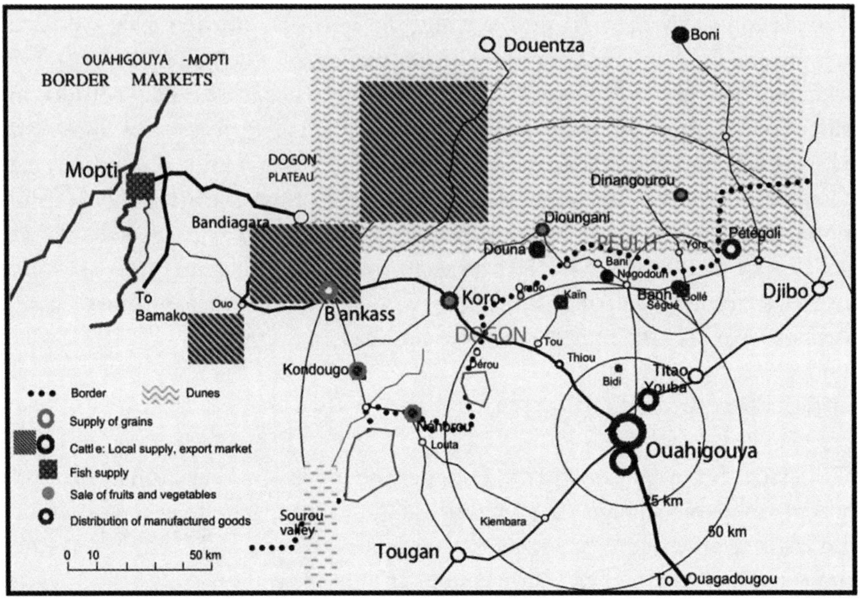

Figure 4.2 Case study Burkina Faso and Mali

Source: Trémolières (2007)

These elements did not come about all at once, but instead have joined the micro-region over time, with the pre-existing elements in a very real sense facilitating the entry of later elements. This borderlands area has a long history of transportation—the comings and goings of people, livestock and goods—which then laid the cross-border trading foundation for subsequent elements of the micro-region to join.

Another pre-existing element in the Mali–Burkina Faso case is that the Fulbe, Mossi and other ethnic groups can be found on both sides of the border. This has led to customary chiefs living on one side of the border being approached by the local population to resolve issues in their group's cultural area on either side of the border. Interestingly, Malian government authorities now seek and comply with decisions by such elders. With transportation and cross-border ethnicity as a foundation, other cross-border elements have then joined. In the education sector, children from Mali regularly are admitted to schools on the Burkina Faso side of the border, with no formality and no issues raised by school authorities. In the health sector, there is considerable cross-border interaction, with citizens of one country crossing the border to use the health clinics and hospitals of the neighboring country depending on distance, ailment, and how well equipped the various health centers are. Hospitals themselves also regularly transfer patients back and forth across the border in the micro-region depending on the medical problem and the expertise resident at the different institutions. In addition, the continuity of the expanding agro-pastoral farming systems across the border area and the ease with which fertilizer, pesticides, and other farming and pastoral practices can cross the border has led to a significant increase in production that is then traded to the larger urban centers of both countries. Building on this, a broader strategy for micro-regional agro-pastoral development is seen as quite likely (apart from the application of national policies). For example, an arrangement for the balanced management of livestock utilization of different lands on both sides of the border according to the capacities of the lands in question has been developed, with cattle-breeders, herders and animals of both countries being able to use water resources and lands with no restrictions, irrespective of whether they are in Mali or Burkina Faso (Trémolières 2007).

The development of land rights in this micro-region has followed the cross-border attributes of other elements. Farmers from Burkina Faso farm land in the Sobangoma, Tongourou, Gourty and Yorou villages on the Malian side, and the inhabitants and authorities of these villages to not oppose the farming of this land by citizens from the villages of Bani, Miyeti and Sabéré in Burkina Faso (Figure 4.2). Likewise, the local governments on either side of the border, recognizing the micro-region as a robust functioning area on its own, have come to engage in land dispute resolution along international border that gives rights to specific pieces of land to one country or another, depending on the details of the dispute—in essence, altering the international border to suit the needs of the micro-region. In one case, the Malian village of Ombo transferred land to the neighboring village of Kain in Burkina Faso (Figure 4.2). More broadly, the dynamics of the micro-region are such that the agricultural hinterland of Ouagadougou is in Mali, with Mopti closer to Ouagadougou than Bamako. As such, the micro-region's actors have robustly made the most of this hinterland-to-urban center trade induced by the elements of transportation and cross-border ethnicity, as opposed to emphasizing divisiveness of the international border (Trémolières 2007).

The Burkina Faso–Mali micro-region now has numerous actors that have joined to pursue many different social and economic cross-border initiatives and ideas: border markets, conflict prevention, mediation structures, health centers, a system of micro-regional cross-border transportation routes and joint management of grazing areas and transhumance trails. Such initiatives are strongly supported by the population of the micro-region and, as a result, these are able to develop over time (Trémolières 2007). Such bottom-up micro-regional development would benefit from supportive national and regional policies that could reinforce opportunities and minimize constraints (Torero 2011; Söderbaum 2004; Neumann 2003).

Patterns of Constraints—Challenges Faced

Overcoming constraints to micro-regional development should become a priority for local-to-national development efforts. Several authors have looked at a variety of constraints operating at different scales and how these can be dealt with (Kenfack 2013; Tavares and Tang 2013). Significant constraints include national policies aimed at strengthening international borders, thus making more problematic the flow of people and goods across borders. For reasons of security, economy, revenue generation, disease, agricultural pests, and migration flows and labor, a state can create a "thick" border, thereby making it difficult to cross for people, goods, and livestock and for the establishment and building of economic relationships that span borders. In addition, certain revenue generating systems can use such border constraints to favor a subset of actors who are in positions to variably enforce these policies. As an example, in the Kenya–Ethiopia borderland region there are significant cross-border trade opportunities involving the movement of livestock from Ethiopia to Kenya. However, policies that seek to regulate the movement of livestock across the border, combined with attempts by herders to circumvent such policies, and the actions of a subset of actors purporting to engage in questionable forms of enforcement, result in a significant deterrent to the development of cross-border trade. Attempts by herders to cross the border from Ethiopia to Kenya so as to sell livestock on the Kenyan side frequently result in capricious confiscation of herds, fines and imprisonment—all with the objective of revenue seeking. In this case, the absence of effective local governance and customs infrastructure, together with problematic enforcement, significantly deters the realization of micro-regional opportunities.

Micro-regions' development can also be constrained due to disparities between economic policies on either side of a border. These can have undue focus regarding the pursuit of purely national goals for economic sectors and their management. Such a focus can act to deter local cross-border activities (Trémolières 2007). For example, such a focus can result in burdensome custom constraints, poorly regulated traffic, and high tariffs. However, these conditions are not uniformly a constraint to the development of micro-regions; in certain circumstances, they can encourage the development of specific micro-regional trade opportunities. The existence of cross-border disparities in prices and differences in the availability of commodities can lead to economic opportunities to exploit such disparities. In such a context, the prospect of engaging in forms of smuggling can also become attractive, particularly if customs tariffs and policing are seen to be unreasonable.

Also within the policy domain, the gap between official regional integration policies and the local informal realities can act as a constraint. This can result in the lack of a genuine relationship between local, national, and larger regional scales. For example, as Trémolières (2007) notes, in West Africa a juridical framework that encourages cross-border cooperation does not exist, but could. This could be the role of a larger regional body such as ECOWAS: encouraging member states and their sub-national micro-regions to engage in effective cross-border interaction, thereby allowing greater convergence between micro- and macro-regions. Notably, however, certain international NGOs such as The Africa Progress Panel (APP) and macro-regional organizations such as the African Development Bank (ADB) are putting significant effort into establishing coalitions and cooperation at a number of levels, and this certainly has great potential (APP 2013; AfDB 2013). In addition, the UN has a research and training unit specifically dedicated to regionalism and its development called The United Nations University Institute on Comparative Regional Integration Studies (UNU-CRIS). This organization brings together scholars and practitioners to share knowledge on regionalism, among other topics (UNU-CRIS 2013). Particularly noteworthy within this effort is the Regional Integration Knowledge System (RIKS), which is a joint initiative between UNU-CRIS and a variety of organizations and networks.

However, the lack of institutions that can facilitate micro-regional development is also important. In this context North (1990) argues that the presence of such institutions is important because they include the structure of market relations, which contain actors involving producers, consumers and the state, as well as sets of rules—among them the more common definition of institutions in a development context (Ostrom 2001). Institutions can play five roles in terms of interacting with markets: 1) reducing transactions costs; 2) building social capital; 3) redressing missing markets; 4) managing risk; and, 5) enabling collective action (North 1990; Torero 2011).

Political and economic antagonism between central and local elites, as well as poorly implemented decentralization, can obstruct the development of micro-regionalism (Karim 2013). Likewise, if economic centers are seen by more peripheral local actors as a threat, instead of an opportunity, then this can create a significant hindrance to the development or deepening of cross-border or other sub-national forms of cooperation (Karim 2013). This can be the case when sub-national regions and national centers have inferiority–superiority perceptions of one another.

Development and Capacity Building in Support of Micro-regionalism

Connecting Micro-regions to Macro-regions

The new regionalism theories (Lombaerde 2010; Söderbaum 2002) have promoted the value of the interaction between micro- and macro-regions nested as they are within one another and frequently crossing borders. Of particular significance in pursuing greater connectivity between micro- and macro-regions is the international nature of many micro-regions. In this regard, it is thought that micro-regions would be able to operate on a certain international plane alongside macro-regions. Such international relations include region-to-state relations, inter-regional relations, and interactions between micro-regions and global institutions such as UN agencies, bilateral donors, and G-20 initiatives (Lombaerde 2010). For micro-regions, these interactions can take various forms: financing programs and projects, partnering, coordinating voting, attempts at formal representation and, increasingly, in sub-national diplomacy (Lombaerde 2010). In what Duran et al. (2009) describe as an evolution toward more international "actorness" by micro-regions, two phases of development can be articulated. The first period began in the, 1980s, as certain micro-regions in Africa and elsewhere began to get involved in the promotion of foreign direct investment schemes and tourism. The second period began in the, 1990s, when some micro-regions came to possess certain legal and diplomatic instruments that enabled them to conduct their own relations across borders and at different scales. Thus, with regard to the connections between micro and macro-regions, the coinciding objectives such as political goals, commercial interests, and identity issues, along with the challenges and other common problems faced in pursuit of these common interests, become important linking mechanisms (Lombaerde 2010). Thus, micro-regions and macro-regions can be seen as emerging international actors operating in a similar and connected way (Lombaerde 2010).

Three additional ways that micro- and macro-regions are connected can be described. The first has to do with complementarity, where certain processes underway in specific micro- and macro-regions occur in concurrent fashion. The second relates to "top-down" efforts in which macro-regions pursue cross-border micro-regionalism through specific incentives and approaches that target border areas. In a similar vein, macro-regional efforts can lead to more trust at the cross-border micro-level so that cross-border cooperation to address common challenges or pursue common opportunities becomes increasingly likely (Schiff and Winters 2002). Macro-regions can also enhance or create micro-regionalism when border zones become less peripheral and more central in a new macro-regional context (Schiff and Winters 2003). The third is "bottom-up" complementarity, such as when intense micro-regional cross-border interaction reaches a point where a certain regulatory framework (formal or informal) is needed, thus inducing a demand for specific macro-institutional arrangements (Lombaerde 2010). Abdoul and Trémolières (2007) note that the Benin–Niger–Nigeria border micro-region serves as an engine for the development of broader macro-regional development. In this regard, robust cross-border cooperation at the micro-regional level serves as a catalyst for a wide variety of macro-regional integrative processes.

In still a different type of connection, both micro and macro-regionalism can move in the same direction due to a systemic relationship affected by a larger set of variables: cultural, historical, institutional, political or economic. The growth corridors and growth triangles noted earlier are examples of this type of connection (Lombaerde 2010). A further type of connection or relationship between the micro- and the macro-regional levels occurs as the two become substitutes of or competitors with one another along certain lines. One regionalism, for example, can fill a governance or other institutional gap left by the other, or the two can end up pursuing opposed, incompatible, or competing development models, encouraged by different political agendas or interests. Overall, however, it is acknowledged that the two regionalisms respond to similar sets of variables and logics that are related to globalization; hence the systemic framework that both are thought to reside within (Lombaerde 2010).

The Local and the Center

There appear to be four broad types of relationship between sub-national regions and the economic centers of countries that can contribute to the success of micro-regions. The first is the nature of the overall relationship between local and central governments. One of the most supportive relationships is decentralization—depending, of course, on how such decentralization is experienced by sub-national groups and regions.

Positive experiences can occur as local governments take on a greater role in managing cross-border cooperation with counterparts. At the same time, the increase in private sector activity that can come about with decentralization can support the development and functioning of micro-regions (Karim 2013).

The second type of relationship occurs when the center initiates or supports specific projects in certain sub-national regions to enhance micro-regional development in that location. This can come about at the behest of development agendas, or in response to the activities of local actors, or as an outcome of the desire to gain the support of a local population, or even to make the micro-region more competitive, prosperous, or politically active in comparison with a neighboring population. The third type is geographical and exists when a peripheral area of one country is closer to the national capital of a neighboring country than it is to its own capital. This can foster significant cross-border activity (Trémolières 2007). The fourth type of relationship is simply neglect. Often this is a negative relationship. But while neglect is not seen as overtly supportive, if the relationship is otherwise antagonistic, confrontational, experiences corruption, or has a problematic history, then neglect of sub-national regions by the center, and the reverse, can be the best relationship that can be hoped for in the near- to mid-term.

Areas that Require Capacity Building

Local Actors

There are several forms that capacity building for local (non-state) participants can take in support of micro-regions. In examining how innovative micro-regionalism begins, certainly an important aspect is local actors' degree of confidence not only in their ability to carry out certain activities, but in estimations that the state(s) will not (or cannot effectively) deter their efforts through neglect, incompetence or support. This confidence is an important form of capacity, particularly in new non-state initiatives and innovations. While there can be specific approaches to supporting and building this form of capacity, certainly one of the most important factors is simply the experience of local actors in (and knowledge of) previous successes and failures at building micro-regions, or attempting to engage in or initiate micro-regional processes or relationships. One approach that would be of considerable utility in building this "confidence capacity" would be for local actors to see successes elsewhere and learn how these came about. Thus, visits to locations where viable micro-regions exist would be valuable in sharing ideas, exploring how common challenges were overcome, and seeing how opportunities were realized. Such visits could be organized by the state, subnational governments, NGOs, donors, or even the micro-regions themselves.

A second capacity building component useful to local actors wishing to initiate, develop, or become more aware of the potential of micro-regions is simply knowledge of any existing supporting financial, legal, logistical, institutional, or organizational constructs that would apply to their situation. If NGOs, the state, or donors offer micro-grants for cross border activities; if the state (including neighboring states) has facilitating laws, policies, and legal incentives, that may be supportive; if there are infrastructure plans, transportation facilities, or unused logistical arrangements that can be exploited; if there exist institutional, organizational, or legal assistance—all of these can be very useful in helping actors to engage in micro-region development, but only if they know of them. Thus radio, traveling workshops, printed matter, and other forms of information dissemination can all be useful in building this kind of capacity among local actors.

Of course, smugglers comprise one set of local actors who already have significantly high capacity at operating within micro-regions. Often, however, smuggling activity takes place with commodities that could be regarded as not harmful, dangerous or otherwise detrimental to society at large, such that prohibitions exist to protect certain economic or political sectors. Relaxing prohibitions against trading such commodities would contribute to the development of micro-regional economies and potentially bring a certain element of "smuggling talent" into the legal domain. Apart from this, accessing the talents of certain small-scale smugglers in order to tap into networks and approaches for enhancing cross-border micro-regional activity would likely be difficult, especially when the commodities traded are detrimental to society, as with weapons or drugs.

Sub-national Government

Enhancing the capacity of sub-national governments so that they are able to operate for the benefit of micro-regional development—particularly local governments that sit across international borders from one another—would be particularly worthwhile. Such governments are at the forefront of local service provision, policy, and law enforcement and are central to the way micro-regional commerce occurs. Decentralization policies and processes would greatly assist local governments in developing micro-regions, but additional capacity building needs to accompany decentralization so that the negative trends of local corruption, heavy-handedness in policy and law enforcement, and the derivation of local policies that favor some groups and disadvantage others are avoided. In this regard, specific training, in the form of workshops conducted by government, macro-regional organizations, NGOs, or donors that focus on how to build micro-regions and micro-regional relationships, would be valuable, as would networking exercises that bring together actors from across borders, sectors, and needs in order to establish relationships and explore opportunities.

National Government

Capacity building at the level of the central government would do well to focus on policies and processes of decentralization. Governments could ask specifically which policies would enhance micro-regional development and could review existing policies, laws and practices that are detrimental to micro-regions. Because national governments usually reside in national capitals, which operate as market destinations for many commodities involved in micro-regional trade, finding ways to encourage this trade, or at a minimum not overtly discourage it, could contribute significantly to the center's connection to micro-regions.

While micro-regional initiatives can solidify peaceful relationships, construct economic and social interdependencies and contribute significantly to a regional civil society, in general they do not possess the organizational capacity that would enable them to have entry into the policy-making level of the countries in which they operate (Abdoul and Trémolières 2007). This reveals two capacity needs. One exists at the level of the local actors who attempt the construction of micro-regional relationships; the other is the capacity need of neighboring states at the national and sub-national levels of government to interact with and support micro-regional initiatives while managing apprehensions about porous borders, customs controls, and micro-regional political aspirations that differ from those of the state. Such state capacity further needs to translate into macro-regional efforts to integrate micro-regional processes into macro-regional development.

While there are indications that some institutional and political leaders believe that micro-regional efforts should be encouraged, these are at present few. Significant capacity building is needed so that macro-regional and state policies become synchronized with the realities of micro-regional processes (Abdoul and Trémolières 2007). In this regard, the capacity needed is that which is able to facilitate linking formal state and macro-regional development with the dynamism of informal micro-regional development (Abdoul and Trémolières 2007).

Macro-regional Organizations

While macro-regional organizations are primarily concerned with functioning at their level, capacity building that seeks to coordinate or synchronize with existing or potential micro-regions within their area of influence would be quite valuable. At a minimum, the recognition of the role micro-regions play in the macro-region, and a consideration of the needs of micro-regions as macro-regional organizations conduct their activities and interact with heads of state, ministers, donors and other macro organizations and actors, would go a long way toward raising awareness of the value of micro-regions. One of the obstacles that capacity building could attend to at this level is how to deal with the informality of micro-regions given the highly formalized mode of operation of macro-regional organizations. This would require a different view of the need for and role of bureaucracies, leadership, laws, and borders.

Conclusion

Micro-regions in Africa contain myriad identities, peoples, and purposes that have evolved throughout history in a process that is ongoing (Grant 2003). The existence and success of a wide variety of "people-centered," flexible, cross-border micro-regions in Africa has the potential to teach much in the way of micro-regional functioning, the prospects for their emergence and development, and the capacity needed to support this process. In a number of micro-regions, civil society associations resolve disputes, health clinics serve patients and coordinate resources, students attend schools, herders utilize transhumance corridors, and traders construct markets, all within an area that traverses state boundaries (Abdoul and Trémolières 2007). Such initiatives demonstrate the dynamism, fluidity, and innovation borne of a combination of the existence of specific needs and a confidence and capacity to attend to such needs in a way that reflects and utilizes the local fabric of the human landscape to realize effective micro-regions (Abdoul and Trémolières 2007). The trick will be how to realize the full potential of this important vehicle for development.

References

Abdoul, M. and Trémolières, M. (2007), "Cross-Border Cooperation between Niger and Nigeria: The Case of the Maradi Micro-Region." In F. Söderbaum, and I. Taylor (eds). Uppsala: Nordiska Afrikainstitutet.

Africa Progress Panel (2013), "About The Africa Progress Panel." (Online) Available at: http://www.africaprogresspanel.org/about/ (accessed November 20, 2013).

African Development Bank (2013), "Mission and Objective." (Online) Available at: http://www.afdb.org/en/about-us/mission-objective/ (accessed November 20, 2013).

Alao, A. (2007), *Natural Resources and Conflict in Africa: The Tragedy of Endowment.* Rochester: University of Rochester Press.

Albert, M. and Brock, L. (1996), "De-bordering the state: new spaces in international relations," *New Political Science* 35: 69–107.

Bach, D. (2008), "Beyond Parochialism: Cross Border Regionalism as a Gateway." In F. Söderbaum and I. Taylor (eds), *Afro-Regions: The Dynamics of Cross-Border Micro-Regionalism in Africa.* Stockholm: Nordiska Afrikainstitutet.

Boas, M. and Jennings, K. (2008), "War in the Great Lakes Region and Ugandan conflict zones: micro-regionalisms and meta-narratives." In F. Söderbaum and I. Taylor (eds), *Afro-Regions: The Dynamics of Cross-Border Micro-Regionalism in Africa.* Stockholm: Nordiska Afrikainstitutet.

De la Torre, A. and Kelly, M. (1992), "Regional Trade Arrangements." International Monetary Fund Occasional Paper No. 93. Washington, D.C.: International Monetary Fund.

Grant, J.A. (2003), "New Regionalism and Micro-Regionalism in South-Western Africa: the Oil Rich Enclave of Cambinda." In J.A. Grant and F. Söderbaum (eds), *The New Regionalism in Africa.* Aldershot: Ashgate.

——— (2008), "Informal Cross-Border Micro-Regionalism in West Africa: The Case of the Parrot's Beak." In F. Söderbaum and I. Taylor (eds),

Afro-Regions: The Dynamics of Cross-Border Micro-Regionalism in Africa. Stockholm: Nordiska Afrikainstitutet.

Hyden, G. (2000), "The Governance Challenge in Africa." In G. Hyden, D. Oluwu and H. Okoth-Ogendo (eds), *African Perspectives on Governance.* Trenton: Africa World Press.

Jessop, B. (2003), "The Political Economy of Scale and the Construction of Crossborder Microregions." In F. Söderbaum and T. Shaw (eds), *Theories of New Regionalism: A Palgrave Reader.* New York: Palgrave.

Jönsson, C., Tägil, S.S. and Törnqvist, G. (2000), *Organizing European Space.* London: Sage.

Johnston, R., Gregory, D., Pratt, G. and Watts, M. (2002), *The Dictionary of Human Geography*, 4th ed. Oxford: Blackwell Publishers.

Karim, M. (2013), *Local Politics and the Limits of Micro-Regionalism in Border Areas.* Ottawa: ASEAN-Canada Partnership.

Kenfack, J. (2013), "Constraints to Regional Integration in Central Africa." In E. Fanta, M. Shaw and V. Tang (eds), *Comparative Regionalisms for Development in the 21st Century: Insights from the Global South.* Aldershot: Ashgate.

Linde, H., Oglethorpe, J., Sandwith, T., Snelson, D. and Tessema, Y. (2001), *Beyond Boundaries: Tansboundary Natural Resource Management in Sub-Saharan Africa.* Washington, D.C.: Biodiversity Support Program.

Lombaerde, P. (2010), "How to 'connect' micro-regions with macro-regions? A note," *Perspectives on Federalism* 2 (3): 29–37.

Neumann, I. (2003), "A Region-Building Approach." In F. Söderbaum and T. Shaw (eds), *Theories of New Regionalism: A Palgrave Reader.* Basingstoke: Palgrave.

North, D.C. (1990), *Institutions, Institutional Change and Economic Performance.* Cambridge: Cambridge University Press.

Ostrom, E. (2001), *The Drama of the Commons.* Washington, D.C.: National Academy Press.

Peace Parks Foundation (2013), "Peace Parks." (Online) Available at: http://www.peaceparks.org (accessed November 20, 2013).

Sabot, R. (1979), *Economic Development and Urban Migration: Tanzania, 1900–1971.* Oxford: Clarendon Press.

Schiff, M. and Winters, L.A. (2002), "Regional Cooperation and the Role of International Organizations and Regional Integration." World Bank Policy Research Working Paper 2872. Washington, D.C.: World Bank.

Schiff, M. and Winters, L.A. (2003), *Regional Integration and Development.* Washington, D.C.: World Bank-Oxford University Press.

Schmidt-Kallert, E. (2005), "A Short Introduction to micro-regional planning." Food and Agriculture Organization of the United Nations, Sub-regional Office for Central and Eastern Europe: Budapest.

Shaw, T., Grant, J. and Cornelissen, S. (2012), "Introduction and Overview: The study of New Regionalism(s) at the start of the second Decade of the Twenty-First century." In T. Shaw, J. Grant and S. Cornelissen (eds), *The Ashgate Research Companion to Regionalisms*. Farnham: Ashgate.

Slocum-Bradley, N. (2008), "The Zambia-Malawi-Mozambique Growth-Triangle (ZMM-GT): Discursive Region-Building in Africa and Consequences for Development." In F. Söderbaum and I. Taylor (eds), *Afro-Regions: The Dynamics of Cross-Border Micro-Regionalism in Africa*. Stockholm: Nordiska Afrikainstitutet.

Söderbaum, F. (2010), "With a Little Help From My Friends: How Regional Organizations in Africa Sustain Clientelism, Corruption and Discrimination." Paper presented at the Political Science Association annual Meeting in Gothenburg, 30 Sept–2 Oct.

——— (2004), *The Political Economy of Regionalism. The Case of Southern Africa*. Basingstoke: Palgrave Macmillan.

——— (2002), "Micro-Regionalism and the Construction of Development in South Africa: The Case of the Maputo Corridor." In M. Perkmann and N. Sum (eds), *Globalization, Regionalization, and Cross-Border Regions*. Basingstoke: Palgrave.

Söderbaum, F. and Taylor, I. (2008), *Afro-Regions and the Dynamics of Cross-Border Micro-regionalism in Africa*. Stockholm: Nordiska Afrikainstitutet.

Söderbaum, F. and Shaw, T. (eds) (2003), *Theories of New Regionalism: A Palgrave Reader*. Basingstoke and New York: Palgrave Macmillan.

Tache, B. (2000), "Changing Patterns of Resource Control Among the Borana Pastoralists of Southern Ethiopia: A Lesson for Development Agencies." In L. Manger and A. Ahmed (eds), *Pastoralists and the Environment: Experiences from the Greater Horn of Africa*. Addis Ababa: OSSREA.

Tavares, R. and Tang, V. (2013), "Regional Economic Integration in Africa: Impediments to Progress?" In E. Fanta, M. Shaw and V. Tang (eds), *Comparative Regionalisms for Development in the 21st Century: Insights from the Global South*. Aldershot: Ashgate.

Torero, M. (2011), "A Framework for Linking Small Farmers to Markets." Paper presented at the IFAD Conference on New Directions for Smallholder Agriculture, Rome, Italy, January 24–25.

Thiollet, H. (2007), "Refugees and Migrants from Eritrea to the Arab World: The Cases of Sudan, Yemen and Saudi Arabia, 1991–2007." Paper presented at Migration and Refugee Movements in the Middle East and North Africa, The American University in Cairo, Egypt, October 23–25, 2007.

Trémolières, M. (2007), "Regionalisms in the Sahel: The Mopti-Ouahigouya Cross-Border Area." In F. Söderbaum and I. Taylor (eds), *Micro-Regionalism in West Africa: Evidence from Two Case Studies*. Uppsala: Nordiska Afrikainstitutet.

United Nations Office for the Coordination of Humanitarian Affairs (UNOCHA) (2004), West Africa: ECOWAS seeks means to recover eight million illicit arms in region. Integrated Regional Information Network (IRIN) News Briefs, March 26.

United Nations University Institute on Comparative Regional Integration Studies (UNU-CRIS) (2013), Comparative regional integration. (Online) Available at: http://www.cris.unu.edu/Comparative-Regional-Integration.15.0.html (accessed November 20, 2013).

Unruh, J.D. and Abdul-Jalil, M.A. (2012), "Land rights in Darfur: Institutional flexibility, policy and adaptation to environmental change," *Natural Resources Forum* 36: 274–84.

Vanrooyen, M., Leaning, J., Johnson, K., Hirschfeld, K., Tuller, D., Levine, A. and Hefferman, J. (2008), "Employment of a livelihood analysis to define genocide in the Darfur region of Sudan," *Journal of Genocide Research* 10 (3): 343–58.

Yeates, N. (ed.) (2007), "The Social Policy Dimensions of World-Regionalism," *Global Social Policy* 7, no. 3: 249–385.

Chapter 5
The Impact of Informal Cross-border Trade on Regionalism and Poverty Reduction in West Africa

Barassou Diawara and Kwabena Agyei Boakye

Introduction

Informal cross-border trade (ICBT) in West Africa is as old as the creation of the countries and is deeply rooted in the region's cultural history (Golub and Hansen-Lewis 2012; Afrika and Ajumbo 2012). The trade is not accurately recorded, but is nonetheless significant, accounting for a large proportion of GDP in some countries in West Africa, with estimates ranging between 20 and 90 percent (ECA/AU/AfDB 2010). Though having numerous definitions (ECA 2013), ICBT is considered throughout this chapter as trade that passes through unofficial routes and avoids customs controls, as well as exchange that traverses official border crossing points and customs posts but is involved in illegal practices such as under-invoicing, mis-classification and mis-declaration (Lesser and Moisé-Leeman 2009).

Informal transnational trade has attracted many actors and infiltrated many sectors in West Africa including illicit activities in drugs, guns, money, people, etc. For example, informal cross-border movements, such as transactions of weapons, militants, and resources, have played a significant role in the emergence of Boko Haram (Oftedal 2013). Informal cross-border trade has facilitated the smuggling of cocaine from South America to Europe via West Africa which has expanded to the extent of endangering the stability and development of entire states (UNODC 2013). In fact, many experts argued that the crisis in Mali and the 2012 coup in Guinea-Bissau are both partly connected with the drugs trade, particularly in terms of the involvement of state actors (Vorath 2013). Examining informal cross-border trade in the Tanzanian Tarime District bordering Kenya, Nixdorf (2013) identified three factors that can explain why ICBT of small-scale actors persists in spite of deepened formal integration steps of the East African Community. These include: lack of implementation by the member states, imperfect information on the micro-traders' side, and corrupt staff within the customs structures, who take advantage of traders' ignorance.

Nevertheless, informal cross-border trade constitutes a great proportion of trade in Africa. The trade is an important component of intra-African trade and mainly patronized by women (mostly less educated) and operating at small to medium scale levels. Afrika and Ajumbo (2012) estimated that women constitute nearly 60 percent of informal traders in the Western and Central parts of Africa. In West Africa, the trade is very dynamic and well organized. The products exchanged via ICBT in the region are mainly foodstuff, livestock; low-quality manufactured and processed goods; low-quality goods from Asia, contrabands, counterfeits and substandard goods (Afrika and Ajumbo 2012).

The literature on ICBT in West Africa is relatively scarce. However, studies have shown that informal trade, in general, and ICBT, in particular, are factors of development and must be encouraged and incorporated into poverty reduction schemes and development strategies of countries. Besides, research also shows that ICBT is a phenomenon on the fringes of state law of which the challenges of regulating it, in addition to tax evasion that it promotes, makes it an unfair competitor to the formal sector (Nkendah 2010). Generally, the positive impacts of ICBT outweigh the negative ones (Afrika and Ajumbo 2012).

Besides the relative scarcity of the studies, the existing literature used surveys that mainly focus on a particular border without necessarily paying attention to the integrating and poverty reducing dimensions of the informal cross-border trade (Lesser and Moisé-Leeman 2009; Economic Commission for Africa, African Union and African Development Bank 2010). The focus of this chapter is to use case studies to document regionalism at the micro-level which is less explored compared to studies conducted within the formal framework of the Economic Community of West African States (ECOWAS). Such an approach has the advantage of capturing the dynamisms of regionalism at the grassroots given that informal cross-border trade features prominently among individuals' strategies for self-employment, poverty reduction and wealth creation.

The chapter pays special attention to ICBT in West Africa and, through a number of case studies and initiatives from different borders, it examines the impact of informal cross-border trade on regionalism and poverty reduction in the geographical areas of interest. The cross-border basin of Karakoro (Mali-Mauritania), the Sénégambie Méridional and the Malanville market (Benin border) are among the case studies used to illustrate the impacts and dynamics of ICBT on regionalism and poverty reduction in West Africa.

The rest of the chapter is organized as follows: Section 2 describes the socioeconomic context and the development of ICBT in the region. Section 3 presents the state of ICBT in West Africa and the proposed conceptual framework for analyzing the impacts on regionalism and poverty reduction.

Section 4 questions issues related to the level and profoundness of integration in West Africa. Section 5 examines the impacts of informal cross-border trade on regionalism and poverty reduction. Section 6 highlights the capacities needed to make ICBT work for regionalism and poverty reduction. The last section concludes the chapter.

Socioeconomic Context of West Africa and Development of Informal Cross-border Trade

ICBT in West Africa as well as other regions of the world does not take place in a vacuum. It happens within the broader context of trade and development processes of the countries and is the results of economic, political, historical and social factors. The extensive development of ICBT in West Africa can be attributed to the high poverty rates and poor economic conditions, the weak institutions, the historical legacy and the strong social ties across the borders.

Despite the recent high economic growth of Africa (known as the second fastest growing region), West African countries are facing higher poverty rates (Figure 5.1) and lower GDP per capita (Figure 5.2) than the average of sub-Saharan African countries. In fact, Figure 5.1 shows that the percentage of poor people has decreased over time. West Africa by contrast still has a higher poverty headcount ratio than the average of sub-Saharan Africa. Moreover, Figure 5.2 shows that since the 1960s, there is only modest increase of per capita GDP in West Africa which is still lower than the average of sub-Saharan African countries.

The low economic performance of the region can be considered as a reason as well as an opportunity for survival. It also represents a treat because well exploited by criminals. UNODC (2013) estimated that West Africa is prone to informal cross-border trade of drugs (mostly cocaine from South America to Europe), cigarettes, weapons and ammunition, people (destined for illegal migration or the sex trade), counterfeit medicines, toxic waste, oil, and natural resources (like hardwood and diamonds). The value of the flows of such illegal cross-border trade tends to dwarf local economies in some cases.

The main challenge facing countries in West Africa is poverty in all its forms. Besides, it is also to be noted that the countries in the West African region lag far behind in terms of human development (health and education) and basic infrastructure (transport and energy) and security (ECOWAS Executive Secretariat and WAEMU Commission 2006). Given the percentage of poor people and the relatively poor economic performance of West African countries, ICBT can be an opportunity for the poor to improve their welfare. ICBT can thus be considered as a survival as well as a wealth accumulation strategy.

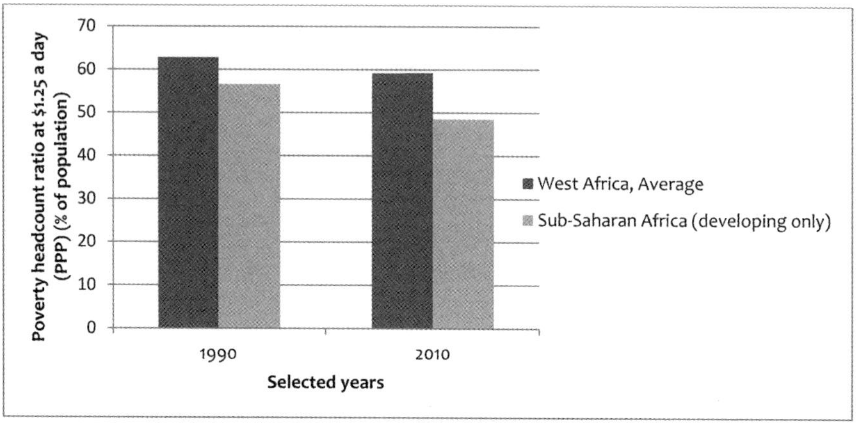

Figure 5.1 Poverty headcount ratio at $1.25 a day (PPP) (% of population)

Note: Data for West Africa are from Benin, Burkina Faso, Cape Verde, Cote d'Ivoire, the Gambia, Ghana, Guinea, Guinea Bissau, Liberia, Mauritania, Mali, Niger, Nigeria, Senegal, Sierra Leone and Togo.

Source: Generated by authors using data from World Bank (2014)

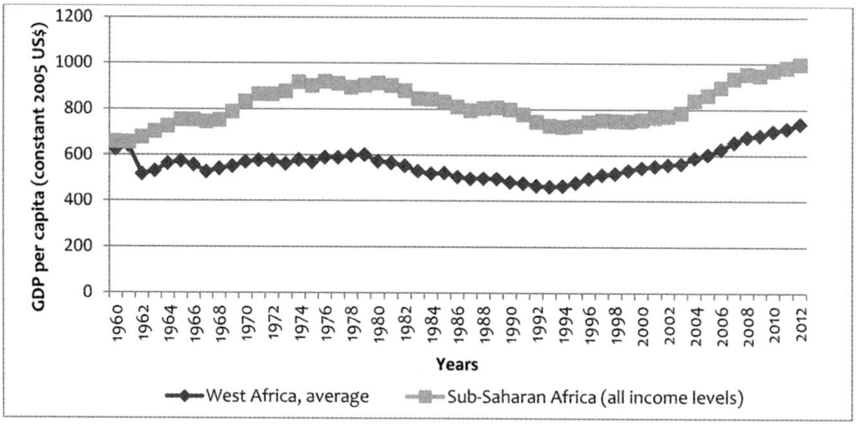

Figure 5.2 GDP per capita in West Africa and sub-Saharan Africa

Note: Data for West Africa are from Benin, Burkina Faso, Cape Verde, Cote d'Ivoire, the Gambia, Ghana, Guinea, Guinea Bissau, Liberia, Mauritania, Mali, Niger, Nigeria, Senegal, Sierra Leone and Togo.

Source: Generated by authors using data from World Bank (2014)

The economic conditions therefore partly encourage the development of informal cross-border trade in West Africa.

Weak political and institutional framework in West Africa remains a critical underpinning for the development of ICBT activities in the region. As argued by Benjamin, Golub and Mbaye (2014), the proliferation of ICBT activities in West Africa are rooted in the following institutional and governance challenges:

- Uncoordinated and often highly interventionist policies, particularly with regard to trade policies;
- Weak state institutions, which undermine the effectiveness of the enforcement of the policies, and widespread corruption; and
- Inability of governments to control movements of people and goods across the artificial borders.

Figure 5.3 presents the political context of West African countries in 2010. Though the situation was generally good in 2010 as compared to the average of African countries, it is to be noted that the stability of West Africa has been compromised mainly because of the 2012 crisis in Mali and Cote d'Ivoire and the frequent terrorist attacks in Nigeria and across the whole region (African Development Bank, Organisation for Economic Co-operation and Development, United Nations Development Programme and Economic Commission for Africa 2013).

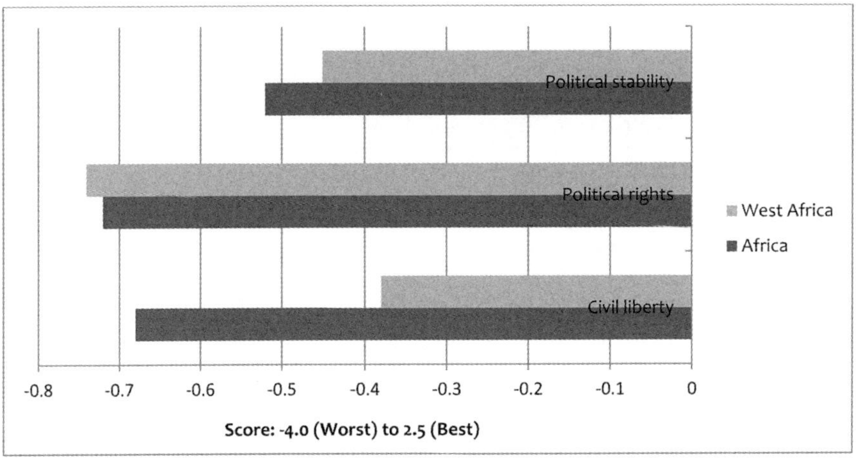

Figure 5.3 Political and institutional context of West Africa in 2010

Source: Generated by authors using data from African Development Bank (2011)

Corruption affects many Africans on a daily basis and can be considered a factor facilitating and nurturing the development of ICBT activities. Table 5.1 shows the International Transparency's rankings of West African countries in terms of corruption perception index. In West Africa, only Cape Verde (ranked 39) is ranked among the world top 50 less corrupted countries. Ghana is the second best country in West Africa. However, West African countries scored below the symbolic 50 pass mark, meaning that there is still a lot to be done by the countries of the regions.

Table 5.1 Corruption perception index

Country	Global rank 2012	Corruption perception index 2012
Cape Verde	39	60
Ghana	64	45
Liberia	75	41
Burkina Faso	83	38
Benin	94	36
Senegal	94	36
The Gambia	105	34
Mali	105	34
Niger	113	33
Mauritania	123	31
Sierra Leone	123	31
Togo	128	30
Cote d'Ivoire	130	29
Nigeria	139	27
Guinea Bissau	150	25
Guinea	154	24
Angola	157	22

Note: A country or territory's score indicates the perceived level of public sector corruption on a scale of 0—100, where 0 means that a country is perceived as highly corrupt and 100 means it is perceived as very clean.

Source: Transparency International (2012) © Transparency International. All Rights Reserved. For more information, visit http://www.transparency.org

Besides the economic situation and the institutional context, social factors namely the strong ethnic and religious ties uniting people across the borders explain also the development of ICBT activities in West Africa. Golub and Hansen-Lewis (2012) described the importance of ethnic and religious ties in ICBT using the case of the Mourides in Senegal and the Gambia and the Yoruba in Benin and Nigeria. They showed that group solidarity and mutual trust have enabled the expansion of commercial activities of the Mourides and Yoruba across the region.

Historical legacies can also be considered a key factor that has encouraged and helped to maintain the ICBT activities in West Africa. In fact, the long traditions of regional trade preceding the colonial era, and the artificial borders imposed by the colonial powers (and largely maintained after the independences) are viewed as key explanatory factors (Benjamin, Golub and Mbaye 2014). Before independence, communities and people from the region interacted and traded without need of interfering with traditional laws or requiring formal registration for such trade. They continued the same practice after the countries gained their sovereignty (ECA/AfDB 2009).

Informal Cross-border Trade, Regionalism and Poverty in West Africa: State and Proposed Conceptual Framework

Brief Review of the Literature

The literature on the impact of informal cross-border trade on regional integration and poverty reduction in West Africa is scarce. Studies done on West Africa include, but are not limited to Afrika and Ajumbo (2012), Economic Commission for Africa, African Union and African Development Bank (2010), Meagher (2001), Grant (2008) and Lesser and Moisé-Leeman (2009).

With respect to the impacts of ICBT on poverty, studies on other regions of Africa, mainly Southern and Eastern Africa, show that the trade is an important mechanism for poverty alleviation. In fact, the analyses of informal cross-border trade activities have unanimously showed that ICBT is a major income earning activity for small scale entrepreneurs hence a mechanism of addressing poverty. It is also to be recognized that, given the significant proportion of women involved in this trade, ICBT represents a real and efficient empowerment instrument (Southern African Research and Documentation Centre 2008). The trade can, in the short/medium terms, contribute to greater food security; however Lesser and Moisé-Leeman (2009) have warned of the potential negative effects in the longer term: loss of competitiveness and weaker formal private sector development; lower efficiency of health, safety and environmental protection measures; erosion of state revenues; and difficulty to formulate appropriate trade and macroeconomic policies.

The literature also shows that the impacts of informal cross-border trade on regionalism are ambiguous. On the one hand, some of the studies see informal cross-border trade as a factor to a more viable, legitimate and authentic regional integration (Abrahamsson 2000). In fact, informal cross-border trade activities are outward-looking, dictated and shaped by real economic processes and necessities. Going beyond the fixation with trade and production, ICBT strengthens the integration process and is even considered as the natural, easy and best way to integrate African economies because it fully embraces the social and cultural aspects of economic development. ICBT activities and initiatives can therefore play the role of economic integration factors from "below."

ICBT has on average a positive impact. Focusing on West Africa and using the case of Nigeria, Afrika and Ajumbo (2012) showed that informal trade in petroleum products has helped make Nigeria the major economic power in West Africa by supplying areas (especially rural ones) which are shunned by traditional international companies such as Total, Shell and BP but also national distribution companies.

On the other hand, some studies have considered the development of ICBT activities as inadequate and a hindrance to the viability of regional economic integration in West Africa (Meagher 2001). Without an institutional framework to direct and incorporate ICBT in support of national and regional economic activities, informal cross-border trade would certainly erode trust, cooperation and stability at the national as well as regional level (Meagher 2001).

Conceptual Framework

It is possible to conceptually link informal cross-border trade to regionalism and poverty reduction when relating the framework to formal activities. More importantly, the approach should be placed within the framework of international trade which has failed to explain ICBT. The literature shows that the neo-liberal economic reforms argument (Azuma and Grossman 2002) and the lack of growth models (Todaro 1997) are two main theoretical frameworks that enable one to link informal cross-border trade to regionalism and poverty reduction.

The neo-liberal economic reforms argument supposes that given the reasonable growth rates in developed countries and the lower barriers to developing countries' exports, it is expected that participation of the latter in world trade will flourish. However, national policies (heavy burden of taxes, bribes, and bureaucracy) have contributed to the emergence of cross-border trading as a survival strategy in reducing poverty. The lack of growth models assumes that a high productivity modern urban industrial sector exists, into which labor from the subsistence sector is gradually transferred. The existence of informal cross-border trade activities is the result of a lack of growth in the urban industrial sector.

With that background in mind, the proposed conceptual framework for analyzing the impacts of informal cross-border trade on regionalism and

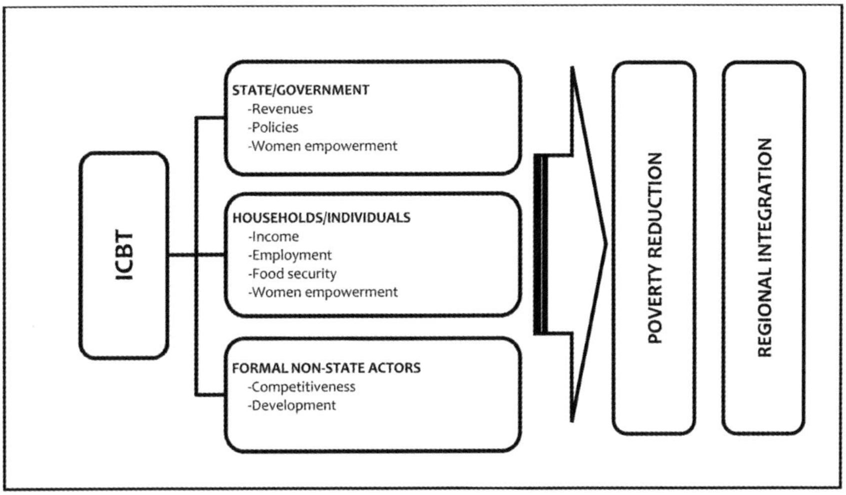

Figure 5.4 From ICBT regionalism and poverty reduction

Source: Authors' construction

poverty is summarized in Figure 5.4. The idea underlying the interrelationship is that ICBT affects all the players in the trade sector, namely the State, the private sector in formal activities and individuals. The impacts on individuals lead in the short/medium terms to poverty reduction and closer interactions across the borders.

Informal Cross-border Trade and Regionalism in West Africa: Integration in the Air and not on the Ground?

Informal cross-border trade is seen as a natural instrument for strengthening regional integration. In West Africa, regional integration schemes have mainly focused on promoting official trade (Benjamin, Golub and Mbaye 2014). A number of initiatives have been implemented across the region aimed at accelerating regional integration. This section intends to assess some of the different cross-border initiatives undertaken to promote and/or strengthen regionalism in the region.

The introduction of the ECOWAS common passport is among the efforts made by the ECOWAS (Economic Community of West African States) member countries to accelerate regional integration. The member States are Benin, Burkina Faso, Cape Verde, Cote d'Ivoire, the Gambia, Ghana, Guinea, Guinea Bissau, Liberia, Mali, Niger, Nigeria, Senegal, Sierra Leone and Togo. The ECOWAS' Protocol on Free Movement, relating to free movement of persons, residence and establishment, signed in Dakar, Senegal on 29th May 1979, was concretized by the introduction in 2000 of the ECOWAS common passport which aims at easing the free movement of persons, essential for regional integration (Economic Commission for Africa, African Union and African Development Bank 2010). The common passport was created to facilitate intra-regional travel of member states' citizens (for a maximum period of 90 days without a Visa); it is also recognized for international travel.

It is, however, to be noted that the free movement of persons and goods within the sub-region has not been fully realized. Incompatibilities in immigration and customs policies and monetary zones among member states have obstructed migration and integration within the sub-region (Oyedele 2013; Economic Commission for Africa, African Union and African Development Bank 2010). This again confirms the perception of ECOWAS citizens as captured by Oyedele (2013): "travelling through the air is a better option in West Africa because of bottlenecks at the borders when travelling by road" … "travelling through the roads in West Africa is hectic, with too many checkpoints and harassment by border officials."

It is against the above background that ECOWAS, since 2005, has attempted to transform the processes of the border regions into pilots units to facilitate the free movement of persons living along these borders. These pilots units include the civil society, judges, parliamentarians and the media. During the ECOWAS Heads of State and Government Conference in January 2006, the Program of Cross-Border Initiatives and the Cross-Border Cooperation Facilitation Fund were adopted (Economic Commission for Africa, African Union and African Development Bank 2010). The Cross-border Initiatives Program aims at promoting the development of concrete projects led by action and dialogue structures in all of the ECOWAS border zones. Implemented by ECOWAS, this program is based on four levels of interventions: 1) "close" cross-border relationships between authorities and/or local/regional communities; 2) bi- and tri-lateral relationships between States that share a common border, often necessary to develop the relationships mentioned above; 3) regional multilateral interventions, whether they be intergovernmental or supranational; and 4) relationships between regional blocks eager to solidify relative relations in the context of their internal and external integration (Cross-Border Diaries 2005).

Projects under the Cross-border Initiatives Program include the Sikasso-Korhogo-Bobo Dioulasso (Mali-Cote d'Ivoire-Burkina Faso), the Senegambia Meridional (Senegal-the Gambia-Guinea Bissau), the Karakoro Basin (Mali-Mauritania), and the Kano-Katsina-Maradi (Nigeria-Niger-Benin) zones (Cross-Border Diaries 2005). Instead of "ready-made" projects served up by institutions, the Cross-border Initiatives Program backs locally-initiated ones that sometimes also cost less. For instance, in the Senegambia Meridional zone, beekeeping professionals from Guinea Bissau, Senegal and the Gambia have set up a network to harmonize their production techniques, set the sale price of their products as well as developed joint marketing strategies. Besides, local associations of Diouloulou (Senegal) and Brikama (the Gambia) have succeeded in mobilizing community manpower in order to repair a cross-border route linking their localities (Cross-Border Diaries 2007b).

With respect to the Karakoro initiative, its implementation has helped support the local economies and more importantly improve local trade and thus strengthen relations between Mali and Mauritania. Thanks to the Karakoro basin, actors from Mauritania supply cereals, hand-made products (cooking rings, kitchen utensils, etc.) as well as natural resources by-products to their Mali partners. In a similar way, Malian economic actors supply cereals, palm and vegetable to Mauritanians via the Kayes (Mali) and Baediam (Mauritania) markets (Cross-Border Diaries 2009). Also, the Kano-Katsina-Maradi corridor (Nigeria-Niger border) represents a crucial and active axis for the exchange of cereals across the borders (Cross-Border Diaries 2007a). The box below shows the importance of the corridor for local populations and food security.

Trade of Cereals Across the Borders at the Kano-Katsina-Maradi Corridor

The Kano-Katsina-Maradi area is at the heart of the Hausa land which covers over 83,000 km² with more than 50 million inhabitants between Nigeria and Niger. They share 1,500km of common border and are often related by family, religious and lineage links. The three main towns of Kano, Katsina and Maradi make up one of the oldest trade corridors.

Trade across the border mainly focuses on cereals and meat. More importantly during the periods of abundant productions, significant volumes of Nigerian cereals are exported towards the neighboring regions of Niger, which are structurally deficient in cereal production. On the other hand, the Nigeriens bring meat and its by-products to Nigeria.

In both sides, the marketing of cash "products" allows the populations to earn revenue, which can be used to buy cereals on the market. Livestock is the principal cash "earner" of Niger and 97% of its livestock exports are to Nigeria.

Source: Cross-Border Diaries (2007a)

The various initiatives (common passport and Cross-border Initiatives Programme) undertaken in West Africa show that informal cross-border trade has mixed effects on poverty reduction and regionalism. Regional integration is yet to be fully realized. The next sections clarify the impacts of ICBT and dwell on the capacity imperatives for informal cross-border trade to work for regionalism and poverty reduction.

Informal Cross-border Trade and Poverty Reduction in West Africa: What are the Impacts?

Positive Impacts of ICBTs

Informal cross-border trade generates a number of direct and indirect impacts on the individual traders and their families, consumers, producers and the economy at large with broader ramifications on economic growth and poverty reduction. The effects are also manifested in terms of the time horizon (short to medium term and long term). This section of the chapter attempts to dissect the different impacts of informal cross-border trade on poverty reduction in Africa.

In the short to medium term, informal cross-border trade provides significant benefits to the traders—women and poor households—by promoting food security, employment, wealth creation and sustainable livelihoods (Lesser and Moisé-Leeman 2009). Women constitute about 60 percent of informal traders in West Africa. According to Plunket and Stryker (2002), over 4 million women are engaged in the shea butter trade in West Africa. Informal trade is the source of over 80 percent of the income of women involved in the shea butter value chain and employs between 300,000 and 400,000 women in Burkina Faso (Harsch 2001). In addition, the trade increases consumer's access to and choice among different varieties of products at relatively cheaper cost. This is mainly because informal traders are able to bring in diverse products at cheaper cost as a result of the fact that they do not go through formal border posts and custom processes—do not pay or underpay custom duties, taxes and VAT—as a result of which they are able to sell their products at cheaper prices compared to the formal traders. Informal trading in foodstuffs across neighboring countries in West Africa is an important source of maintaining balance between demand and supply. The traders buy and sell depending on the demand dynamics and price variation along the border countries. This phenomenon tends to ensure food security and price efficiency among countries in the region by bringing foodstuff from the countries where there is excess supply to where there is shortage. For example, the trade in vegetables such as tomatoes and onions and seafood across the borders of Ghana and Burkina Faso has helped to ensure continuous supply of the products throughout the year and at a reasonable price.

Informal cross-border inflows can be an important source of government revenue. According to Afrika and Ajumko (2012), the trade's contribution to GDP in West Africa ranges as high as 75 percent in Benin to 20 percent in Nigeria. The positive impact of the informality on national income is very significant in countries such as the Gambia and Benin where trade tax constitutes about 50 percent of their tax revenue. Also in coastal countries such as Benin and Togo where imported goods are resold in neighboring countries, taxes and custom duties from re-export tend to constitute an important source of government revenue. The box below briefly presents the Malanville market (Benin border), known as a "market without borders," illustrating the short/medium terms impacts of cross-border trade in West Africa.

Malanville (Benin), a Market Without Borders

Malanville is a town with fewer than 200,000 inhabitants in the borders of Benin and Niger and geographically very close to Nigeria. The market is a platform for sellers from Benin, Niger, Nigeria, Togo and Ghana. They all contribute to the dynamism of a commercial center which is now regional in scale.

Every week, an average of 2,000 tonnes of cereals, tubers, fruits and vegetables are sold at the Malanville market. For example, Beninese sell agricultural products such as tubers (yams, manioc and its derivative products, e.g. gari and tapioca), vegetables (okra and tomatoes), fruits (pineapples, mangoes, oranges), corn and Sahelian grains from North Benin (millet, cashew and sorghum); Nigeriens supply beans, nut-grass, Bambara ground-nut, tomatoes, mandarins, and livestock products; and Nigerians deal mainly with manufactured goods, and also supply garlic, ginger and pepper.

Because of the market, the local authority gets its cut by levying fees which is still considered as paltry gain in comparison with what could be collected by a watertight customs authority. Schools, other related businesses (transport, accommodation, etc.) and employment opportunities have developed around the markets, ensuring better living standards to local populations.

Source: Cross-Border Diaries (2004)

Negative Impacts of ICBTs

Notwithstanding the fact that informal flows may have noticeable short to medium term benefits, the trade can generally have serious negative effects (Lesser and Moisé-Leeman 2009). It may have direct impact on the health and safety of individual consumers, negative effect on competition, property right and business development and severely erode government revenue as well as reduce the capability and effectiveness of states to provide and maintain public goods and services. Informal cross-border trade can also curtail governments' ability to undertake strategic investment (telecommunication, power, and infrastructure) that are critical for regional integration, economic growth and poverty reduction (Lesser and Moisé-Leeman 2009). For the specific case of West Africa, ICBT creates a threat mainly because of its possible links with transnational trade of drugs, exotic goods and cheap labor which are being smuggled via and within the region (UNODC 2013). Grant, Mitchell, Nyame and Yakovleva (2013) also showed that ICT, by creating winners and losers, might have contributed to the development of ICBT.

Loss of Government Revenue and Curtailing of Public Sector Investment

Informal cross-border trade accounts for about 25 percent of tax revenue in sub-Saharan Africa and represented about 4 percent of the regions GDP in 2004 and 2008 respectively (Walsh 2006; Gupta and Tareq 2008). Since informal traders operate entirely outside the formal economy (avoid official custom duties and taxes or are engaged in illegal practices such as under-invoicing, misdeclaration and misclassification of imports), they deny the State of significant amount of revenue for national development. The situation is exacerbated by the fact that a sizeable amount of imports especially agricultural inputs are re-exported into neighboring countries leading to losses in foreign exchange receipts (Lesser and Moisé-Leeman 2009). The high incidence of informal flow on the continent, especially in West Africa leads to erosion of millions of dollars of government revenue resulting from unpaid custom duties and taxes. As indicated by Afrika and Ajumbo (2012), the economies of Benin and Togo tend to suffer from macroeconomic imbalances due to the high incidence of re-export of imported merchandise. The countries spend foreign exchange to import the merchandise that is re-exported across the border in local currencies.

Further, the erosion of government revenue reduces the States' potential and capability to develop and or maintain public goods and services such as roads, schools and hospitals that are already overstretched in most parts of West Africa. The erosion of government revenue due to the informality partly explains the low economic growth and ineffectiveness of poverty reduction initiatives across the region. The trade has a direct implication on the effectiveness of governments to initiate and implement policies and programs that are of strategic importance to the countries (PAAP's Electronic Newsletter 2009). Meager (2003) argues that the ineffectiveness of agricultural initiatives implemented by the government of Nigeria can be attributed to the high incidence of informal cross-border trade in agricultural products (key subsidized inputs are sold across the border to neighboring countries) along the borders of Nigeria.

Unfair Competition and Private Sector Development

Informal cross-border trade poses a critical danger to fair competition and business development. The high incidence of informality erodes fair competition (Afrika and Ajumbo 2012). Evidence from surveys indicates that a sizeable number of businesses and firms are folding up because of the growing informal inflows. They avoid or underpay taxes which makes it easy for the traders to sell their merchandise at a lower price than their counterparts in the formal sector who have to contend with high custom duties, value added tax and other taxes including the delays at the ports and road blocks. This negative competition and the fact that the formal sector is not able to compete against cheaper good have led to many formal traders being crowded out of the market space. The problem is exacerbated by the influx of cheap and counterfeit products from Asia and other parts of the world due to weak regulatory framework and border control in a majority of the countries. The failure to control the trade brings in its wake copyright violations and counterfeiting. All these impact negatively on the ability and willingness of entrepreneurs to invest or new businesses to be created (PAAP's Electronic Newsletter 2009).

The trade, as indicated earlier, impacts on governments' ability to mobilize adequate resources, which has a direct bearing on the state's ability to support private sector development by investing in policies and initiatives that will boost cross-border trade, as well as ensure effective implementation of strategies and frameworks to optimize benefits and outcomes that accrue from formal trade.

Low Effectiveness of Health, Safety and Environmental Protection Measures

Ensuring that cross-border trade is conducted in a healthy, safe and environmentally conducive manner is important for sustainable economic growth and poverty reduction. Goods traded across borders can be carriers of plant, animal and human disease, pests and insects that may be harmful to people, animals and hazardous to the environment including the flora and fauna. The fact that informal traders are not subjected to Sanitary and the Phytosanitary (SPS) controls, they become a potential source of health, safety and environmental risk (Lesser and Moisé-Leeman 2009). As well stated by Afrika and Ajumbo (2012), most consumers are at risk since informal traders generally fail to subject their merchandise, especially foodstuffs, to standard inspection. A number of agricultural products traded informally can be contaminated and may be a carrier of diseases and insects that may be harmful to consumers and hazardous for the environment. The non-compliance of the SPS and technical barriers to trade (TBT) requirements which are conducted at the border posts impacts negatively on the ability of the state to ensure food safety and prevent the spread of human, animal and plant disease across border (Lesser and Moisé-Leeman 2009).

Ineffective Trade and Macroeconomic Policies

One of the important effects of the informality is the loss of data and information on the traders and the dynamics of the trade, which is very crucial for policymaking, design of targeted interventions, monitoring and evaluation of impacts of cross-border trade. The inability of governments to adequately capture data on informal inflow in official records is a great loss and can significantly affect the relevance, quality and impact of trade and macroeconomic policies (PAAP's Electronic Newsletter 2009). One is not sure of the actual numbers and dynamics of the trade since it mostly occurs outside the radar of the State. The situation poses a serious threat to the effectiveness of government policies and interventions aimed at promoting cross-borders trade. The sheer volume and magnitude of the informality means that it has serious implications on balance-of-payment and national income dynamics. As advanced by Ndlela (2006) cited in Lesser and Moisé-Leeman (2009), missing data on informal trade can greatly influence the conceptualization, effectiveness and outcomes of policies and targeted interventions.

Making Informal Cross-border Trade Work for Regionalism and Poverty Reduction: What Capacities are Needed?

The benefits of informal inflow can be optimized only when measures are put in place to ensure that the formal sector becomes attractive, secured and yield better returns both in the short and the long run. Capacities at individual, organizational and institutional levels should be enhanced to reduce trade barriers and prop up the attractiveness and returns on formal trade so as to encourage more traders to formalize their business. This section of the chapter details some of the capabilities that are required to leverage the benefits of cross-border trade in West Africa.

Enhanced Regulatory and Trade Facilitation Services

Complex, non-transparent and inconsistent regulatory requirements have been identified as some of the key underpinnings and drivers of informal cross-border trade in the region. High taxes, fees, custom duties and large numbers of road blocks coupled with complex and inconsistent documentation processes reduces the returns from trade by increasing the transaction costs. Policies and initiatives that reduce tax burden should be implemented and where possible statutory requirements harmonized across the countries. Customs procedure, formalities and charges in the region are laborious involving an average of 20–30 customs transactions encompassing different parties, 200 data elements, 30 of which are duplicated at over 30 times and the re-inputting of over 60 percent of the data more than once (Lesser and Moisé-Leeman 2009). To motivate traders to comply, such cumbersome and complex customs procedures and formalities should be simplified and unnecessary and duplicative steps and processes should be removed to speed up and ease clearance of goods through the ports and beyond so that traders are able to optimize the benefits from the trade. In addition, import and export documentation and clearance processes should be automated to reduce the turnaround time and customer service centers with hotline manned by capable staff should be established especially along the borders to provide timely technical support to traders.

The enhancement of trade facilitation will also mean that relevant institutions and agencies are properly organized and well equipped to carry out the duties. Porous borders and inefficient control measures should be strengthened and corruption curtailed. Systems must be developed to ensure that border officials and traders are motivated to comply with formal trade procedures and requirements.

Improved Border Infrastructure

Effective and fit for purpose border facilities are critical for safe and profitable cross-border trade. Evidence from a number of surveys points to the fact that a majority of informal traders do not use the border facilities because of a number of challenges that impact the cost, safety and security of the merchandise and their own lives. Inadequate access to proper warehousing, accommodation facilities, transport networks and community markets coupled with weak and dysfunctional border institutions and agencies tend to increase the cost of the trade across the borders in West Africa. This situation partly explains the growth of informal inflows in the region. To increase utilization of the borders and the services of the state institutions, the infrastructure at the borders needs to be improved. Well-equipped warehousing facilities should be developed along the borders to ensure that there are secured and convenient places for traders to keep their wares especially perishable goods. Road networks should be improved and community markets established. Proper lodging facilities should be developed and relevant institutions and agencies strengthened to ensure the security and safety of traders especially women (Afrika and Ajumbo 2012).

Enhanced Collection, Management and Use of Data on Informal Trade

Capacity of public, private and civil society organizations should be built to effectively collect, analyze and use information on informal cross-border trade for policymaking and programing. One of the critical challenges faced by governments in the region is how to adequately capture the volume and dynamics of informal flows. Data and information on the trade is mainly estimated because the sector is not incorporated into the national data collection system. This approach has serious implications on the relevance and outcomes of government policies and initiatives aimed at improving the sector. There is the need therefore to identify and develop tools and strategies that will enable countries and other players along the value chain to collect, analyze and use reliable information to drive policies and interventions in the sector including mobilization of tax and customs revenue. Processes and arrangements should be developed for periodic review and refinement of data collection methodologies and tools. Across the region efforts should be made to harmonize data collection to remove duplication and complexities as well as make it easy to complete without compromising quality. This can serve as an added incentive for traders to provide the requisite information once they get to the border post. Effective collection, analysis and utilization of timely and accurate data will greatly enhance the formulation, implementation and achievement of trade policy outcomes.

Increased Access to Trade Information

Access to timely, accurate and reliable data and well-packaged information on trade regulations, duties and taxes and other dynamics are crucial for the profitability of the trade. Easy access to trade information can reduce the cost of doing business, enhance predictability of the trading environment and can serve as incentive for traders to formalize their business. Capacities of key actors including relevant government institutions and agencies should be built to enable them collect and share information on trade dynamics in the country including government regulations and custom requirements such as new procedures, duty and tax rates, import and export restrictions, tariffs classifications and appeal and grievance procedures on trade (Lesser and Moisé-Leeman 2009). There should also be systematic investment in trade policy research and analysis capabilities in the oversight institutions and trade associations to provide actors along the trade value chain with timely information to update and increase their knowledge and understanding of the nature and dynamics of trade across the region including the incentives and opportunities. The information should be processed and made available to traders and other stakeholders in a user-friendly and non-discriminatory manner. Moreover, border institutions and agencies should be equipped with capable personnel and tools to enable them provide timely and relevant information and support to traders. Strategies such as the use of mass media should be deployed to make it easily accessible to the traders in a timely manner (Dada 2012).

Increased Access to Finance

Trade finance is one of the critical challenges faced by informal traders. The trade is mostly at small-scale levels and the main source of financing is either self or from family members (Afrika and Ajumbo 2012). The traders are mostly not bankable and are unable to expand their businesses due to lack of collateral and documentation that are acceptable to formal banks. There is the need to develop customized financial products that will enable the traders to secure working capital and funds, and financial services can motivate informal traders to join the formal sector. Also, traders must be sensitized, educated and supported to formalize their trade as well as join associations that will enhance their legitimacy. Rural and community banks should also be established in rural and remote areas especially in small communities along the border to increase traders' access to banking services which will also help reduce the risk of carrying a lot of money by traders.

Enhanced Knowledge and Skills of Traders and Other Players Along the Value Chain

All the above capacities can be fully utilized only if the traders themselves are aware, knowledgeable and skilled enough to take advantage of the opportunities and improvements along the border. Traders should be supported to formally register their business and provided with requisite business management skills. Border communities should be sensitized on the basic custom requirements and procedures (Afrika and Ajumbo 2012). Enhanced capability, including increased understanding of the trade rules and market dynamics, will empower the traders and boost their confidence in engaging in formal trade. Moreover, the traders will be able to reduce the direct and indirect costs of formal trade by avoiding the payment of illegal fees and bribes at the border post. Officials and staff of border institutions and agencies should be capacitated to improve the turnaround time for completing import and export clearance processes and to respond to the needs of traders.

Conclusion

Since independence, African leaders have striven to promote regionalism as a viable strategy to unite the continent both politically and economically (Lee 2002). A number of strategic policy instruments, such as the creation of the African Economic Community (AEC) as an offshoot of the Abuja Treaty signed in 1991, have been developed aimed at facilitating the total integration of African Economies.

Until recently, the majority of the efforts have targeted the formal sector without adequate attention to informal inflows. The informal trade constitutes a significant proportion of cross-border trade on the continent and holds a lot of promise in promoting intra-African trade and poverty reduction through wealth creation, employment, food security and as a source of income and economic empowerment for the poor, especially women who constitute a greater proportion of the traders. The trade can also serve as a significant source of government revenue and means of mobilizing resources for national development (Afrika and Ajumbo 2012). Notwithstanding the prospects of the sector, its potential and value have not been fully harnessed due to a number of challenges such as unwieldy custom valuation and cumbersome and time consuming clearance procedures (Benjamin, Golub and Mbaye 2009) that serve as a major reason for keeping informal traders outside the radar of government and a motivation for circumventing and evading taxes and regulations.

The chapter has analyzed the potentialities offered by informal cross-border trade using case studies from mainly the Karakoro cross-border area, the Malanville market, the Senegambia Meridional and the Kano-Katsina-Maradi corridor. Case studies all show that ICBT has positive impacts on income generation and regionalism. It is, however, to be noted that informal cross-border trade has negative impacts while the positive impacts might not be sustainable in the long run. It is therefore necessary to strengthen individual, organizational and institutional capacities to make ICBT a real instrument for regional integration and poverty reduction. Enhanced regulatory and trade facilitation services; improved border infrastructure; enhanced collection and management of data on informal trade; increased access to trade information; increased access to finance; and enhanced knowledge and skills of traders are the capacity imperatives for beneficial informal cross-border trade in West Africa.

References

Abrahamsson, H. (2000), "Hegemon, Region and Nation-State: The Case of Mozambique." In B. Hettne, A. Inotai and O. Sunkel (eds), *National Perspectives on the New Regionalism in the South*. London: Macmillan in association with UNU/WIDER.

African Development Bank, Organisation for Economic Co-operation and Development, United Nations Development Programme and Economic Commission for Africa (2013), *African Economic Outlook 2013: Structural Transformation and Natural Resources*. AfDB, OECD, UNDP and ECA.

African Development Bank (2011), "Regional Integration Strategy Paper for West Africa 2011–2015." Regional Integration and Trade Department. African Development Bank.

Afrika, J-G. K. and Ajumbo, G. (2012), "Informal Cross Border Trade in Africa: Implications and Policy Recommendations." *Africa Economic Brief* 3 (10). African Development Bank.

Azuma, Y. and Grossman, H. (2002), "A Theory of the Informal Sector." Working Papers 2002–2007. Department of Economics. Brown University.

Benjamin, N., Golub, S. and Mbaye, A.A. (2014), "Informality, Regional Integration and Smuggling in West Africa." 4th WTO Chairs Programme Annual Conference Overcoming Supply Side Constraints: Issues for Policy Makers. World Trade Organization.

Cross-Border Diaries (2009), "Emersion in the Karakoro Bassin," *Bulletin on West African Local-Regional Realities* Issue 10, January.

Cross-Border Diaries (2007a), "Cross-border Networks." *Bulletin on West African Local-Regional Realities*. Special Edition, February.

Cross-Border Diaries (2007b), "Cross-border Networks." *Bulletin on West African Local-Regional Realities* Issue 6, June.

Cross-Border Diaries (2005), "One Park, Three Countries." *Bulletin on West African Local-Regional Realities* Number 02, September.

Cross-Border Diaries (2004), "Kanollywood, Video-mania without Borders." *Bulletin on West African Local-Regional Realities* Number 00, October.

Dada, E. (2012), "Special Report: Cross Border Trade and Women in West Africa." *West Africa Insight* June 2012: Cross Border Trade. Available at: http://westafricainsight.org/articles/PDF/183 (accessed July 3, 2014).

ECA (Economic Commission for Africa) (2013), "Report on the Magnitude of and Tools for Measuring Informal Cross Border Trade in Africa's Regional Economic Communities." Eighth Session of the Committee on Trade, Regional Cooperation and Integration. Addis Ababa: ECA.

ECA/AU/AfDB (Economic Commission for Africa, African Union and African Development Bank) (2010), *Assessing Regional Integration in Africa IV: Enhancing Intra-African Trade*. Addis Ababa: ECA.

ECOWAS Executive Secretariat and WAEMU Commission (2006), "Regional Integration for Growth and Poverty Reduction in West Africa: Strategies and Plan of Action." Technical Steering Committee, Regional Poverty Reduction Strategy for West Africa.

Golub, S. and Hansen-Lewis, J. (2012), "Informal Trading Networks in West Africa: The Mourides of Senegal/Gambia and the Yoruba of Benin/Nigeria." In Nancy Benjamin and Ahmadou Aly Mbaye (eds), *The Informal Sector in Francophone Africa: Firm Size, Productivity and Institutions*. Washington, D.C.: World Bank and Agence Française de Développement, pp: 173–93.

Grant, J.A. (2008), "Informal Cross-border Micro-regionalism in West Africa: The Case of the Parrot's Beak." In Fredrik Soderbaum and Ian Taylor (eds), *Afro-regions: The Dynamics of Cross-Border Micro-regionalism in Africa*. Stockholm: Elanders Sverige AB, pp: 105–20.

Grant, J.A., Mitchell, M.I., Nyame, F.K. and Yakovleva, N. (2013), "Micro-regionalisms, Information and Communication Technologies, and Migration in West Africa: A Comparative Analysis of Ghana's Diamond, Cocoa and

Gold Sectors." In Ulrike Lorenz-Carl and Martin Rempe (eds), *Mapping Agency: Comparing Regionalisms in Africa*. Farnham: Ashgate, pp: 149–74.

Gupta, S. and S. Tareq (2008), "Mobilizing Revenue: Strengthening Domestic Revenue Bases is Key to creating Fiscal Space for Africa's Developmental Needs." *Finance and Development* (September). Available at: https://www.imf.org/external/pubs/ft/fandd/2008/09/pdf/gupta.pdf (accessed June 7, 2014).

Harsch, E. (2001), "Making Trade for Poor Women, Villagers in Burkina Faso Discover an Opening in the Global Market." *Africa Recovery* 15(4).

Lee, M. (2002), "Regionalism in Africa: A Part of Problem or a Part of Solution." Polis/R.C.S.P. /C.P.S.R. Vol. 9, Numéro Spécial, 2002, p. 5, Available at: http://www.polis.sciencespobordeaux.fr/vol10ns/lee.pdf (accessed June 12, 2014).

Lesser C. and Moisé-Leeman, E. (2009), "Informal Cross-Border Trade and Trade Facilitation Reform in Sub-Saharan Africa." OECD Trade Policy Working Paper No. 86.

Meagher, K. (2001), "Throwing out the Baby to Keep the Bathwater: Informal Cross-Border Trade and Regional Integration in West Africa." In Nordiska Afrikainstitutet (ed.), *Regionalism and Regional Integration in Africa: A Debate of Current Aspects and Issues*. Discussion Paper 11, pp: 40–53.

Meager, K. (2003), "A Back Door to Globalization? Structural Adjustment, Globalization and Transborder Trade in West Africa." *Review of African Political Economy* 95. pp: 57–75.

Nixdorf, L. (2013), "Regional Integration and Informal Cross-border Trade in the East African Community." In Ulrike Lorenz-Carl and Martin Rempe (eds), *Mapping Agency: Comparing Regionalisms in Africa*. Farnham: Ashgate, pp: 133–48.

Nkendah, R. (2010), "The Informal Cross-Border Trade of Agricultural Commodities between Cameroon and its CEMAC's Neighbours." Paper presented at the NSF/AERC/IGC Conference (December 4).

Oftedal, E. (2013), "Boko Haram: A Transnational Phenomenon?" Master's Thesis. The Department of Political Science University of Oslo. Spring.

Oyedele, A. (2013), "A Journey inside ECOWAS through Hearts and Minds." *This Day Live*. Available at: http://www.thisdaylive.com/articles/a-journey-inside-ecowas-through-hearts-and-minds/157306/ (accessed June 7, 2014).

PAAP's Electronic Newsletter (2009), "Informal Cross-Border Trade and Trade Facilitation Reform in Sub-Saharan Africa." *PAAP's Electronic Newsletter* 12(8).

Plunkett, D.J. and Stryker, J.D. (2002), "Regional Interventions to Improve Crossborder Trade and Food Security in West Africa." Agricultural Policy Development Program, USAID AFR/SD, December.

Southern African Research and Documentation Centre [SARDC] (2008), *Optimising Regional Integration in Southern Africa: Assessing Informal Cross-border Trade in SADC*. Harare: SARDC.

Todaro, P.M. (1997), *Economic Development 6th Edition.* Longmans: New York University.

Transparency International (2014), *Corruption Perception Index.* Available at: http://www.transparency.org (accessed June 17, 2014).

United Nations Economic Commission for Africa and African Development Bank (2009), *Assessing Regional Integration in Africa IV: Gender and Intra-African Trade, The Case of West Africa.* Tunis, Tunisia.

UNODC [United Nations Office on Drugs and Crime] (2013), *Transnational Organized Crime in West Africa: A Threat Assessment.* United Nations Office on Drugs and Crime: Vienna.

Vorrath, J. (2013). "Transnational Organized Crime in West Africa: More Than a Problem of Terrorism and Law Enforcement." *SWP Comments* 24 (August).

Walsh, J.T. (2006), "New Customs." *Finance and Development* 43(1). A Quarterly Magazine of the IMF.

World Bank (2014), *World Development Indicators Online.* Washington, D.C.: World Bank.

Chapter 6
Enhancing Regionalism for Intra-African and African Inward Foreign Direct Investment

Abbi M. Kedir

Introduction

The regional integration process in Africa is increasingly becoming fundamental in the promotion of intra-African foreign direct investment (FDI). Intra-Africa foreign direct investment has been on the rise in the past five years (Ernst and Young 2012). South Africa is expanding investment beyond its borders to other African nations but its recent muted growth limits this expansion (Kedir 2013). Regional economic integration can expand Africa's market access, attract intra-regional FDI flows, enhance private sector activities and increase potential economies of scale for investing firms. It is believed that harmonization of regional policies and infrastructures projects will hasten regional integration by increasing market openness and capital flows, which in turn could stimulate trade and investment among African states, the movement of productive resources and the interaction of people. Given the fact that Africa is endowed with natural resources (both renewable and non-renewable) coupled with recent discoveries in different countries, if it continues to pursue appropriate economic policy reforms backed by effective policy implementation, political goodwill, sustained investment in infrastructure, maintain peace and security, there is a huge potential to attract increased regional FDI. This call will elucidate the potential of regionalism and regional economic communities (RECs) in fostering intra-African FDI. The chapter will discuss the conditions necessary for Africa to boost intra-regional FDI and explore the effect of regionalism on investment strategies by the private sector from within but also outside Africa. Building on previous work,[1] we will highlight the current state of African

1 This chapter is informed by our works presented in the African Economic Conference in October 2011 (Addis Ababa, Ethiopia) on net FDI inflows to Africa; and the intra-Africa investment and trade study presented in the May 2013 at the Annual Meetings of the African Development Bank (Marrakech, Morocco).

inward FDI using dynamic panel models for selected African countries and examine the trends and issues surrounding intra-Africa FDI. In recent years, the encouraging development within Africa and the presence of growing emerging economic partners outside Africa (e.g. China, India, Brazil, Turkey) is diversifying the sources of capital inflows (UNCTAD 2013; AfDB 2011; McKinsey Global 2010).

In this chapter, we explore the following key issues. What determines FDI inflows in Africa? With the variation in size, market structure and exchange rate regimes among African nations, what measures need to be in place to ensure consistent and equitable intra-Africa FDI between richer and poorer nations? What capacity do African governments, regional institutions, NGOs and private sector have to enhance an environment that supports intra-African FDI? What areas need capacity enhancement?

With regard to capital inflows, the growth of African economies is not independent of what is happening elsewhere particularly in the European Union (EU). Following the 2008 global financial crisis, Africa faced declining foreign direct investment (FDI) inflows. But there are glimpses of recent recovery in inflows mainly due to resource seeking investments. The 2012 African Economic Outlook shows the overall declining trend in investment to Africa in recent years (i.e. 2008 to 2012). Despite this trend, FDI still remains as an important external financial flow in Africa and has the potential for employment and growth generation (Ibrahim et al. 2011). South Africa is the largest investment recipient in the continent. In terms of source of FDI for 2010, Africa still receives most from developed economies (68 percent) followed by Asia (24 percent). However, emerging economies (e.g. the BRICS) are increasing their investments in the continent. For instance, in 2011 out of the total FDI outflow 4.3 percent was destined to Africa (UNCTAD 2013).

The remainder of this chapter is organized as follows. Section 2 provides a review of relevant literature on the determinants of FDI flows followed by details of the econometric methodology in section 3. Section 4 describes the dataset and the descriptive statistics while section 5 provides the discussion of results. Section 6 shows the trends in intra-Africa investment flows. In section 7, we discuss the capacity issues and constraints that need to be addressed to attract intra-Africa investment. Then the chapter concludes with a focus on recommendations.

Determinants of FDI Inflows to Africa

This section provides a brief review of the literature on the determinants of FDI in Africa. The focus of the section is essentially influenced by the data used to conduct our empirical work. As we use aggregate data at country level to compare our results to those used by previous work in this area, studies on the industry and firm levels as well as literature focusing on bilateral data will not be covered.

Classical Determinants of FDI

The categorization of the plethora of factors influencing FDI location decisions has been a central question in international economics. Dunning (1993) divided the FDI motives into four main types—resource seeking, market seeking, efficiency seeking and strategic asset seeking or knowledge seeking. The most influential motives for transnational corporations have been market seeking and resource seeking (Dunning 1998). The large host country's market size and high growth prospects are the main drivers of FDI. If it is resource-seeking, FDI is drawn to the location endowed with abundant natural resources (Asiedu 2013; Wernick et al. 2009; Buckley 2008; Bevan and Estrin 2004 and Blonigen 2005).

Further, a number of recent studies have attempted to identify the role of structural reforms as key determinants in attracting FDI inflows in developing countries (Morisset 2000, Ali Fiess and Macdonald 2010; Asiedu and Freeman 2009; Asiedu 2004 and 2006). This strand of literature focuses on the impact of business environment and trade and financial liberalization. Other important factors include inflation, exchange rate effects, taxes, tariffs, trade openness and financial liberalization, the size of the manufacturing sector and economic policy changes over time. In empirical modelling, exchange rate variables are included to see the impact of bilateral exchange rate and its volatility. The tax elasticity of FDI is also of interest. Trade protection or tariff jumping FDI is also well investigated.

Sound macroeconomic management focuses on low inflation, industrial and trade policies that move away from subsidies and tariffs. Thus, they give investors protected markets. Therefore, Morisset (2000), for example, claims that African countries with more liberal investment environments are able to attract more substantial FDI flows than countries with bigger local markets and/or natural resources. Other researchers show that high inflation rate would impact negatively on investors' confidence and profitability (Yartey and Adjasi 2007; Onyeiwu and Shrestha 2004). Note also that in addition to inflation targeting, nominal GDP targeting, fiscal consolidation and liberalized trade are used as macroeconomic stability indicators (World Bank 2002).

RECs and Investment

Progress in regional integration improves competitiveness and attractiveness of member countries for investment. Multinational corporations (MNCs) would like to take advantage of liberalized policies across borders such as openness to imports and reduced/zero tariffs. Regional blocs play a pivotal role in expanding market. It is not only RECs that may potentially drive the presence of increased FDI and intra-Africa investment but it is also the expansion of the cross-border private sector that may drive the process of regionalism and regional integration. For instance, there is an increasing role of South African corporations in Southern African Development Community (SADC) and non-SADC member countries. This leads to encouraging competitiveness in market share among the SADC countries (Goldstein 2004). However, some members can attract more FDI funds than others. For instance, most MNCs are attracted to the SADC bloc mainly to take advantage of the big market size, good physical and human capital of South Africa.

The Role of Governance and Institutions

Over the last three decades African governments have undertaken major economic reforms that potentially facilitate higher volumes of FDI inflow. Despite these reforms, the level of FDI has been low relative to other developing regions, and is mainly concentrated in the oil and mineral rich countries. Low FDI inflow is partly due to poor institutions, governance, ad hoc policies and unpredictable political uncertainty. Few countries pursue sensible macroeconomic management policies (Addison and Heshmati 2003; Asiedu 2002). Trade openness, infrastructure, absence of conflicts, low transaction costs, respect of property rights, absence of corruption and law and order promote FDI (Busse and Hefeker 2005; Jensen et al. 2010; North 1990). Other important issues include "perception bias" as driver of FDIs and broader investments (Kararach and Léautier 2012). Asiedu (2002) highlights the importance of geography and the detrimental effect of country "remoteness" from world markets. The seminal work by Wei (2001) highlights a close linkage between the structure of capital flows to a country and its degree of corruption, arguing that a country with a more severe problem of crony capitalism is more likely to have a distorted structure of capital flows that makes it more vulnerable to a sudden reversal in international capital flows.

Econometric Methodology

This section presents the econometric framework adopted to examine the main determinants of FDI inflows to Africa. Specifically, we investigate the role of market size, infrastructure, the macroeconomic environment, and the various institutional factors and structural reforms. The empirical strategy makes maximum use of both the time-series and cross-sectional aspects of our data. First, we adopt a baseline fixed effects (FE) panel model for a static analysis which can serve as a robustness check for our findings. This is followed by a dynamic generalized method of moments (GMM) specification suggested by Arellano and Bond (1991). By employing the GMM estimator, we attempt to address some common empirical problems in the cross country FDI literature such as the unobserved country heterogeneity and the dynamics of the FDI process. Other benefits of the GMM estimation framework also include the ability to correct for omitted variable bias and endogeneity.

Fixed Effects Model

First, we consider a baseline static panel model (i.e. FE estimator) which is given as:

$$FDI_{it} = \beta_0 + \beta_1 x_{it} + \beta_2 I_{it} + u_{it} \quad (1)$$

where FDI is net FDI inflow to country i at time t expressed as a percentage of GDP. The last term in the equation is the error term which is normally distributed. X stands for a vector of explanatory variables which includes GDP, share of natural resources in exports, domestic credit and inflation. I_{it} representsa vector that consists of all the institutional, governance and political risk variables from the International Country Risk Guide (ICRG) database for all the selected countries across time (t). GDP conventionally is used to represent economies of scale and a proxy for market size. Despite the availability of opportunities to access global markets, immobility of labor makes host market size relevant. In many African countries, multinational companies are attracted to countries with natural resources often with the purpose of exporting. Hence, we include in our model a variable that shows the share of natural resources (e.g. fuel and ores) in exports. Another important factor for FDI inflows is financial development[2] of a given economy. Institutional quality matters and to capture all the governance related aspects we include variables such as corruption and bureaucratic quality as obtained from the ICRG database (Asiedu 2013). Infrastructure availability is another important consideration for multinationals. In our estimation, this is captured by telephones per 1000 population. Inflation is included to examine the likely impact of macroeconomic stability (Goldstein 2004).

The error term u_{it} contains both country and time fixed effects and can be represented as follows:

$$u_{it} = \mu_i + \varepsilon_t + \eta_{it} \quad (2)$$

2 There are a variety of financial development indicators. Here, we use domestic credit to the private sector.

We assume that there are some country specific factors (or country heterogeneity) why levels of inward investment vary across countries. For instance some African countries have historical reasons such as colonial ties with certain countries which underlie economic ties including via FDI. There are also factors that are specific to a given country or region within Africa that cannot easily be measured and observed by the researcher. However they can be important heterogeneity factors driving FDI inflows. In such a case, the proper estimating framework is the fixed effects model. The country FE are represented by the unobservable μ_i. Taking the first differences of equation (1) removes these country fixed effects.

Note that η_{it} is a well-behaved error term with a zero mean and constant variance. Hence, $\eta_{it} \sim iid\,(0, \sigma_{\eta}^2)$. In the final set of results reported in the results table below, we did not include random effects model estimates after conducting a Hausman test which suggests the use of fixed effects estimator.

Dynamic Panel GMM Estimator

In the dynamic model, we include the lagged net inward FDI as an explanatory variable. This entails that there is a correlation between the explanatory variables and u_{it-1}. Given equation (2) above, the lagged error term (i.e. u_{it-1}) is a function of the country fixed effects μ_{i-}. As Baltagi et al. (2009) argue, this correlation causes the dynamic version of equation (1) to suffer from the Nickell (1981) bias. The bias is eliminated if T is large. The appropriate and preferred estimator for the dynamic model is the GMM estimator which removes the country fixed or time-invariant effects via differencing.

The dynamic version of equation (1) after taking first difference including a lagged value of net inward FDI, is given as follows:

$$\Delta FDI_{it} = \gamma \Delta FDI_{it-1} + \beta_1 \Delta x_{it} + \beta_2 \Delta I_{it} + v_{it} \qquad (3)$$

The lagged independent variable captures state-dependence or agglomeration effects. Li et al. (2010) found these effects to be strong drivers of FDI. This suggests the tendency for FDI to concentrate in certain locations where there is skilled manpower, input and transport cost advantage (Dunning 2009). If μ_i is purely random, then v_{it} is AR (1), and using OLS or a linear random effects panel model will be appropriate. The Arellano and Bond GMM estimator is the relevant estimator and it involves the first differencing shown in (3) above to eliminate the fixed effect. However, differencing makes the lagged FDI variables endogenous and this problem should be handled using appropriate instruments. The dynamic estimator used further lags (of course with automatic determination of the optimal number of lags) of the FDI variables ΔFDI_{i2}, ΔFDI_{i3} … etc., as instruments.

Data

Our FDI data set along with the key explanatory variables of interest are generated from Global Development Finance of World Bank (GDF_WB) and the period covered ranges from 1980 to 2009. This is a panel data on a number of countries and our focus is only on the African sub-sample. The panel data on Africa is merged with the institutional variables obtained from International Country Risk Guide (ICRG). ICRG has an index based on institutional variables divided into 12 components such as government stability, socioeconomic conditions, investment profile, internal conflict, external conflict, corruption, military in politics, religion in politics, law and order, ethnic tensions, democratic accountability and bureaucracy quality.

In our analysis, we considered a range of other sources of governance and institutional indicators from other sources. For instance, there are aggregate measures of institutional strength from Fraser Institute and Polity IV and Freedom House but the ICRG indices are appealing due to their disaggregated nature that help us to capture some interesting country specific heterogeneity. From a technical perspective, it is useful to recognize the difficulty of measuring institutional quality. Often, researchers use a composite index of a country's political, legal and economic institution (Wei 2000). Another technical problem is the lack of variation across time in variables that capture institutional features. Country risk is an important element affecting business/investment risk (Goldstein 2004). Therefore, in our analysis we merged two data sources to investigate which aspects of country risk guide indicators are associated with attracting or deterring inward FDI in Africa. Our primary data source, the Global Development Finance (GDF) of the World Bank, has variables such as FDI, inflation, market size (GDP), infrastructure and share of natural resources in exports. The second data source merged with the GDF has 12 components of country risk from IGRG. We also use additional financial and trade liberalization indicators based on data from Thortsen Beck and Asli Demirgüç-Kunt. This is a World Bank's financial liberalization data for African and non-African countries[3].

Table 6.1 below provides descriptive statistics of the key variables used in the models estimated. The indices are from IGRG and the rest of the variables are generated from World Development Indicators database of the World Bank.

---

3 The source for this data is, "Financial Institutions and Markets Across Countries and over Time: Data and Analysis," World Bank Policy Research Working Paper No. 4943, May 2009.

Table 6.1 Summary statistics of key variables

FDI inflows (% of GDP)	2.97	0	90.5
Log of GDP in constant prices	21.9	18.6	27.8
Telephone per 1000 population	2.2	0.01	29.7
Log of domestic credit to the private sector	3.2	0	5.77
Inflation	71.8	-100	24411.03
Share of ores in exports	10.9	0	88.8
Share of fuel exports	19.1	0	100
Bureaucratic quality index	1.3	0	6
Law and order index	2.8	0	6
Corruption index	2.4	0	6
Religion in politics index	4.06	0	6

Results

The econometrics estimates are generated for all African countries with relevant and available data, including sub-Saharan Africa and North Africa, for a period of 26 years (i.e. 1984–2009).[4] In Table 6.2, we provide the baseline fixed effects estimates using two different specifications. The first model in column 2 shows the model of key FDI determinants that are conventionally controlled for. These include variables such as market size (proxied by log of GDP), natural resources (captured by the share of fuel and mineral ores in exports), infrastructure (proxied by the log of the telephones per 1,000 population in a given country), financial development or financial liberalization (proxied by the log of domestic credit provided by the banking sector), inflation, corruption, bureaucratic quality and law and order.

The results reported in the last column are based on the same set of variables as in the second column but we interacted the bureaucratic quality indicator with the proxy for financial development/liberalization and trade liberalization. This is based on the premise that trade and financial markets work in conjunction with institutions and that the latter has an important role to play in the performance of the former. The inclusion of the interactive term is an attempt to provide evidence on the hypothesis that economic reforms, which are unaccompanied by improved quality of civil servants are likely to be ineffective.

4 In relation to the institutional, policy and political risk variables, we used International Country Risk Guide dataset.

Table 6.2 Baseline fixed effects (FE) estimates of FDI determinants in Africa

Variables	Without interaction	With interaction
Log of GDP	7.816*** (0.089)	7.902*** (0.912)
Share of fuel in exports	0.049*** (0.013)	0.049*** (0.013)
Share of ores in exports	-0.002 (0.020)	-0.004 (0.019)
Log of phones per 1000 population	-0.168 (0.475)	-0.273 (0.475)
Policy variables		
Log of credit	-0.264 (0.224)	-1.366*** (0.502)
Log of credit *bureaucratic quality	-	0.678** (0.277)
Inflation	0.002 (0.003)	0.003 (0.003)
Political risk and institutional variables		
Bureaucratic quality	-0.147 (0.256)	-2.361** (0.941)
Reduced corruption	0.541*** (0.218)	0.398* (0.225)
Law and order	-0.275 (0.199)	-0.307 (0.199)
Religion	0.388*** (0.150)	0.394*** (0.149)
Constant	-176.69*** (20.41)	-174.79*** (20.30)
R-squared	0.33	0.34
Sigma_u	11.98	12.12
Sigma_e	2.61	2.59
Rho	0.96	0.96
No of observations	458	458

Note: ***, **, *=significant at 1%, 5% and 105 respectively. Based on Hausman test, the fixed effects model was preferred to random effects of model. We found trade openness insignificant. Similar to the interaction of the financial development proxy with the bureaucratic quality index, we estimated the model by interacting the institutional quality indicator with the trade openness measure. The results neither change qualitatively with this interaction nor do we observe significance of the trade liberalization proxy and the interactive term.

Table 6.3 provides the dynamic model of FDI inflows in Africa using the GMM estimator and has a similar set of variables in each of the two result columns as in Table 6.2 above. The GMM estimator allows for dynamics and we can clearly see the strong state dependence FDI inflows. With the 2nd lagged value of FDI being insignificant, we used only one lag for the final estimates reported here. Except for some changes in levels of statistical significance, the GMM estimates are qualitatively similar to the fixed effects model estimates. Again our interesting result of interacting the proxy for financial liberalization policy with the volume of credit suggests the effectiveness of the policy measure only if it is accompanied with good institutional structures as indicated by bureaucratic quality.

Table 6.3 Dynamic panel GMM estimates of FDI determinants in Africa

Variables	Without interaction	With interaction
Lagged FDI net inflows	0.529*** (0.046)	0.512*** (0.046)
Log of GDP	4.856*** (1.097)	5.108*** (1.096)
Share of fuel in exports	0.026* (0.015)	0.027* (0.015)
Share of ores in exports	0.011 (0.019)	0.016 (0.019)
Log of phones per 1000 population	-0.209 (0.523)	-0.293 (0.522)
Policy variables		
Log of Credit	-0.284 (0.218)	-1.433** (0.592)
Log of Credit*Bureaucratic Quality	-	0.663** (0.316)
Inflation	-0.002 (0.003)	-0.001 (0.003)
Political risk and institutional variables		
Bureaucratic Quality	0.012 (0.297)	-2.185** (1.091)
Reduced Corruption	0.434** (0.243)	0.357 (0.249)
Law and order	-0.145 (0.205)	-0.160 (0.204)
Religion in politics	0.273** (0.112)	0.333*** (0.130)

Constant	-110.09*** (24.98)	-112.09*** (24.85)
AR(1), p-value	-2.70(0.007)	-2.919 90.004)
AR(2), p-value	0.47(0.64)	0.63(0.53)
Sargan test statistic (chi-squared value)	531.2(0.000)	547.2 (0.000)
No of observations	386	386

Note: ***, **, *=significant at 1%, 5% and 10% respectively. Neither interacting trade openness with bureaucratic quality nor controlling for it change the results reported above qualitatively.

We now discuss the statistically significant results, which were found to be robust across different specifications. In all models, market size, share of fuel in exports and corruption and religion tension risk indictors were found to be important drivers of net FDI inflows to Africa. Without interacting them, both the bureaucratic quality indicator and credit provided by the banking sector of the host economy are found to be insignificant determinants of FDI and the volume of credit has a negative sign. The sign of this variable turned positive when interacted with bureaucratic quality. This is an interesting finding because it suggests that the role of expansion of loans by the banking sector in the host economy is instrumental to attracting FDI only if it is accompanied by good bureaucratic quality. Without this complementary institutional set up, the financial development/liberalization variable is associated with declining net FDI inflows as the significant and negative coefficient of the log of credit variable indicates in the last column. In cases where the log of bank credit is negative and significant, one may argue that there is lack of complementarity between domestic credit in the host economy and FDI. The domestic credit finances domestic investment which is potentially playing a substitution role.

Our key findings have the expected signs and our results agree with other work done on the continent on FDI determinants (Asiedu 2006). FDI inflows to Africa are concentrated in the relatively resource-rich countries and in countries with a larger market size. This implies that productions of affiliate transnational corporations in Africa mainly target local sale rather than opting for an export platform, and that market seeking FDI is still dominated by the traditional horizontal mode with less emphasis on vertical integration and value addition. Such FDI is not beneficial to employment creation in the continent.

It is also evident that FDI inflows are strongly associated with natural resource presence. However, instead of treating all natural resources together, we treated the share of fuel and mineral ores in total exports separately to investigate their relative importance. This clearly shows that it is not all natural resources that are the drivers of FDI inflows to Africa as we saw from the insignificant coefficient associated with ores. But FDI inflows are still positively and significantly influenced by the presence of oil. Yet, the positive and significant coefficient of the market-size variable suggests the importance of market-seeking FDI on the continent and calls for intensification of efforts by African countries to accelerate regional integration and enhance their global competitiveness.

The corruption risk indicator in the ICRG database is constructed in such a way that the higher the indictor, the lower the corruption risk. Thus, according to the results, the positive coefficient indicates that as the corruption risk declines, the volume of net FDI inflows increases. The disaggregated components of the weighted corruption risk indicator include financial corruption, which takes the form of demands for special payments, bribes in relation to export and import licenses, exchange controls, tax assessments and bank loans. The indicator also takes into account corruption in the form of patronage, secret funding, and nepotism and job reservations (Hayakawa et al. 2010).

Our findings with regard to country risk variables support the pattern of existing mixed evidence in the literature. Similar to Gastanaga et al. (1998) and Wei (2000), we find that lower corruption is associated with greater FDI inflows. In cases where we include all country risk variables from ICRG, corruption's significance dropped. Most of the other political risk and institutional variables are not significant determinants of net FDI flows in Africa. Likewise, Asiedu (2002) concludes that neither political risk nor expropriation risk has any significant effect on FDI. Further, Noorbakhsh et al. (2001) also report that democracy and political risk are not significantly related to FDI.

Increased religious tensions (e.g. domination of governance by a single religious group) are found to lead to lower FDI inflows and this result is robust across different specifications. The positive coefficient indicates an increase in FDI inflows as the risk of religious tension declines. Religious tensions often lead to political uncertainty and intense rent-seeking behavior on the part of public servants, creating uncertainties that disrupt economic activity and discourage investment. Hence, it is necessary to encourage social goals such as participation, open societies with freedom and remove religious repressions.

Patterns of Intra-Africa Investment Flows

There are investment outflows from Africa with North and Southern African countries leading the way. Relative to Africa, investments within other continents is higher. For instance, intra-regional FDI in Europe, Latin America, Asia and Africa are, respectively, 82 percent, 17 percent, 10 percent and 5 percent. However, there is an increasing trend in intra-African investment flows. For instance, intra-African investment increased by 21 percent between 2003 and 2010 (Ernst and Young 2011; Johnson et al. 2012). In terms of the major players, investment from South Africa continues to play a major role in the continent followed by Kenya and Nigeria. According to the Vale Columbia Centre on Sustainable International Investment between 2002 and 2004, average annual flows of intra-African FDI were estimated to be US$2 billion with a decline in 2005 and 2006. However, there is an upward trend in 2007. There is also an increase in the share of number of projects originating in Africa in the value of FDI projects with a growth of 8 percent in 2003 to 17 percent in 2011.

The focus of intra-Africa investment is in primary sector but there is also a success story in terms of services sector (e.g. bank related) driven investment. Intra-Africa investment is often triggered via merger and acquisition (M&A) deals. According to Johnson et al. (2012), the challenge facing intra-Africa investors include lack of capital, technology, competitive strength, skilled labor, access to markets, supportive policies of home/source countries, and the presence of persistent gaps in infrastructure and integration. These challenges are inherent capacity challenges that persist over the years and it is imperative to channel efforts to tackle them to unlock investment and growth potential of the continent. South Africa has contributed to private investment in Africa and is credited to increasing productivity, competitiveness and overall improvements of various sectors such as banking, telecommunications, pay-tv, hotels, the retail sector, business services, construction, mining, farmers and agribusiness.

In recent years, there is an increasing trend in intra-Africa investment and trade. Between 2003 and 2011, there has been 23 percent compound growth in intra-African investment into new FDI projects. This growth is accelerating and remarkable since 2007 with a recorded growth rate of 42 percent. In 2011 intra-African investment accounted for 17 percent of all new FDI projects on the continent. A study by Ernst and Young in 2012 shows the growing trend in intra-Africa investment inflows in terms of investment projects. As indicated earlier, the major intra-Africa investors are South Africa, Nigeria and Kenya for the period from 2007 to 2011 and have registered investment growth rates in cumulative FDI projects of 64.8, 73.2 and 77.8 percent respectively. However, there are opposite trends in the context of investment growth rates in FDI project for North African countries such as Egypt which registered -38.5 percent and Tunisia with a very depressing figure of -100 percent (Ernst and Young 2012). The political turmoil and the subsequent growth decline in North African countries most likely underlines the negative growth rates.

Capacity Issues

In this sub-section, we address capacity issues in relation to attracting investment within the continent. However, our discussion has direct implications for the promotion of capital flowing from outside Africa. The key questions that we attempt to answer are: "What capacity do African governments, regional institutions, NGOs and private sector have to nurture an environment that supports intra-African FDI?" and "How does intra-Africa investment encourage FDI flows from outside Africa?"

Strong and sustained growth in Africa over the last decade urged developed countries to see the continent with optimism. This led to increases in FDI flows into the continent. But it is not only investors from outside that see the growth, trade and investment opportunities of the continent. As shown earlier, the volume of intra-Africa trade is encouraging and is progressively increasing even if it is at its low level compared to other regions of the world such as Latin America and Asia. Intra-African investment flows and intra-Africa trade depend on the intensity of regional integration within the continent. For Africa to fully realize its intra-regional trade and investment potential, there is a need for harmonization of regional trade agreements and the inclusion of investment regimes. Since investment has a positive multiplier effect on trade, it is imperative to encourage it for sustainable development and less reliance on other sources of growth such as foreign aid (Seyoum et al. 2013). Through FDI-induced trade particularly exports, countries can enhance their competitiveness. There are some encouraging developments in terms of coordinating regional investment policy reforms. The Economic Community of West African States (ECOWAS) has been developing the ECOWAS Common Investment Market since 2008 (see Mobolaji and Kedir 2013 for details). Likewise the Southern African Development Community established its Regional Action Plan for Investment (RAPI) in 2012 and the East African Community (EAC) urged its members to harmonize national laws according to the EAC Common Market Protocol.

Infrastructure and technology challenges (such as infrequent electricity supply) are major impediments to intra-Africa investment as much as they are for investment coming outside of the continent. To increase, Africa's share of investment within the continent and its share in the overall global stock of flow of capital increases if these bottlenecks are tackled. Given the heterogeneous nature of the structure of African economies, investors can exploit potential complementarities. For instance, coastal countries (e.g. Ghana, Senegal, Tanzania, etc.) have a comparative advantage in attracting an African country with a sound refrigerator technology (e.g. long-haul vehicles with cooling systems to transport fish and vegetables across borders) and countries with large arable land can be a target by another African country that can invest in commercial agriculture with food security in mind.

Ensuring central bank independence and having a pragmatic monetary and fiscal stance are essential macroeconomic policies that create conducive environment for investment. In recent years, FDI flows to Africa improved precisely for these reasons (Elumelu and Oppenheimer 2013).

Africa has a young population and this is a huge asset for investors. However, the human capital quality and capacity need to be developed further. As in the case of FDI coming from outside Africa, intra-FDI is also attracted to large markets and where there are educated young people such as in South Africa (Goldstein 2004). Hence, the supply side consideration of improving education quality for the young and future generation is an important component of a strategic policy to attract and retain investment to which governments should give sufficient attention. Focus on quality is also needed for the development of skills and technology which is acutely lacking right now in Africa. This gap is often filled by FDI from outside Africa.

Evidence shows that investors follow those who invest before them. Hence, we argue that the increasing trend in intra-Africa investment is the basis for further investment by other investors within the continent and also outside the continent. Big foreign investors will invest behind local investors in the continent and feel confident if there is increasing activity via intra-Africa investment projects. Hence intra-Africa investment has a direct positive spillover effect in attracting capital flows from outside Africa. In terms of institutional implementation, African governments should treat investors from the continent in identical terms as those coming from outside the continent.

Conclusion and Policy Recommendations

African governments are increasingly engaged in mobilizing resources via intra-Africa investment and public finance reforms for better tax collection within their shores. In this study we saw the trends in intra-Africa investment descriptively and net FDI inflows to Africa in a multivariate setting. The growth records of the recent past and the future prospects present opportunities for investment. Our study identified key capacity challenges in the bid to attract investment funds both within and outside the continent. To attract FDI, African countries need to improve governance (e.g. by reducing corruption), fight financial corruption at all levels and address religious tensions. Depending on the quality of bureaucracy, financial liberalization can help African countries induce increased FDI inflows, but financial development alone might have a negative effect, suggesting the potential substitution between domestic and foreign investments.

The econometric findings have important policy implications for African countries in a bid to attract more FDI. While the resource factor remains an important determinant of FDI flows, other factors such as market size are assuming an increasing importance in stimulating investment on the continent. Africa needs to attract increased and diversified market-seeking investment in order to promote high-level and sustainable growth that spurs economic transformation, job creation and poverty reduction. Market-seeking FDI normally flows to such labor-intensive sectors as services and processing that add value and create jobs. Therefore, in addition to policies aiming to expand markets, including regional integration and economic partnership arrangements, growth and development strategies of African countries should include specific policies aimed at attracting FDI. These measures would range from institutional reforms that improve the business environment to targeted/increased public spending on infrastructure and human capital development.

In this context, many African countries have adopted international codes and standards and put in place policies aimed at improving the investment climate along with special incentives for foreign investment. However, owing to implementation gaps these policies remain ineffective for African countries to attract the desired amounts and quality of FDI despite their huge untapped economic potential and resource abundance. Strengthening policymaking and implementation is therefore essential especially in relation to the quality of civil servants and the fight against corruption.

Well-trained and adequately paid bureaucrats contributed to high levels of investment and economic take-off in emerging economies in East Asia and Latin America (Blomstrom and Kokko 2003). The evidence provided by this chapter calls for more and effective efforts by African countries to improve the quality of bureaucracy in order to ensure that financial development is conducive to FDI. In the absence of quality bureaucracy, financial development may create a bias in resource allocation that discourages foreign investment and perhaps domestic investment as well.

Despite notable improvements in economic governance, corruption remains a serious development challenge in Africa owing to institutional weakness and declining economic and living standards of public servants, among other factors (2010 Transparency International's Corruption Perception Index [CPI]). The results of this chapter show that corruption has a significant adverse effect on FDI inflows to Africa and should therefore remain a priority policy area especially if African countries are to attract competitive market-seeking foreign investments. Many African countries have identified corruption as "public enemy number one," but the methods they use to fight corruption remain ineffective.

Governments often lack commitments and/or the means to implement anti-corruption codes and standards they have already ratified and many of the anti-corruption bodies fail to meet the basic minimum requirements (independence; jurisdiction, powers and scope of activities of the institution; and cooperation between national authorities and non-state actors) to be effective (UNECA 2009). To be effective in combating corruption in the context of good economic governance, African governments need to establish inclusive and transparent anti-corruption institutions that have the legal framework as well the human and financial resources to implement their mandate. A well-trained and adequately compensated bureaucracy and an independent judiciary system are essential in stemming corruption, enforcing laws and regulation and attracting FDI.

Weak political governance institutions in Africa allow the domination of special interest groups including religious and ethnic groups that undermine existing economic, political and social institutions. The evidence provided by this chapter strongly underscores the disruptive effect of religious tensions that deter the flow of FDI. Governments should pay special attention to these religious tensions not just for attracting FDI but also for promoting political stability as a prerequisite for broader economic and social development. Future work can focus on compiling a long series of intra-Africa investment data and investigating analytically unique drivers of intra-Africa investment.

Though it is not borne out an empirical exercise, RECs can promote policy predictability and liberalized markets. Hence, facilitating the formation of well- functioning RECs has an important role to play to attract FDI to Africa (Goldstein 2004).

References

Addison, T. and Heshmati, A. (2003), "The new global determinants of FDI flows to developing countries: the importance of ICT and democratization." WIDER.

AfDB (2011), "African Economic Outlook 2011: Africa and its emerging partners." Tunis, Tunisia: African Development Bank.

Ali, F., Fiess, N. and Macdonald, R. (2010), "Do Institutions matter for foreign direct investment?" *Open Economies Review* 21 (2): 201–19.

Arellano, M. and Bond, S. (1991), "Some Tests of Specification for Panel Data: Monte Carlo Evidence and an Application to Employment Equations," *Review of Economic Studies* 58: 277–97.

Asiedu, E. (2013), Foreign Direct Investment, Natural Resources and Institutions, working paper, International Growth Centre, London School of Economics (LSE), UK.

——— (2006), "Foreign Direct Investment in Africa: The Role of Natural Resources, Market Size, Government Policy, Institutions And Political Instability," *The World Economy* 29 (1): 63–77.

______ (2004), "Policy Reform and Foreign Direct Investment in Africa: Absolute Progress but Relative Decline," *Development Policy Review* 22 (1): 41–8.

______ (2002), "On The Determinants Of Foreign Direct Investment To Developing Countries: Is Africa Different?" *World Development* 30 (1): 107–19.

Asiedu, E. and Freeman, J. (2009), "The Effect of Corruption on Investment Growth: Evidence from Firms In Latin America, Sub-Saharan Africa And Transition Countries," *Review Of Development Economics* 13 (2): 200–214.

Baltagi, B., Demetriades, P. and Law, S.H. (2009), "Financial Development and Openness: Evidence From Panel Data," *Journal of Development Economics* 89 (2): 285–96.

Benassy-quere, A., Coupet, M. and Mayer, T. (2007), "Institutional Determinants of Foreign Direct Investment," *World Economy* 30 (5): 764–82.

Bevan, A. and Estrin, S. (2004), "The Determinants of Foreign Direct Investment into European Transition Economies," *Journal of Comparative Economics* 32 (4): 775–87.

Blonigen, B.A. (2005), "A Review of the Empirical Literature on FDI Determinants," A*tlantic Economic Journal* 33: 383–403.

Blomstrom, M. and Kokko, A. (2003), "Human Capital and Inward FDI." Working paper 167. Sweden: Stockholm School of Economics.

Blundell, R. and Bond, S. (1998), "Initial Conditions and moment restrictions in dynamic panel models," *Journal of Econometrics* 87: 115–43.

Bond, S., Hoeffler, A. and Temple, J. (2001), "GMM estimation of empirical growth models." Economics Papers 2001-W21, Economics Group, Nuffield College, University of Oxford.

Buckley, P.J. (2008), "Do We Need A Special Theory of Foreign Direct Investment for Extractive Industries?" *Journal of Chinese Economic and Foreign Trade Studies* 1 (2): 93–104.

Busse, M. and Hefeker, C. (2007), "Political Risk, Institutions and Foreign Direct Investment," *European Journal of Political Economy* 23 (2): 397.

Chakrabarti, A. (2001), "The Determinants of Foreign Direct Investment: Sensitivity Analyses of Cross-Country Regressions," *Kyklos* 54 (1): 89–113.

Dunning, J. (2009), "Location and the multinational Enterprise: a Neglected Factor?" *Journal of International Business Studies* 40 (1): 5–19.

——— (1998), "Location and the Multinational Enterprise: A Neglected Factor?" *Journal of International Business Studies* 29 (1): 45–66.

______ (1993), *Multinational Enterprises and the Global Economy*. Harlow: Addison-Wesley.

Elumelu, T. and Oppenheimer, J. (2013), "Africans investing in Africa: Building prosperity through intra-African trade and investment." Discussion paper #2; The Brenthurst Foundation and the Tony Elumelu Foundation, Lagos, Nigeria.

Ernst and Young (2012), "Growing Beyond Building Bridges," Africa Attractiveness survey.

Gastanaga, V., Nugent, J. and Pashamova, B. (1998), "Host Country Reforms and FDI Inflows: How Much Difference Do They Make," *World Development* 26: 1299–314.

Hayakawa, K., Kimura, F. and Lee, H-H. (2010), "How Does Country Risk Matter for FDI?" Mimeo, Division of Economics and International Trade, Kangwon National University, South Korea.

Goldstein, A. (2004), "Regional Integration, FDI and competitiveness in Southern Africa." Development Centre Studies, OECD, Paris.

Ibrahim, G., Elhiraika, A., Hamdok, A. and Kedir, A. (2011), "Revisiting the Determinants of Foreign Direct Investment in Africa: the role of Institutions and Policy Reforms." Paper presented at the 2011 African Economic Conference (AEC), Addis Ababa, Ethiopia.

Jenson, N.M. (2002), "Economic Reform, State Capture, and International Investment in Transition Economies," *Journal of International Development* 14 (7): 973–7.

Kedir, A. (2013), "African transforming Africa: Intra-Regional Investment for growth." Paper prepared for the Annual Meetings of the African Development Bank, Marrakech, Morocco.

Kolstad, I. and Tøndel, L. (2002), "Social Development and Foreign Direct Investments in Developing Countries." Report R 2002: 11, Chr. Michelsen Institute Development Studies and Human Rights, Bergen, Norway.

Li, Q., Vashchilko, A. and Vashchilko, T. (2010), "Interstate Political Relations and Bilateral FDI flows." Paper presented at the International Political Economy Society Meeting. Cambridge, MA: Harvard University.

McKinsey Global (2010), "Lions on the Move: the Progress and Potential of African Economies." South Africa.

Mobolaji, H. and Kedir, A. (2013), "Financial Integration and Common Investment Market among ECOWAS countries," *Journal of West African Integration* 1 (2): 96–137.

Morriset, J. (2000), "Foreign Direct Investment in Africa: Policies also Matter," *Translational Corporations* 9 (2): 107–25.

Naude, W. and Krugell, W. (2007), "Investigating Geography and Institutions as Determinants of FDI in Africa Using Panel Data," *Applied Economics* 39 (10): 1223–33.

Nickell, S. (1981), "Biases in Dynamic Models with Fixed Effects," *Econometrica* 49: 1417–26.

Noorbakhsh, F., Paloni, A. and Youssef, A. (2001), "Human Capital and FDI Inflows to Developing Countries: New Empirical Evidence," *World Development* 29: 1593–610.

North, D. (1990), *Institutions, Institutional Change and Economic Performance.* Cambridge: Cambridge University.

Onyeiwu, S. and Hemanta, S. (2004), "Determinants of Foreign Direct Investment," *Journal of Developing Societies* 20 (1): 89–106.

Seyoum, M., Wu, R. and Lin, J. (2013), "Foreign Direct Investment and Trade openness in Sub-Saharan Economies: A Panel Data Granger Causality Analysis," *South African Journal of Economics*, DOI: 10.1111/saje.12022.

UNECA (2009), *The Governance Report*, UNECA. Addis Ababa, Ethiopia.

Wei, S.J. (2000), "How Taxing is Corruption on International Investors?" *Review of Economics and Statistics* 82 (1): 1–11.

Wernick, D.A., Haar, J. and Singh, S. (2009), "Do Governing Institutions Affect Foreign Direct Investment Inflows?" *International Journal of Economic and Business Research* 1 (3): 317–32.

World Bank (2002), "Global Economic Prospects." Washington, D.C.: World Bank.

Yartey, C.A. and Adjasi, C.K. (2007), "Stock Market Development in Sub-Saharan Africa: Critical Issues and Challenges." IMF Working Paper No. WP/07/209. Washington, D.C.: International Monetary Fund.

UNCTAD (2013), "Global Investment Trends Monitor, The Rise of BRICS FDI and Africa," Special Edition, unedited version, Geneva.

Chapter 7
Infrastructure and Capacity Development as a Catalyst for Regionalism and Economic Integration in Africa

Kobena T. Hanson, Francis Owusu and Korbla P. Puplampu

Introduction

The development prospects of any country or region requires a complex interaction of internal and external factors, as well as the availability and optimum combination of necessary and sufficient conditions, specifically human and physical resources. One particular variable and the source of intense interest has been the state of infrastructure, its quality within and beyond the national context. This interest has assumed a particularly significant place in the face of the growing relevance of regionalism in the development prospects of Africa. Indeed, infrastructure is of immense significance to regionalism, especially in the environment of contemporary globalization.

Infrastructure is the "capital that provides public goods" (Hirschman 1958, p. 63) or capital goods (Gramlich 1994) that, in principle, are non-exclusive and accessible to all. Infrastructure can also be classified as economic (e.g. transport, communications, power generation, water supply and sanitation facilities) or as social (e.g. educational and health-care facilities), although there are overlaps between these categories. The meaning of infrastructure has expanded to focus on physical fixed assets or "hard" infrastructure as well as regulatory or "soft" infrastructure (AfDB 2010). Aspects of the former include the state of the facilities and their interconnectedness, while the latter involve the policy framework and its practical implications, for example excessive red tape. Taken together, the hard and soft aspects of infrastructure are keys in any program on regionalism that seeks to promote trade in particular and economic development in general.

Regionalism is the desire by countries to seek the betterment of each other by working together. Such togetherness, which involves changing roles of the state, is consistent with attributes of globalization. Contemporary globalization calls for, among other things, a minimal role of the state in the political and economic sectors; including opening up the productive space to the active participation by non-state actors and other private entities, some of whom could be non-profit or for-profit and located within and beyond the nation-state. Infrastructure occupies an essential place in regionalism and economic integration. Its major components, energy, telecommunications, and transport, serve as architecture connecting countries in the regional context and beyond. The essence of regionalism is to enlarge the development possibilities, and infrastructure is the anchor forging those possibilities.

There is growing literature on the state of infrastructure in Africa (Ranganathan and Foster 2011a, b, c, d; AfDB 2010; Schiere and Rugamba 2011; Kuroda, Kawai and Nangia 2007; Mbekeani 2010; Mafusire et al. 2011). The literature stresses what has become known as the infrastructure gap or deficit in Africa. This gap involves not only the state of the region's infrastructure, but also the financial commitments necessary and required to close the gap, if the goals of unleashing the productive potential and integration for human development are to be met. There seems to be a consensus in the extant literature that African governments have to adopt a different model in financing improvements in the infrastructure sector. Put differently, the historical role of the state in financing infrastructure is not, in view of its changing role in the political and economic spheres, sustainable. While some promising and tangible cases of infrastructure dot the continental landscape, the depth of the infrastructure deficit requires sustained attention in the region's development agenda.

This chapter examines the extent to which infrastructure can aid productivity growth, enable and deepen regionalism and economic integration. Specifically, the chapter identifies and discusses the state of infrastructure in Africa and reviews ongoing attempts to upgrade the infrastructure network in the region. The study is divided into three sections. The first section presents an overview of infrastructure, regionalism and economic integration in Africa. Section two addresses the state of infrastructure in Africa and focuses on some notable contemporary initiatives while section three draws attention to capacity development imperatives, opportunities, and possibilities for multi-sector and multi-actor participation. This section also presents the concluding remarks.

Regionalism, Infrastructure and Development: An Overview

A sufficient and quality infrastructure foundation, such as development of ports, logistics systems, and road conditions and maintenance of transit corridors in collaboration, are vital to fostering regional integration and sustainable economic development. According to the ECLAC (2009, p. 1), "Regional integration is the process by which diverse national economies seek mutual gains by complementing one another more." Regional integration can help countries to overcome their locational constrains and facilitate their participation in regional and global economies. For the purpose of this discussion, it is helpful to breakdown the regional integration process into the following three dimensions: economic and trade integration, which includes different degrees or stages of integration (preferential trade agreements; free trade area; customs union; common market and economic and monetary union); political integration, which implies greater depth, coordination and harmonization of actions among members in the governmental and institutional sphere; and physical integration, featuring infrastructure and its services as the protagonists (ECLAC 2009, p. 1). We focus on physical integration as a way of actualizing economic, trade, and political integration. Regional infrastructure development is a critical component of physical integration (Mbekeani 2010; Kessides and Benjamin 2012).

While this chapter is not about the definitional debate over the term "infrastructure," it is still important to note that physical infrastructure takes on multiple forms in regional and economic integration (Fourie 2006; Torrisi 2009). With the exception of bridges and tunnels that connect two countries, or power lines, pipelines, and fiber optic cables that may span several countries, most infrastructure are national in nature. Kessides and Benjamin (2012: 10), define regional or cross-border infrastructure as "projects that involve physical construction works and/or coordinated policies and procedures spanning two or more neighboring countries; and national infrastructure projects that have a significant cross-border impact." The potential benefits of regional infrastructure for developing countries are therefore enormous and significant, hence the strong reciprocal relationship between regional integration and infrastructure (Kessides and Benjamin 2012). This is the basis of the argument that "integrating physical infrastructure is both a precursor to and enabler for deeper economic integration" (World Bank 2009, p. 143).

Infrastructure development promotes regional integration and globalization. Cross-border infrastructure, such as improvements in transportation and the application of modern information and communication technologies, improve the physical connectivity between countries, facilitate geographic division of production processes, and provide opportunities for individual economies to participate in international production networks. Increased regional integration also creates demand for infrastructure. Transportation and communication infrastructure, for instance, are the glue that hold regional integration together. The former facilitates trade and factor mobility and the latter is necessary for increasing trade, facilitating transboundary transactions, and linking the region with the rest of the world. Other benefits of regional integration include harmonization of legal, regulatory, and institutional frameworks among the countries involved, a reduction in cross-border transaction costs and a rational use of resources due to coordinated development of infrastructure (Kessides and Benjamin 2012).

Given the poor state of infrastructure in many developing countries, it is obvious that they cannot achieve their development goals, including poverty alleviation, without significant improvements in the physical infrastructure (Kessides 1996; Kessides and Benjamin 2012; Calderòn and Servèn 2004). The availability and quality of a country's physical infrastructure significantly influences its international competitiveness, regional trade, investment, poverty reduction and development potential (SELA 2011). As argued by Mbekeani (2010, pp. i88–i89), "whether each country's priorities are defined as enhancing international trade, stimulating private investment or diversifying the industrial base, the ability to meet these objectives depends on the performance of an interrelated set of infrastructure services such as transport, energy, [and] telecommunications." Specifically, investments in infrastructure contribute to GDP growth through transport services, telecommunications, potable water, power supply, and sanitation services; create externalities on production and investment leading to long-term growth; and influence the overall productivity level of the economy. Regional integration also allows for coordinated investments for development of infrastructure which, in turn, sustains economic, social and political integration, including the establishment of common development areas through border integration (SELA 2011).

Infrastructure is primarily important given the low intra-African trade. Over 80 percent of Africa's exports are destined for, and over 90 percent of imports originate from, markets outside Africa (Hartzenberg 2011). Meanwhile, the trade flows (both imports and exports) within the various regional economic communities (RECs) have recently increased significantly. ECA analysis also showed that between 2000 and 2007, exports between the RECs saw an average growth rate of 15 percent, with imports also recording 18 percent growth rate within the same period (Hartzenberg 2011). These growth rates are impressive and point to the benefit of RECs and the need for effective regional integration efforts.

Infrastructure does not contribute to improvements in macroeconomic situation of countries alone. There are qualitative improvements in the living standards of the people as well. For instance, as Willoughby (2004) argued, infrastructure investments at the national level underpin virtually all the millennium development goals (MDGs), including halving income poverty. It also affects the non-income aspects of poverty, contributing to improvements in health, nutrition, education and social cohesion. In sum, regional infrastructural development efforts are critical for achieving the development and poverty eradication objectives of developing countries.

Regionalism and the State of Infrastructure in Africa: Historical and Contemporary Survey

Discussions on infrastructure in African development require a historical context. First, in the colonial era, the nature of the infrastructure was, not unexpectedly, tied to the movement of primary commodities (agricultural produce and minerals) to the ports for export. Hence, of the major forms of infrastructure, there was an intense interest on transport, while others, such as energy and telecommunications did not receive the desired attention. Second, the colonial state was at the helm of establishing the transport infrastructure (railways, roads, ports and harbors) to enable mostly expatriate trading companies to profit from the export and import trade. Take the case of the railway systems in colonial Africa. Given the bulky nature of primary produce, it was not surprising that railways and, to some extent, roads were from production sites in the interior to ports and harbors on the coast and thus the focus of budgetary considerations and priority (Prior 2013; Kay 1972). Another remarkable aspect of the colonial development trajectory was the recognition that the transport network was one way to integrate the colonies, especially the hinterlands and the urban areas and therefore significant in the urbanization process (Prior 2013; Havinden and Meredith 1993).

The postcolonial African state continued with the role of financing infrastructure development and became a dominant player in the overall development process. However, the efforts of the postcolonial state at regional integration predate the independence struggle. For instance, the South African Customs Union (SACU) was established in 1910. Similarly, there was the Customs Union between Kenya and Uganda in 1917, which Tanganyika (now Tanzania) later joined in 1927; this ultimately led to the creation of the East African Community in 1967. During the struggle for independence, the pan-African leaders aggressively pushed the idea of a unified Africa as a way of counteracting the effects of colonialism and promoting economic and political cooperation in the region. The establishment of the Economic Commission for Africa (ECA) in 1958 and creation of the Organization of African Unity (OAU) in 1963 laid the initial blue print for contemporary discussions on regionalism and also reiterated the significance of infrastructure in economic integration and regional development.

Specifically, the 1991 Abuja Treaty and the subsequent establishment of the African Economic Community (AEC) were watershed moments in terms of how African countries would "coordinate and harmonize polices among existing and future regional economic communities" (Kessides and Benjamin 2012, p. 4) with the ultimate goal of enhancing free trade and the free mobility of relevant factors of production. The AEC has legitimized eight regional economic communities: Union de Maghreb Arabe (Arab Maghreb Union,

AMU); the Economic Community of West African States (ECOWAS); East African Community (EAC); Common Market for Eastern and Southern Africa (COMESA); Economic Community for Central African States (ECCAS); Intergovernmental Authority on Development (IGAD); the Community of Sahel-Saharan States (CEN-SAD); and Southern African Development Community (SADC) (Thonke and Spliid 2012).

In 2002, African leaders officially established the African Union (AU) as a way of expediting the process of economic and political integration on the continent. By converting the OAU and the AEC into one unified institution, the AU envisions the RECs as the building blocks for the AEC in a process to be completed by 2028 (Kessides and Benjamin 2012). The African Union-sponsored New Partnership for African Development (NEPAD) launched in 2002 gave further impetus to a continental approach to regionalism and economic integration. It is important to note that while political motivations prompted early regional integration attempts, current initiatives are driven more by the forces of globalization as African countries respond to global competitive pressures and strive to attract foreign direct investment. The key question is how the state of infrastructure across Africa underpin the continental and regional approaches to economic integration

There are significant variations among most African countries and their respective regional economic communities (RECs) on the state of their energy, telecommunications and transport infrastructure (NEPAD 2013; Kabele-Camara 2012; AfDB 2010; Ranganathan and Foster 2011a, b, c, d). As Foster and Briceno-Garmendia (2010) point out, in terms of energy, more than 30 African countries continue to experience power shortages and irregular service delivery in addition to a significantly high cost of generating electricity. The unavoidable outcome of this state of affairs is the lack of reliable and steady electricity systems to power industries and households.

In comparative terms, although the power transmission network in SADC is relatively advanced and has the highest generation, it has poor outcomes in terms of access to power (Ranganathan and Foster 2011d). While the EAC has the smallest generation capacity and the lowest access to power in Africa, the performance of its utility system is encouraging with the lowest system loses after SADC (Ranganathan and Foster 2011a). On one hand, ECOWAS performs relatively well when it comes to electrification, but on the other hand, it experiences shortfalls in generation capacity, service reliability, and the overall performance of the electricity system (Ranganathan and Foster 2011c).

There has been growing interest in the extent to which the breakthroughs in information and communication technologies (ICTs) can contribute to Africa's development (NEPAD 2013; Akpan-Obong 2006). Beyond the traditional radio and television, the contemporary telecommunications envelope includes phone services, both fixed-landlines and mobile facilities and broader changes in line with the advances in computerization. SADC has made significant strides in ICTs in Africa by way of access, but prices are still very high in the region (Ranganathan and Foster 2011d). ECOWAS is closely behind SADC in the relative performance of ICTs in Africa and like SADC has to contend with high prices for services, but boasts of better broadband prices compared to SADC (Ranganathan and Foster 2011c, p. 55). A noteworthy aspect of ICTs in ECOWAS is the high cost within member countries compared to calls to distant locales such as the United States of America. Perhaps, another feature of ICTs in ECOWAS is the widespread nature of regional roaming arrangements, compared to the SADC region.

ICT features in EAC mirror those in SADC and ECOWAS, but at different levels of efficiency (Ranganathan and Foster 2011a). First, the cost of services are high, penetration of internet services, for example, is low, even though there is a strong global system of mobile communication (GSM) coverage around Lake Victoria, engulfing countries such as Burundi, Rwanda, Uganda and Kenya. While ICT coverage is not extensive in Tanzania, and is limited in Ethiopia, Sudan has high mobile signal coverage. The NEPAD (2013) portfolio on ICT infrastructure is spearheading the East Africa Submarine Cable System (EASSy) to connect East African countries, eventually tapping into the optical fibre submarine network running from South Africa to Sudan.

Transport infrastructure involves roads, railways, ports as well as airports. It is imperative to stress that the interdependence that all forms of infrastructure manifest is better demonstrated by transport infrastructure. Seaports and airports, as points of exit to and entry from external regional and global markets, cannot adequately function without a commensurate efficiency in roads and railways in the first place. By and large, roads are ubiquitous in the movement of freight and passengers in Africa. The relevant features of African roads include the following: toll roads are not widespread with all such roads (about 0.1 percent based in South Africa); and there are significant differences in road quality between rural and urban areas (AfDB 2010). The continental picture is further reflected differently across the RECs in Africa.

SADC has about 75 percent of its road regional network in relatively good condition compared to only 57 percent of such roads in EAC (Ranganathan and Foster 2011d). In the ECOWAS subregion, national governments have given significant attention to the state of the regional road network and thus, 93 percent of the network has been paved (Ranganathan and Foster 2011c). In view of the pivotal role of the road network, there has been a growing interest in linking African trade and transport corridors. The result is the nine interlinked sections as part of the Trans-African Highway Network: the Cairo–Dakar Highway; Algiers–Lagos Highway; Tripoli–Windhoek–Cape Town Highway; Cairo–Gaborone–Pretoria-Cape Town Highway; Dakar-Ndjamena Highway; Ndjamena–Djibouti Highway; Dakar–Lagos Highway; Lagos-Mombasa

Highway; and Beira–Lobito Highway (AfDB 2010). These interlinked highways crisscross the various RECs in Africa and demonstrate the potential that a holistic approach to road transport on the continent can bring to regional integration and economic development.

Railways, if properly aligned, can help facilitate the movement of freight and passenger traffic and introduce a degree of competition with the road network (Bullock 2009). The railway system in the SADC region is not only the most connected across the region, but also the most extensive and well developed in Africa (Ranganathan and Foster 2011d). The railway systems in both ECOWAS and EAC do not constitute a regional network (Ranganathan and Foster 2011a; 2011c). Ports and waterways are indispensable in linking global markets, and that places serious barriers on the development prospects for landlocked African countries such as Burkina Faso, Zimbabwe and Ethiopia. African ports and waterways have experienced significant increases in volume within the last decade, however inadequate physical infrastructure resulting in congestion and delays as well as different institutional capacities relative to the goods they handle continue to pose challenges (AfDB 2010).

The types of ports and waterways in Africa range from general cargo ports (Port Elizabeth in South Africa), hub ports (Port Said in Egypt and Durban in South Africa), feeder ports (most of the ports on the West African coast), bulk ports (Buchanan, Liberia and Sort Saco, Angola), transshipment ports or terminals (Algiers, Algeria; Mombasa, Kenya; Durban, South Africa; and Djibouti, Djibouti); dedicated oil terminals (Durban and Cape Town, South Africa); to river ports (Matadi, DRC). To place the above in a regional framework, the ports and waterways within SADC are the most actively utilized; and Durban is the second busiest African port, given its various roles (hub, transshipment, dedicated oil terminal) (AfDB 2010). The ports in the ECA, although behind those in SADC and ECOWAS, have been undergoing substantial increases in growth of container traffic within the last two decades (Ranganathan and Foster 2011a). Ports in the ECOWAS sub-region, when compared to others regions, are behind those in the SADC region, but ahead of their counterparts in the EAC. While the ports in ECOWAS generally continue to experience significant infrastructure deficit, their performance, like their other regional counterparts, varies.

Air transport, like the other forms of infrastructure, has been the focus of growing pains and structural changes in all the RECs across Africa. However, SADC has “the largest and most advanced air transport market in Africa, with South Africa … [as] the most important international gateway” (Ranganathan and Foster 2011d, p. 31). Johannesburg, has emerged as a strong hub-and-spoke center, with Nairobi and Addis Ababa playing a similar role, but at a lesser level of intensity. The EAC’s air transport system mainly revolves around Kenya Airways, a reflection of Kenya’s dominant role in the economic affairs of the sub-region (Ranganathan and Foster 2011a).

Notwithstanding the foregoing, below are three notable illustrations of regional infrastructure in Africa: West African Gas Pipeline (WAGP); Dakar–Ndjamena–Djibouti (DND) Road and Rail Project; and the Maputo Development Corridor (MDC).

Infrastructure, Regionalism and Development: Selected Case Studies

West African Gas Pipeline (WAGP)

The Governments of Benin, Ghana, Nigeria and Togo, within the setting of the ECOWAS, conceived the West African Gas Pipeline (WAGP) in the early 1980s as a vehicle for facilitating clean, natural gas and supply security, as well as a tool to advance regional integration (World Bank 2006). However, following recent oil and gas discoveries in Ghana, it is projected that the WAGP could in the future be extended beyond Ghana, further strengthening opportunities for improved sub-regional integration, and shaping new regionalism in the ECOWAS sub-region (Shaw and Fanta 2013). The US$690 million offshore pipeline project, covering 681 km, is designed to carry 474 MMscf/d of gas from Nigeria to Benin, Togo and Ghana and should complement the existing hydro power systems in these countries. Current market forecast suggests an expansion schedule to increase from the presently installed capacity of 170 MMscf/d to 474 MMscf/d by 2026. The WAGP also serves as a "feeder" into the West Africa Gas Pool which involves the four countries but also benefits the entire Gulf of Guinea sub-region. Aside from the four governments, other key stakeholders in the project are private sector oil companies such as Chevron Texaco, and Shell.

This micro-regional project is driving an open, unified economic space through the integration of markets for goods as well as financial and other services (World Bank 2006). The project is also spurring the essential building blocks of a sustainable energy infrastructure network. Particularly, when Ghana's Volta River Authority (VRA) in April 2009 generated its first electricity using natural gas from WAGP, it ushered in a new era with vast opportunities and possibilities.

To further enhance cooperation, participating nations and private sector stakeholders set up the West African Gas Pipeline Company limited (WAPCo), a limited liability company, to manage and operate WAGP. WAPCo is a joint venture between public and private sector companies from Nigeria, Benin, Togo and Ghana. Jointly owned by Chevron West African Gas Pipeline Ltd (36.9 percent); Nigerian National Petroleum Corporation (24.9 percent); Shell Overseas Holdings Limited (17.9 percent); Takoradi Power Company Limited (16.3 percent); Societe Togolaise de Gaz (2 percent); and Societe BenGaz S.A.

(2 percent), the company's main mandate is to transport natural gas from Nigeria to customers in Benin, Togo and Ghana in a safe, responsible and reliable manner, at prices competitive with other fuel alternatives (WAPCo 2014). The project is reflective of contemporary regionalism in its "fluid, multi-dimensional, multi-level" nature (Söderbaum 2003; Söderbaum and Taylor 2008); with its headquarters in Accra, Ghana; an office in Badagry, Nigeria; and field offices in Cotonou, Benin; Lome, Togo; as well as Tema and Takoradi, both in Ghana. To further drive regionalism, participating countries have set up commercial and regulatory terms; and a comprehensive and harmonized investment regime to enable WAPCo operate as a single business entity across all four countries (WAPCo 2014).

The above notwithstanding, and as with all regional initiatives, the WAGP also has its vulnerabilities, the primary one being the illegal maritime navigation activities along the project route and the perennial issues around institutions, their capacity and leadership. Accordingly, while the rise of this, and other, regional projects hold much potential and promise (Draper and Ismail 2014; Besada et al. 2013), attention needs to be paid to the sequencing of implementation, and the capabilities of all stakeholders (Tavares and Tang 2013), to ensure successful regionalism.

Dakar-Ndjamena-Djibouti Road and Rail Project

The Dakar-Ndjamena-Djibouti (DND) project is another initiative with distinctive features and a number of commonalities with micro-regional strategies and transport corridors (national and transboundary SDI). The 8715 km project, as part of the larger proposed Trans-Africa Highway, connects Dakar (Senegal in the west) to Djibouti (Djibouti in the east) will traverse 10 African countries (i.e. Burkina Faso, Cameroon, Chad, Djibouti, Ethiopia, Mali, Niger, Nigeria, Senegal and Sudan). Connecting African countries in the west, central and the east, the project is consistent with the seven regional infrastructure projects within the framework of the Presidential Infrastructure Promotion Initiative (IPPI) launched by the AU and NEPAD (NEPAD 2013). The project is also in line with the African Development Bank's Program for Infrastructure Development for Africa (PIDA), a series of initiatives aimed at addressing infrastructure needs in key sectors (transport, energy, ICT and transboundary water) by 2040 (AfDB 2011).

The DND transportation corridor is expected to bolster cross-border regionalisms and the road network will facilitate the free movement of people, improve imports and exports across land-locked countries such as Burkina Faso, Chad, Ethiopia, and Niger while strengthening intra-Africa trade and encouraging complementarity between the road and rail sectors (African Manager 2014). As a cross-border and domestic transportation infrastructure,

DND is expected to reduce trade costs, resulting in increased trade, heightened "foreign direct investment (FDI) in the form of intra-firm vertical integration across borders" (Fujimura 2004, p. 3). As Bach (2008, p. 179) also points out, "trans-state networks mobilize … bonds … [and] promote regionalization through their exploitation of the opportunities offered by the customs, fiscal, normative or monetary disparities that are found along boundary line."

The flurry of cross and transboundary regional schemes is not entirely new. However, such cross-border initiatives "offer privileged insights into the dynamics of micro-region-building" and reflect situations where "opportunities for survival and accumulation associated with cross-border interactions are vital to large section of the population and sometimes the state itself" (Bach 2008, p. 180). Yet, to do so meaningfully, the quest for an efficient provisioning of such a regional public good must ensure a degree of non-excludability and non-rivalry. After all, aside from the international, regional and national players involved in the DND project, a second tier of varied actors notably from civil society as well as the private and non-governmental sectors, to criminal gangs concerned about the potential to make money, are all in their own dynamic ways helping to give life to the DND, "albeit mostly as part of micro-regionalization processes than as promoters of [the] micro-regionalist project" (Breslin and Hook 2002, p. 226).

Once finalized, the DND initiative will form a seamless east-west crossing of the continent giving rise to myriad micro and cross-border relationships both formal and informal which, individually and collectively, will advance intra-African trade and regionalism. The DND project highlights "the complex dynamics" of transboundary regionalism, "primarily in the economic realm, but also considering [the] political, security and social dimensions" (Breslin and Hook 2002, p. 218). Also worth paying attention to are the complex entanglements of different channels of rules and regulation and mirroring the "Bhagwati Spaghetti Bowl" (Bhagwati and Panagariya 1996).

Maputo Development Corridor

The Maputo Development Corridor (MDC) is part of the broader Spatial Development Initiative (SDI) established by South Africa in 1995 as a way of expanding global reach and interconnectedness following the end of apartheid (Söderbaum and Taylor 2008). SADC has been supportive of the MDC, which is regarded as a key strategy for ensuring that the necessary transportation infrastructure was in place to implement SADC's economic policies, particularly concerning the trade and investment requirement for the movement of goods. The MDC is the "flagship of the SDI program" (Söderbaum and Taylor 2008, p. 38), and illustrates the interplay between "South Africa driven multi-scalar regionalization and lean institutionalization" (Bach 2008, p. 177).

Although the Corridor is an agreement between the governments of South Africa and Mozambique, it is a worthwhile case of regionalism in Africa, as it is largely dependent on public-private partnerships and networks (Lewis and Bloch 1998, p. 730). Since its inception, the project's focus has been on generating skills and jobs with the support of private sector investors. The MDC has "given rise to an impressive array of trans-frontier projects, most of [which were] funded through private sector initiatives" (Bach 2008, p. 178). To this end, the MDC "... contains a very comprehensive investment portfolio, and with regard to the rehabilitation of primary infrastructure ... a total estimated value of 661.5 million USD" (Söderbaum and Taylor 2008, p. 38). The variety of private sector investments involved in the project include the US$1.3 billion Mozambique Aluminium Smelter (MoZAL), the US$1.4 billion Maputo Iron and Steel project, the Beluluane Industrial Park (BIP), as well as Pande/Temane Gas. Private investors are involved in all aspects of the project, from mining to forestry to energy to ecotourism (Söderbaum and Taylor 2008).

The MDC sets institutional parameters around a "generalized SDI methodology" premised on cross-border relationships. Any infrastructure development along the borders within the MDC's jurisdiction is discussed by the MDC prior to implementation. Thus, matters relating to research, capacity building, trade, infrastructure projects, and investment must pass through a discussion phase with the MDC. There are several phases of implementation, and the degree to which civil society and public-private partnership voices are engaged throughout these phases presents a positive example for environmental and natural resource governance throughout the continent. The slower process of the phases prior to implementation ensures that a variety of actor voices can be heard. The MDC builds upon the decentralization already evident within the region, utilizing local, provincial, and national authorities alongside the private sector.

The Corridor seeks to expand trade and open access to the Mozambican port, in essence linking the Atlantic and Indian Oceans and providing ocean access to landlocked areas. The Maputo Corridor Logistics Initiative demonstrates the importance of public-private partnerships in creating effective cross-border initiatives. The involvement of the private sector in the decision-making process has extended the perceived importance of regionalism beyond the creation of borders. To be sure, because the private sector invested in the Corridor, they have a recognized interest in ensuring that the border continues to operate efficiently. Thus, the border continues to be viewed as one of the largest and most successful example of regional cooperation continentally and an excellent case of regional cooperation among countries and between the private and public sectors (World Bank 1999). This point warrants particular attention, as the MDC has ignited a shift toward a networked system of governments, whereby decision-making and implementation processes transcend the state (Castells 2005). While this was at first thought perhaps too "ad hoc" to ensure effective implementation, this networked approach is now seen as an important case study that can be mirrored by other countries. Maintaining roads is difficult, especially in cross-border contexts where no one government wants to take ownership of the maintenance investment.

Throughout Africa, transport authorities have been met with conflict, as countries neglect their road maintenance, which, in turn, undermine the road network within the border of member countries. When two countries share a road, it is paramount for each country to maintain their road, to ensure that the road can continue to provide for its functions. In the case of MDC, the transport authorities are not the sole proprietors involved. Rather, road maintenance is handled largely by the private sector, which operates in both South Africa and Mozambique. Consequently, the Maputo Corridor road remains well maintained and, therefore, well travelled.

Lessons, Challenges and Concluding Remarks

The above discussion offers critical lessons in and challenges to infrastructure development, regionalism and integration in Africa. These lessons and challenges revolve around three related themes: a) capacity development imperatives; b) coherence, coordination and complementarity; and finally c) the role of state and non-state actors both within and beyond the African continent. At the heart of capacity development is the allocation of resources and the utilization of resources for maximum impact and outcomes. A common theme about the state of infrastructure in Africa and the three specific case studies reviewed is the dependence on external resources to push the frontiers of infrastructure development. While that by itself is not a problem, the issue has been the inability of several African institutions to be able to timely disburse and utilize available resources for infrastructure development (NEPAD 2013, p. 18). The result is delays or cancellations of proposed projects.

Perhaps, the synergies of involving multi-actors might jolt African countries into action with a new sense of mission. The problem, however, is the role of regional economic communities (RECs) in the push to close the infrastructure gap in Africa. There are significant variations in the relative capacity of RECs in Africa (see other chapters in the volume, notably Puplampu; Arthur; and Hanson and Tang). In cases of relatively strong capacity-infused institutions, the outcomes are obvious. The networked approach to the MDC presents a valuable lesson for African regional integration. Indeed, a networked institutional structure allows for a more fluid approach to cross-border relationships. This is particularly central in cases of environmental and natural resource management, where a variety of actors have vested interests in the outcome of a regional decision-making body. Thus, the MDC is non-bureaucratic in the classical Weberian sense. This has facilitated nuanced planning, especially with the inclusion of a variety of actors in institutional decisions through numerous subcommittees, technical teams, and decision-making processes. The inclusive nature of the institutional framework has enabled more public-private partnerships and civil society actors to be involved in the process.

The MDC also offers valuable lessons on how to address coherence, coordination and complementarity in infrastructure development. MDC validates how private-public dynamics across countries in the sub-region are helping to not only create regional energy trade, but also cross border exchanges between national utility service providers. The involvement of these international, transnational and regional actors, as Breslin and Hook (2002, p. 225) point out "goes hand in hand with that of national and subnational actors. As far as states are concerned, although same in a very basic sense of being sovereign and equal, they differ in terms of political system, power distributions, degrees of integration into the global political economy." The WAGP, for example, also clearly shows that for coherence and coordination to become assets and part of the parcel of these projects, will require attention to the leadership and institutional capacities of member states (Tavares and Tang 2013, p. 230; see also ACBF 2013).

In line with the changing role of the state, it is not surprising that infrastructure developments have taken on the public-private partnership model. The regionalism of the MDC is driven by multi-actors notably "state elites, who have their own agenda, but also by communities and peoples who utilize the micro-region for a heterogeneous set of reasons and motives … and alternative regional strategies" (Soderbaum and Taylor 2008, p. 52). The dynamic entanglements of multiple actors is an effective way to ensure diverse ownership. This model underscores the continuing relevance of the state and how smart states are able to liaise with the private sector. For such a liaison to yield the expected results, however, institutional capacity will be both a necessary and sufficient condition. While the leadership role of the AU through NEPAD and the respective RECs are commendable, the absorptive capacity of institutions, as stated earlier, remains a concern.

There is no question that regional integration and infrastructure development are fundamental to Africa's economic and trade performance as well as poverty reduction and quality of life improvement efforts. One reason for promoting regional integration in Africa is the continent's record of regional trade. Thus, the expectation is that the various regional integration arrangements would help facilitate intra-regional trade and thereby promote growth. One way to promote trade is overcoming Africa's regional infrastructure networks gaps. This can be illustrated with ICT connections in the continent. According to a World Bank (2009) report, African countries, especially landlocked ones, have low access to the global network of submarine cables and intraregional connectivity by fiber-optic cables is also limited. As a result, most countries rely on satellites for international telecommunications, including internet access, leading to high prices for dial-up and broadband Internet. Thus, projects underway to ensure connectivity will also reduce prices and provide better international voice and internet connectivity services.

As part of and flowing from the discussions, it is obvious that private sector institutions are involved in the financing and operationalization of infrastructure projects in the region. Given that private sector involvement is premised on a profit motive, it is essential to have enabling conditions for private sector participation in improving the state of infrastructure in Africa. For example, African countries will have to endeavor to enshrine or have investment processes based on the rule of law, transparency and accountability. Along the same lines, private sector investment entities should be held accountable in paying the appropriate taxes. Then again, the ability to levy the appropriate taxes assumes the existence of an effective tax system. There have been significant changes in the global aid architecture, for example, the increasing role of Chinese investments in infrastructure development in Africa (Schiere and Rugamba 2011). Thus, the need for capable and effective African institutions in policy formation and the regulatory framework cannot be overemphasized.

It is necessary to approach infrastructure development and its capacity dimensions as both a means and an end. As a means, the state of the continental infrastructure network is integral to the objectives of promoting trade as a route to reducing poverty. Infrastructure development entails significant capital overlay. The investment should be contextualized in terms of the long term development prospects of countries. Then again, any long-term development program will depend on capable institutions, institutions that have the required and sufficient human and physical capital to discharge and ensure compliance to the regulatory framework. The bane of African development continues to be that of both political calculations in the development agenda and the dearth of political leaders who are genuinely interested in the development prospects of their citizens beyond the usual platitudes and election cycles. The growing significance of a veritable civil society that could hold governments accountable for the welfare of their citizens is one hopeful sign that needs to be nurtured and enhanced in twenty-first century African societies.

References

ACBF (2013), *Africa Capacity Indicators Report 2013: Capacity Development for Natural Resources Management.* Harare: ACBF.

African Development Bank (AfDB) (2010), *African Development Report 2010*, Oxford: Oxford University Press for African Development Bank.

——— (2011), "AU Summit Identifies Key Priority Infrastructure Projects." Available at: http://www.afdb.org/en/news-and-events/article/au-summit-identifies-key-priority-infrastructure-projects-7684/ (accessed August 11, 2014).

African Manager (2014), "Dakar-Djibouti trans-African highway to traverse 10 African countries." (Monday, 11th August, 2014). Available at: http://www.africanmanager.com/site_eng/detail_article.php?art_id=17873 (accessed August 10, 2014).

Akpan-Obong, P. (2006), "Information and Communication Technologies (ICTs) and African Development." In M.S. Smith (ed.) *Beyond the 'African Tragedy': Discourses on Development and the Global Economy.* Farnham: Ashgate, pp. 247–67.

Asian Development Bank (ADB) (2009), *Infrastructure for a Seamless Asia.* Tokyo: Asian Development Bank.

Bach, D. (2008), "Beyond Parochialism: Cross-border Regionalism as a Gateway." In F. Söderbaum and I. Taylor (eds), *Afro-Regions: The Dynamics of Cross-Border Micro-Regionalism in Africa.* Uppsala: Nordic Africa Institute, pp. 175–80.

Besada, H., McMillan, L. and Sanieipour, A. (2013), "Regionalism, Trade and the Growth of Africa's Economy." ACIR2014 Background Paper No. 6. Harare: The African Capacity Building Foundation.

Bhagwati, J. and Panagariya, A. (1996), "Preferential Trading Areas and Multilateralism—Strangers, Friends, or Foes?" In J. Bhagwati and A. Panagariya (eds), *The Economics of Preferential Trade Agreements.* Washington, D.C.: AEI Press, pp. 1–55.

Breslin, S. and Hook, G.D. (2002), "Researching Microregional Integration: Towards New Framework of Analyses." In S. Breslin and G.D. Hook (eds), *Microregionalism and World Order.* Basingstoke: Palgrave Macmillan, pp. 215–35.

Bullock, R. (2009), *Off Track: Sub-Saharan African Railways.* AICD Background Paper 17, Africa Region. Washington, D.C.: World Bank.

Calderòn C. and Servèn, L. (2004), "The Effects of Infrastructure Development on Growth and Income Distribution." World Bank Policy Research Working Paper 3400. Washington, D.C.: World Bank.

Castells, M. (2005), "Global Governance and Global Politics," *Political Science and Politics* 38: 9–16.

Draper, P. and Ismail, S. (2014), "The Potential Impact of Mega-regionals on Sub-Saharan Africa and Least Developed Countries in the Region." In *World*

Economic Forum Global Agenda Council on Trade and Foreign Direct Investment, Mega-regional Trade Agreements: Game-Changers or Costly Distractions for the World Trading System? p. 8.

ECLAC (2009), "Physical Infrastructure and Regional Integration," *Bulletin Fall* 280, 12: 1–4.

Foster, V. and Briceno-Garmendia, C. (2010), *Africa's Infrastructure—A Time for Transformation*. Agence Française de Développement and Washington, D.C.: World Bank.

Fourie, J. (2006), "Economic Infrastructure: A Review of Definitions, Theory and Empirics," *South African Journal of Economics* 74: 530–56. doi: 10.1111/j.1813–6982.2006.00086.x.

Fujimura, M. (2004), "Cross-border transport infrastructure, regional integration and development." ADB Institute Discussion Papers, No. 16. Tokyo: Asian Development Bank Institute.

Hartzenberg, T. (2011), "Regional Integration in Africa." World Trade Organization, Economic Research and Statistics Division, Staff Working Paper ERSD-2011–14. Available at: http://www.wto.org/english/res_e/reser_e/ersd201114_e.pdf (accessed August 7, 2014).

Havinden, M. and Meredith, D. (1993), *Colonialism and development: Britain and its tropical colonies, 1850–1960*. New York: Routledge.

Kabela-Camara, A.K. (2013), "Achieving Energy Security in ECOWAS through the West African Gas Pipeline and Power Pool Projects: Illusion or Reality?" CEPMLP Annual Review, CAR vol. 16. Available at: http://www.dundee.ac.uk/cepmlp/gateway/index.php?news=32349 (accessed August 15, 2014).

Kay, G.M. (1972), *The Political Economy of Colonialism in Ghana—Documents and Statistics 1900–1960*. Cambridge: Cambridge University Press.

Kessides, C. (1996), "A Review of Infrastructure's Impact on Economic Development." In D.F. Batten and C. Karlsson (eds), *Infrastructure and the Complexity of Economic Development*. Berlin: Springer Verlag, pp. 213–30.

Kessides, I.N. and Benjamin, N.C. (2012), *Regionalizing Infrastructure for Developing Market Integration: The Case of East Africa*. Washington, D.C.: The World Bank Development Research Group, Policy Research Working Paper Series 6113.

Kuroda, H., Kawai, M. and Nangia, R. (2007), *Infrastructure and Regional Cooperation*. Tokyo: Asian Development Bank Institute.

Mafusire, A., Anyanwu, J., Brixiova, Z., Mutambatsere, E., Mubila, M. and Dhib, A. (2011), "Closing Africa's Infrastructure Gap." In K. Mlambo, A.B. Kamara, A. Kateeto and C. Lufumpa (eds), *Telling Africa's Development Story, October 2010 to March 2011*. Tunis: AfBD, pp. 41–59.

Mbekeani, K.K. (2010), "Infrastructure, Trade Expansion and Regional Integration: Global Experience and Lessons for Africa," *Journal of African Economies* 19, AERC Supplement 1, i88-i113.

NEPAD (2013), NEPAD-IPPF: Infrastructure Project Preparation Facility—2012 Annual Report, Midrand: NEPAD (http://www.nepad-ippf.org).

Prior, C. (2013), *Exporting Empire—Africa, Colonial Officials and the Construction of the Imperial State, c. 1900–39*. Manchester: Manchester University Press.

Ranganathan, R. and Foster, V. (2011a), *East Africa's Infrastructure—A Continental Perspective*. Washington, D.C.: World Bank, Africa Region, Sustainable Development, Policy Research Working Paper 5844.

——— (2011b), *ECCAS's Infrastructure—A Continental Perspective*. Washington, D.C.: World Bank, Africa Region, Sustainable Development, Policy Research Working Paper 5857.

——— (2011c), *ECOWAS's Infrastructure—A Regional Perspective*. Washington, D.C.: World Bank, Africa Region, Sustainable Development, Policy Research Working Paper 5899.

——— (2011d), *The SADC's Infrastructure—A Regional Perspective*. Washington, D.C.: World Bank, Africa Region, Sustainable Development, Policy Research Working Paper 5898.

Schiere, R. and A. Rugamba (2011), "Chinese Infrastructure Investments and African Integration." In R. Schiere, L. Ndikumana, and P. Walkenhorst (eds), *China and Africa: An Emerging Partnership for Development?* Tunis: African Development Bank, 91–101.

SELA (2011), *Physical Infrastructure for Integration in Latin America and the Caribbean*. Permanent Secretariat of SELA Caracas, Venezuela, SP/ Di N° 9–11, June.

Shaw, T.M. and Fanta, E. (2013), "Introduction: Comparative Regionalisms for Development in the 21st Century: Insights from the Global South." In E. Fanta, T.M. Shaw and V.T. Tang (eds), *Comparative Regionalisms for Development in the 21st Century: Insights from the Global South*. Farnham: Ashgate, pp. 1–17.

Söderbaum, F. (2003), "Introduction: Theories of New Regionalism." In F. Söderbaum and T.M. Shaw (eds), *Theories of New Regionalism: A Palgrave Reader*. Basingstoke: Palgrave, pp. 1–21.

Söderbaum, F. and Taylor, I. (eds) (2008), *Afro-Regions: The Dynamics of Cross-Border Micro-Regionalism in Africa*. Uppsala: Nordic Africa Institute.

——— (2008), "Micro-Regionalism in Africa: Competing Region-Building in the Maputo Development Corridor." In F. Söderbaum and I. Taylor (eds), *Afro-Regions: The Dynamics of Cross-Border Micro-Regionalism in Africa*. Uppsala: Nordic Africa Institute, pp. 35–52.

Tavares, R. and Tang, V.T. (2013), "Regional Economic Integration in Africa: Impediments to Progress?" In E. Fanta, T.M. Shaw and V.T. Tang (eds), *Comparative Regionalisms for Development in the 21st Century: Insights from the Global South*. Farnham: Ashgate, pp. 209–32.

Thonke, O. and Spliid, A. (2012), "What to expect from regional integration in Africa," *African Security Review*, vol. 21, no. 1, pp. 42–66.

Torrisi, G. (2009), 'Public infrastructure: definition, classification and measurement issues," *Economics, Management, and Financial Markets* vol. 4, no. 3, pp. 100–124.

UN-Habitat (2011), "Infrastructure for Economic Development and Poverty Reduction in Africa." United Nations Human Settlements Programme: Nairobi.

WAPCo (West African Gas Pipeline Company) (2014), "Welcome to Our Company." Available at: http://www.wagpco.com (accessed September 28, 2014).

Willoughby, C. (2004), "Infrastructure and the MDGs." Sponsored by DFID. Available at: http://www.oecd.org/dac/povertyreduction/36567911.pdf (accessed August 3, 2014).

World Bank (2009), "Africa's Infrastructure: A Time for Transformation." Washington, D.C.: The World Bank.

——— (1999), "Southern Africa—A Regional Strategy." Washington, D.C.: The World Bank.

Chapter 8

Innovation, Science and Technology: Regional Networks for Research and Technology Development in Africa

Joseph R. Oppong

Science, Technology and Innovation in Economic Development

Science, technology, and innovation (STI) are universally recognized as important drivers of economic development (UNESCO and African Union, 2009). In fact, the widening economic gap between nations and the international distribution of wealth and power are linked to corresponding gaps in investment in science and technology. Accordingly, African countries have launched several initiatives to use science and technology as a vehicle for achieving rapid economic development, but with little success (Viotti 2002; Bell and Albu 1999). Investment in STI remains low, with only three countries—Malawi, Uganda, and South Africa—devoting more than 1 percent of total GDP to STI research (AU-NEPAD 2010). Consequently, many scientific labs depend on sporadic foreign funding that, understandably, defines research priorities. Science students get little practical research training due to obsolete equipment and a shortage of trained personnel. Even when research is successful, translating the results into market products is problematic because of poor coordination between research institutions and industry and the absence of strong and effective national innovation systems.

This chapter addresses the challenge and promise of STI in African economic development by reviewing the problems, and the role of cell phone technology. It argues that global pressures and African demand and creative energy, particularly from the African youth, make regional integration in science and technology necessary. Properly harnessed, integration promises a bright future in science and technology based economic development for those African countries that create the right environments. The chapter ends by suggesting policy options and regulatory best practices for harnessing the creative energy and potential of African youth in science and technology innovation for national and regional economic development.

Science, Technology and Innovation

Science is concerned with how and why things happen, while technology deals with making things happen. Science explains the reasons behind phenomena; technology translates science into products. It uses tools, machines, materials, techniques and sources of power to make work easier and more productive (Kitetu 2008). Innovation combines resources in new or unusual ways to generate new or improved products (goods and services) and processes. Such innovation may be truly transformative, changing technology systems and economic paradigms, or only a slight improvement in performance.

Creating an environment that supports African STI requires regional integration for two main reasons. First, Africa's many small economies lack the infrastructure and human, physical, and financial resources required for STI and economic transformation. Of Africa's 54 countries, 26 have fewer than 10 million in population; 28 have a GDP under US$10 billion, and 16 are landlocked (Figure 8.1). Thus, with a total population almost the size of China or India, Africa is 54 different markets, while China and India are both single markets. Regional cooperation would enable countries to combine their scarce resources of research and development infrastructure and skilled human capital. Such cooperation could generate economies of scale to undertake scientific research and invest in technological innovation. Regional cooperation in STI is also important for collective technological learning and peer influence. Countries with weak systems of innovation can learn from those with better developed systems.

Second, successful regional integration can provide a wider market for increased trade, larger and diversified investment and production, socioeconomic and political stability, and increased bargaining power for participating countries (Maruping 2005). By facilitating the movement of goods and services, capital and labor, socioeconomic policy coordination and harmonization, and infrastructure development, regional integration will produce expanded markets and greater intra-African trade. Furthermore, improved intra-African trade can enhance regional food security, promote peace and stability by decreasing regional conflicts, achieve economies of scale, and build African countries' supply capacity and competitiveness (Chetty 2012).

Yet, despite the many benefits, few successful African regional integration stories exist; this is a consequence of colonialism, internal structural problems, poor physical infrastructure and other challenges. Colonialism left the African continent with a legacy of fragmented states. Additionally, severe macroeconomic challenges—including huge foreign debt, a narrow tax base,

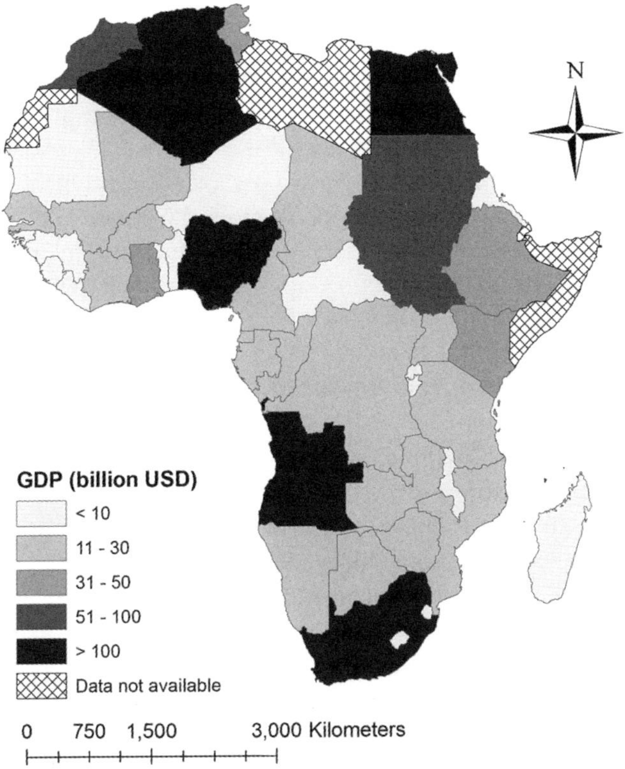

Figure 8.1 2012 GDP of African countries (current US$)

Source: Created by author using data from World Bank (2013a)

and protective import substitution strategies dating back to independence—have produced a hostile environment for regional collaboration and integration (Matthews 2003; Oppong 2010). Thus, fragmentation and an unfavorable economic context hinder regional integration.

According to Qobo (2007), weak national foundations, political conflict, and instability are major obstacles. Integrating incomplete states that struggle with internal insecurities and heterogeneity is inevitably problematic (Nye 2004). Africa's insecure and debt-ridden states are unwilling to yield sovereignty to a supranational body (Mistry 2000). In countries such as Somalia, Sudan, Côte d'Ivoire and Sierra Leone, political conflict and instability impede integration (Qobo 2007). Moreover, poor infrastructure, particularly road network and power supply, is a major obstacle to regional integration in Africa. Much of the sparse road network is in poor condition or passes through fragile or conflict-affected states where basic maintenance is often neglected (Chetty 2012).

Consequently, ideal conditions for successful regional integration are absent in many African countries, and politicians demonstrate little interest in creating them. Apart from the often cited problems related to corruption, instability, undemocratic rule, and civil strife, there is also a lack of private sector activity in regional integration schemes (ECA 2004). In some instances, economic reforms have not been properly designed and implemented. Different countries and regions pursue the goals of integration from the point of view of narrow economic interests, rather than as part of a broader and single vision toward continental unity and development.

Challenges and Prospects of Regional STI Partnerships

Mugabe (2011) identified three major limitations of current regional STI initiatives: funding, focus and coordination. Most initiatives aimed at promoting cooperation in STI through the regional economic communities (RECs) depend solely on temporary external funding from development partners. This is not sustainable. Also, funding instruments such as venture capital are rare, and tax relief and other instruments are not available to universities or research and development institutions. Ensuring adequate and sustainable funding to support innovation is a huge challenge for most countries. Moreover, most initiatives in regional bodies focus largely on research and development, with little emphasis on technological innovation. Finally, poor coordination of the initiatives produces considerable duplication of efforts instead of building robust national and regional innovation systems.

Given these challenges, targeted regional science and technology research networks, such as research or technology parks, may be the vital link. Such development not only exploits synergies across countries, but also presents a bigger market that is more attractive to foreign investment. This is crucial because transitioning from the conduct of science or research to the application of scientific knowledge to generate specific product and process innovations will require the creation and use of business or commercial oriented enterprises for innovation (NEPAD 2006). Such institutional arrangements can take different forms, such as technology parks or innovation hubs. Whatever their form, these are really mechanisms for ensuring that research and development initiatives generate products and services.

Funding Regional STI Programs

Dearth of funding impedes the implementation of regional science and technology innovation programs in Africa. Many AU, NEPAD, EAC, SADC, and other regional initiatives are underfunded (Mugabe 2011). Financial contributions from national governments tend to be low and unpredictable; external donors funding regional programs are few, usually temporary, and frequently have different research priorities. For example, the European Union's (EU) Seventh Framework Program which provides research funding amounting to 8.1 billion Euros (US$10.2 billion) excluded the requirement to collaborate with African colleagues in 2013. Previously, recipients were required to include an African collaborator, a major source of funding for African researchers. Concern exists that the policy shift may also affect the EU's Horizon 2020 framework, a research and innovation program worth approximately US$100 billion (SciDev.Net. 2013). The EU's decision is consistent with mounting austerity measures. As the markets contract Europe tightens its belt. Thus, while initiatives such as the Seventh Framework Program may be effective during good times, they cannot be the core foundation for African science and technology innovation efforts.

Consequently, the success of African regional programs for science, technology, and innovation will depend on new kinds of funding alliances involving governments, bilateral and multilateral donors, private foundations, and businesses. In the past, African governments designed programs and created new institutions without clear agreements on sources and levels of funding. Regional pools of funds to provide competitive research grants to individuals or groups of researchers working on carefully defined research priorities are indispensable.

Capacity Constraints

STI initiatives are hampered by significant capacity constraints. Physical infrastructure—including laboratories for scientific research, electricity, telecommunications and Internet connectivity—is vital for developing new products and processes, or even to use existing technologies. Also, costly and unreliable power supply is a major constraint. For example, more than two thirds of the population of sub-Saharan Africa (in rural areas, more than 85 percent) lacks access to electricity (White House Fact Sheet 2013). Moreover, African prices for electricity are among the highest in the world (World Bank 2012; The World Bank Group 2013), and supply is erratic and unreliable. Improving infrastructure is thus a pressing necessity in most African countries.

In addition, Africa's educational and training institutions are not producing enough skilled manpower to meet market demands for skills in science and engineering. Most African countries have a shortage of skilled scientists and engineers (see box on Expanding GIS Technology in South Africa and Ghana on p. 165). Similarly, innovative policy analysis and development expertise is limited. This is a major barrier to improving national technological performance and growing national systems of innovation.

Patents, Science, and Technology for Africa

Intellectual property (and patenting in particular) has been highlighted as a significant factor limiting the transfer of new technologies to developing countries. In the case of clean energy technologies (CET), a 2013 UNEP and European Patent Office (EPO) report documents that because only 1 percent of CET patent applications have also been filed in Africa, claims that patent rights constitute a barrier in Africa are largely unfounded (EPO and UNEP 2013). The report concludes that the vast majority of CET is not patented in Africa and can be freely exploited. Consequently, international policies may be developed for promotion of CET in Africa without having to consider significant issues relating to patent rights. Moreover, the patent system has made its extensive technical documentation available freely throughout the world via the Internet (EPO and UNEP 2013).

Developing Science, Technology and Innovation (STI) through Research Parks

African policymakers and scientists recognize the importance of regional cooperation in science and technology. But while most regional integration treaties have provisions on science and technology cooperation, little has been done to translate provisions of the treaties into concrete processes and activities.

Technology parks play an incubator role: nurturing the development and growth of new, small, high-technology firms; facilitating transfer of university know-how to tenant firms; encouraging development of faculty-based spin-offs; and stimulating the development of innovative products and processes. These parks also stimulate the formation and development of new technology-based firms by providing an important resource network. Finally, they are known to catalyze regional economic development and to ensure the competitiveness of traditional industries and the growth of new ones through advancement of knowledge-based enterprises.

Successful examples include Egypt's Smart Village and Kenya's Konza. Smart Village, the Egyptian science park opened in 2003, had a total workforce of 35,000 employees in 2013, and has helped to sustain Egyptian economic growth at 4.7 percent a year. Similarly, Kenya established an information, communications, and technology park on a 5,000-acre site at Konza, 60 kilometers south of Nairobi. The government allocated KSh 1 billion (US$12 million) for the initial stages of the KSh 900 billion (US$10 billion) project, modeled after Silicon Valley in California. Additionally, the government created a KSh 400 million (US$4.7 million) STI fund to support research and innovation and provide start-up funds for young innovators. The goal is to close

Expanding GIS Technology in South Africa and Ghana

Geographic Information Systems (GIS) has become widely accepted as an essential decision-making tool worldwide for numerous fields, including natural resource management, disease mapping and monitoring, crime analysis, transport and distribution services planning, and emergency response. Consequently, employment in geospatial technologies is booming (U.S. Department of Labor 2007; 2012). The demand for GIS skills has produced a proliferation of GIS certificate and degree courses in colleges and universities in the developed world. In developing countries, however, GIS access is restricted to urban areas with uninterrupted electricity supply, adequate communication technology, and skilled personnel (Oppong and Ofori-Amoah 2012).

In fact, GIS education in Africa faces significant impediments (Oppong and Ofori-Amoah 2012; Eksteen, Pretorius, and Breetzke 2012). In South Africa, aside from the vagueness of the curriculum description, teaching GIS requires substantial computer resources, trained personnel, and development of new study materials, each of which is a serious impediment (Eksteen, Pretorius, and Breetzke 2012). Although South Africa has introduced GIS technology into its school syllabus and it is now part of the geography curriculum in Grades 10–12, GIS education faces severe impediments—particularly a shortage of resources.

In Ghana, awareness of GIS as a decision-making tool is matched with very little application. Government departments talk unceasingly about the potential uses of GIS but lack the resources to make this work. Computer-based GIS education is offered in only four universities, and only to graduate students; undergraduate students learn only the theory and principles of GIS without actually touching a computer (Oppong and Ofori-Amoah 2012). ESRI runs short-term courses to introduce ESRI products in Ghana, but usually in the major cities. Moreover, despite GIS awareness within the government and the private sector, there is neither demonstrable demand for GIS-trained personnel nor a commitment to create the necessary environment for their hire (Oppong and Ofori-Amoah 2012). Consequently, GIS work in Ghana is done mostly by expatriate consultants; projects are single-tiered, single-layered, and typically unsustainable (Karikari, Stillwell, and Carver 2003; Oppong and Ofori-Amoah 2012).

The real challenge is not simply establishing GIS labs in the universities but equipping, sustaining, and staffing them and creating a market for graduates of GIS programs. A real GIS infrastructure to provide quality spatial data is also required. National standards for collecting, processing, storing, and sharing spatial data must be established, preferably with well-funded regional data repositories. In short, for Ghana and South Africa, sustained and dedicated government leadership is required to ensure successful adoption, development, and ultimately, innovation in GIS technologies. Depending on the goodwill of global leaders in GIS, such as ESRI, is not a viable option and will not propel Africa into global leadership in innovation in GIS.

the innovation–implementation gap in order to increase global competitiveness. Interestingly, global technology giant IBM has launched a research lab in Nairobi, to conduct applied and exploratory research into the grand challenges of the continent by delivering commercially viable innovations. According to the Kenyan government, the IBM lab signals success of government efforts to turn Kenya into a research hub, a bid that would be supported by huge government investment through universities and the Ministry of Education, Science and Technology (Nganga 2013).

Despite these challenges, several major regional science and technology innovation efforts are underway. Table 8.1 lists the goals and major accomplishments of the more successful efforts. Together, they demonstrate clearly that with adequate support, regional integration for STI has great potential for Africa.

Table 8.1 Regional research and development partnerships

Organization	Goals	Accomplishments/Successes
The New Partnership for Africa's Development (NEPAD)	To address critical challenges facing the continent: poverty, development, and Africa's marginalization internationally. To facilitate regional integration in science and technology.	NEPAD's ICT Broadband Infrastructure Network for Africa, one of the key initiatives of the e-Africa program.
The African Academy of Sciences (AAS)	To facilitate the development of research and technology throughout Africa and honor internationally renowned African scientists.	Significant growth in the number of AAS fellows as well as capacity building projects in Science and Technology, Soil and Water Management, and the African Training for Leadership and Advanced Skills (ATLAS) Project.
Network of African Science Academies (NASAC)	To provide advice to governments and regional organizations on scientific aspects of issues of importance to Africa's development. To support existing institutions and encourage the creation of new academies of science in African countries where none exists.	Organizing several scientific conferences, workshops, and seminars on a variety of topics to inform the science policy dialogue in Africa in such areas as sustainability, energy efficiency, climate change, and the African brain drain.
The African Virtual University (AVU)	To significantly increase access to quality higher education and training through the innovative use of Information and Communication Technologies.	The AVU has graduated 43,000 students across Africa and established a wide-ranging network of Open Distance and e-Learning institutions in more than 30 countries in sub-Saharan Africa.

Source: Author

Mobile Phones and Unemployed Digital Natives: Time Bomb or Opportunity?

The unparalleled explosive growth of mobile phone use across Africa over the past decade has revolutionized communications in Africa, and the much-improved connectivity is transforming business and trade transactions. In 2000, Africa had fewer than 20 million fixed-line phones, a number that had accumulated slowly over a century, and a waiting list of a further 3.5 million. By 2012, Africa had more than 500 million mobile phone subscriptions, more than in the United States or the European Union, making Africa the fastest growing region in the world. Driven by falling costs, mobile phones are transforming everything from banking and health care (with text messages used to transfer money and send health advice), to agriculture (farmers can receive guidance, weather forecasts, and market reports) and politics (communications technology has played a key role in recent uprisings; e.g. see Sokari Ekine's 2010 edited volume, *SMS Uprising: Mobile Activism in Africa*).

With 200 million people aged between 15 and 24—a figure that is expected to double by 2045, according to the 2012 *African Economic Outlook*—Africa has the world's largest youth population (Ighobor 2013). It also has a troubling rate of youth unemployment, the highest in the world (World Bank 2013). Youth account for 60 percent of all African unemployed. Africa's growing youth population is well educated, highly energetic, creative, and talented—critical ingredients for future prosperity (Ighobor 2013). They are also *digital natives*: young people who were born into the digital age and are growing up using information and communication technologies (ICTs) in their daily lives. According to Prensky (2001), they are native speakers of the digital language of computers, video games and the Internet. Policymakers are paying increasing attention to digital natives, not only because of the possibilities that ICTs open up for young people all around the world, but also because they play a role in shaping and driving the information society.

Technology has enabled digital natives to rise to prominence on a global scale. They mobilize behind common causes, respond to social concerns and connect across huge geopolitical barriers. To digital natives, access to information means better access to capital, markets and training, as well as increased participation in political processes. This is why the huge unemployment problem among African youth is such a huge concern and has been characterized as a ticking time bomb (Ighobor 2013).

Instead of a ticking time bomb, however, Africa's burgeoning population of digital natives could be empowered as entrepreneurs and innovators for societal transformation. By allowing African youth to work in the digital economy, mobile technology presents an exciting opportunity to address the unemployment challenge in African countries and could facilitate science technology innovation and regional integration (Biteye 2013; Kalan 2013; Kyem 2012).

Digital natives are pioneering the use of ICT and by driving trends in what is a major and dynamic growth industry. Reasons for their great success include their capacity to learn to use ICTs quickly, their natural enthusiasm for new technology (which offers a wide variety of solutions for playing, communicating, and socializing), and the extra spare time they tend to have compared with older people (ITU 2008). Digital natives are often their nation's drivers in terms of getting online, thereby trailblazing a new digital future for their country. They are the tip of the digital spear across much of the globe, so we must be ready to listen, learn, and grow with them. With appropriate support African digital natives could very well be a major key to Africa's STI challenge.

The African continent is bustling with youth full of fresh ideas for creating apps and going into businesses that transcend national boundaries, but investment in these ventures is severely limited (Kalan 2013). Creative training programs for Africa's new entrepreneurs are required. Innovations that began in Africa, such as dual SIM card mobile phones or use of mobile phones for remittance payments, now spreading across the globe (Yonazi et al. 2012), demonstrate the incredible potential. Social networks, such as Twitter, Facebook, and Africa's home-grown MXit, provide a platform for informal learning to take place in an environment of fun and experimentation. As African digital natives enter the labor market and government, they will bring with them the habits of information sharing that they have grown up with. Africa once an ICT laggard, has the opportunity to become an ICT leader. But what is it going to take?

Valuable and sustainable ICT applications are most likely to develop within an environment that encourages experimentation and collaboration between technologists, entrepreneurs and development practitioners. Often, stakeholders may combine their interests in communal projects, such as the creation of the Cape Town Internet exchange. The recent proliferation of local ICT development clusters—such as iHub and NaiLab in Kenya, Hive CoLab and AppLab in Uganda, Activspaces in Cameroon, BantaLabs in Senegal or infoDev's mLabs in Kenya and South Africa—is helping to create new spaces for collaboration, training, application and content development, and pre-incubation of firms (World Bank Group, African Development Bank, and African Union 2012).

The labs serve as an accessible platform for bringing together technologists, investors, tech companies and hackers in the area. Each lab shares a focus on young entrepreneurs, web and mobile-phone programmers, and designers. The technology movement in Africa is being driven by the young people who, through these labs, have the means and foresight to apply new and accessible technologies to solve immediate problems and find useful solutions for common problems. Many youth are in tune with the problems and challenges facing their communities. The labs provide an environment to share experiences, brainstorm and use digital technology to create tech communities that have no borders. This approach to nurturing technology is quite different from the top-down approach that had been tried in the early 2000s of building science parks or government run initiatives to promote business process outsourcing. These initiatives are generally bottom-up and community driven. They may receive the blessing of the government but are not dependent upon it for providing opportunities for training and capacity building.

The Rockefeller Foundation's Digital Jobs for Africa Initiative is an excellent example of the kinds of strategies that are needed (Grady 2013). Led by the Nairobi office, with pilot projects in Kenya, South Africa, Ghana, Nigeria, and Morocco, the program seeks to use digital jobs to help young people build a transferable skill set that makes them resilient in their economies, strengthens their future employment opportunities, and enhances their adaptability to the changing nature of the workplace.

While cell phone communication is an important platform for STI and regional integration, significant challenges remain. In many countries it is still much cheaper to call Europe or the United States than to call a friend in a neighboring country. Because different companies or networks dominate in different countries, excessively high connection tariffs make phone calls across networks too expensive. Reductions in the tax rates and call charges for communication within regional economic communities will facilitate regional integration. High VAT charges leads to prohibitive call charges and discourage intra-regional trading. African governments must reduce their levies on mobile operators and provide incentive pricing to facilitate increased integration. Governments must lead the call to harmonize information communication technologies policies and especially call charges and to ensure more reasonable roaming fees within the region.

Managing and Harnessing ICT for STI and Regional Integration

National ICT/broadband policies can stimulate the market, expand services and lower prices. Governments can therefore play an important role by providing an enabling environment developing the ICT market and deploying broadband infrastructure. Governments should establish policies to stimulate competition and private investment, in particular in advanced ICT networks, because these are long-term investments that foster economic growth and regional integration. This is why countries such as Ethiopia and Sudan need to change their policies of overtaxing and over-regulation (Lubua and Maharaj

2012; Economist 2013a). An increasing number of governments have not only recognized the importance of broadband but also taken active steps to develop a national broadband plan or strategy, or include broadband in their universal access/service definitions.

In its latest *Trends in Telecommunication Reform* report (ITU 2013b), ITU highlights various options for policymakers and regulators to create incentives for the private sector to invest in ICTs, such as adopting enabling policies, simplifying licensing regimes, increasing the amount of available spectrum, reducing regulatory obligations and offering tax incentives. In addition, for a thriving broadband environment, regulatory frameworks need to achieve a balance between the promotion of competition in services and infrastructure to address the challenges associated with access to broadband networks and services.

Governments have an important role to play in creating an enabling environment and in acting as a lead client for large-scale ICT-based programs. They may participate directly in infrastructure investment, as the government of Botswana did when creating an alternative fiber route to the coast via Namibia. But their larger role lies in creating an enabling environment—issuing licenses, making available rights of way, auctioning spectrum or mandating infrastructure sharing and interconnection—that allows a liberalized market to thrive. Beyond that, governments can serve as a leading customer for faster networks and move their own services and data online. When the Kenyan government allowed exam results to go online, it provided a major demand driver for mobile broadband and stimulated further investment in that country's networks.

Cybercrime and Cyber Security

Africa's fast Internet access, the expanding Internet user base, and the lack of effective cybercrime laws in many African countries provide a safe haven for cybercriminals (Trend Micro Incorporated 2013). Faster and better Internet access benefits internet-based science, technology and innovation institutions and users, and also hackers and cybercriminals, posing serious cyber security problems. The burgeoning growth of internet and social network users, smart phones, and greater reliance on credit cards increase the potential number of cybercrime victims. Yet, only 14 of Africa's 57 countries have cybercrime laws in place (Figure 8.2) (Kharouni 2013). Another four countries are in the process of creating their own or adapting other countries' cybercrime laws (Global Centre for ICT in Parliament 2013), but the remaining 38 countries do not have cybercrime laws yet. For some countries, the cybercrime laws are outdated or do not apply to the current threats. Because many of these cybercrime problems facing the African continent are unique to Africa and other developing

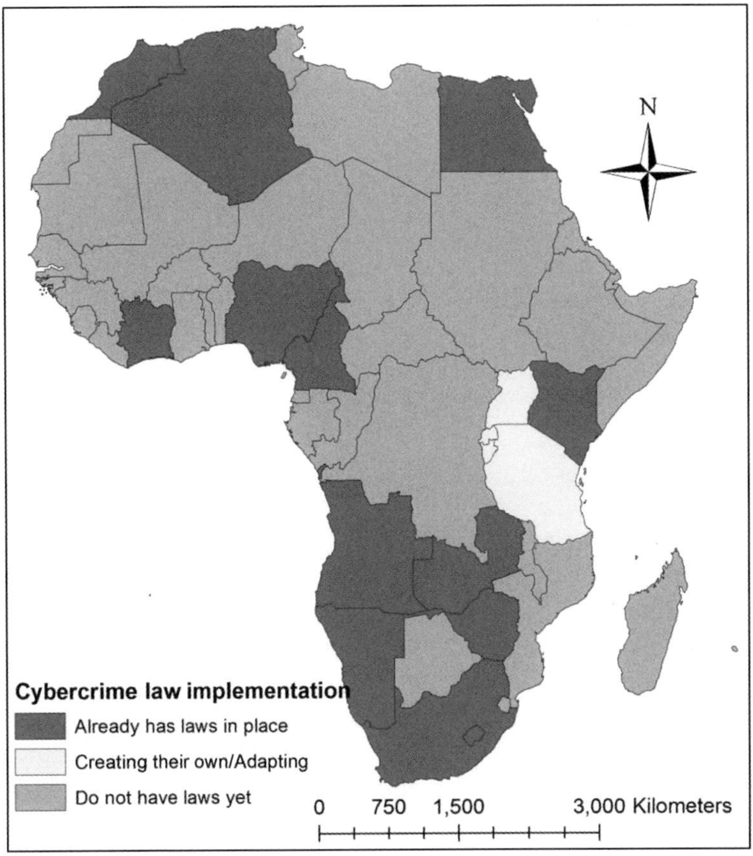

Figure 8.2 State of African countries in terms of cybercrime law implementation

Source: Created by author using data from Kharouni (2013)

countries, solutions imported directly from developed countries are not likely to be effective. In order to control cybercrime, African countries must turn to regional collaboration and integration.

Several efforts are underway to deal with the problem. In 2006, the African Information Security Association (AISA) was established to promote knowledge and create awareness about computer security and cybercrime. The United Nations African Institute for the Prevention of Crime and Treatment of Offenders (UNAFRI) launched the African Centre for Cyber Law and Cybercrime Prevention (ACCP) in Kampala, Uganda in August 2010 in response to mobile phone banking. The ACCP set itself the ambitious task of monitoring cyberspace abuses and the incidence of cybercrime in Africa.

In South Africa, the government declared cyber-security to be a national security priority in 2010. The declaration reinforced the official resolve underlying the three main applicable statutes, namely the Interception and Monitoring Prohibition Act (1992), the Prevention of Organized Crime Act (1998), and the Electronic Communications and Transactions Act (2002).

Successfully combating cybercrime and protecting information infrastructures requires international cooperation to promote the exchange of experience, identification, and application of compatible norms and standards. Fast Internet access to the rest of the world makes African information systems more vulnerable than ever before. Here again, concerted African cyber security solutions, including regional-based efforts, are needed, including proper and relevant laws, policies and practices to fight cybercrime successfully (Akuta, Ong'oa, and Jones 2011).

ICT for African Economic Transformation: Opportunities and Challenges

In the area of information and communications technologies (ICTs), despite increasing acquisition and use, Africa remains a net importer and consumer. The dearth of capacity and expertise in computer science, information systems, and related disciplines in African higher education institutions has precluded significant contributions to global software research (NEPAD 2006). Higher education institutions in Africa that should be leading Africa's participation in the ICT revolution are severely under-resourced, with serious shortages of equipment, software, and trained personnel. Despite these difficulties, a number of higher education institutions in Africa have made significant progress in building ICT infrastructure and developing computer science and other ICT disciplines.

Despite the excitement about the unbridled potential for mobile phone-based e-learning (e.g. mobile technology can provide distance learning programs and access to university education for students away from the university campuses), only a few private organizations provide learning materials, such as exam quizzes, via mobile phones (Parr 2013). Poor network coverage, lack of affordable devices, relatively expensive service costs and the limited nature of the phones that are available are some challenges. For most people, the price of Internet access is just prohibitive.

Another huge challenge is developing online educational resources that can cater to Africa's diverse and multilingual population. There is little on the Internet in many African languages, because no one in those communities has the ability to produce content, but this should change soon with Africa's booming digital natives. As with M-PESA and other applications, we should expect really great educational resources to come out of Africa as more people get mobile and are able to produce content. Different—and perhaps more effective—models of mobile learning could emerge from Africa (Parr 2013).

For a knowledge society to be realized, supported and developed, however, education and innovation should be viewed as interrelated drivers for socioeconomic development in a context where ICT is the enabler. Increased access to broadband networks using suitable technologies (wired and wireless) is necessary. Fully integrating technology into teaching and learning requires well-qualified educators, with a clear focus on both equipping teachers with ICT literacy skills and showing teachers how to use these skills to plan lessons and use technology for teaching and learning.

Balancing legitimate democratic access and national data security needs is a huge challenge for most African countries. For example, systems to enhance e-voting and access government services and statistical data online promote citizen participation in governance (Bannister and Connolly 2011). Yet, despite the need for e-transparency in promoting good governance (Onyach-Olaa 2003), security challenges, including hackers, virus writers and criminals necessitate defensive measures (Van Niekerk, Pillay, and Maharaj 2011). African governments should encourage innovative work in the area of e-transparency while government leaders demonstrate accountability to their citizens through information provision. Governments should recognize the power of social media and exploit it to their advantage, in particular to reinforce democratic processes, drive efficiency, foster innovation, empower public sector workers and expose corruption. Public data transparency should be a basic right of every member of society, which right is enhanced and exercised through e-transparency (Lubua and Maharaj 2012).

Mobile banking has reached a tipping point in Africa, particularly in Kenya, where active bank accounts have grown fourfold since 2007, aided by some 17 million M-Pesa mobile money accounts. Bold government actions in consultation with central banks and the private sector, including commercial banks and mobile money service providers, will facilitate increased growth. Governments need to coordinate with the regional economic communities by introducing favorable regulations to allow mobile operators and other non-bank third parties to offer cross-border mobile financial services.

Conclusion

Africa's lack of infrastructure, at first glance, may be seen as a disadvantage. On closer examination, however, this can be turned into an advantage if properly managed. African countries are not encumbered by extensive networks built on obsolete technology, which will require an evolutionary process of replacement.

The technological inertia is thus quite low. African countries can thus leapfrog several stages and decades in the ICT development process and learn from the experience of more advanced countries how to provide the greatest social benefits to most of the population while reducing unpleasant side effects.

Africa currently has the edge and momentum in mobile phone penetration, usage and innovation. The economic benefits in terms of revenue and much needed employment, particularly for the teeming population of digital natives, await the countries that create the right environment with strategic investment and supportive legislation. Overcoming the digital barriers and making Africa a leader in science and technology innovation for economic development necessitates regional integration. There is no room for lone rangers. Africans, especially the youth, are already engaged in breaking down barriers through their use of social media. They are developing technological innovations to solve African problems and exporting those innovations beyond their immediate geographic borders. It is time for African leaders to follow suit and promote technology-led regional integration for African development.

However, these should not come at the expense of other technologies, such as solar and wind power. The current situation, in which African university administrators brag about their "fully equipped computer labs" even when they lack regular electricity supply, is untenable. Developing apps for farmers, while laudable in increasing farmer profits, cannot replace food production. We cannot eat virtual food. The challenge then is to determine what technologies and what support will facilitate regional integration and regional economic development. For example, agricultural engineering students prioritize information technology rather than building next-generation farm machinery. Can African youth be empowered to develop other technologies, for example, to enhance food production while facilitating regional integration? In short, the continent needs appropriate policy options that support regional technological integration, build on the strength of Africa's youth, and are mutually beneficial.

Global pressures and African demand and creative energy, particularly from the African youth, make regional integration in science and technology necessary. Properly harnessed, integration promises a bright future in science and technology based economic development for those African countries that create the right environments. It is time for the creative energies of Africa's vibrant youth population to be unleashed for African economic development. Regional integration focused on digital natives and science and technology is a critical key. Through NEPAD, the African Union is already taking the right steps, but expedited action is needed. Africa's digital natives want more speed and more power, very quickly, right now.

References

Akuta, E., Ong'oa, I. and Jones, C. (2011), "Combating cybercrime in Sub-Sahara Africa: A discourse on law, policy, and practice," *Journal of Peace, Gender, and Development Studies* 1, no. 4: 129–37.

African Union-New Partnership for Africa's Development (AU-NEPAD) (2010), "African Innovation Outlook 2010." AU-NEPAD, Pretoria, Republic of South Africa.

Bannister, R. and Connolly, R. (2011), "The trouble with transparency: A critical review of openness in e-Government." Policy and Internet 3, no. 1.

Bell, M. and Albu, M. (1999), "Knowledge systems and technological dynamism in industrial clusters in developing countries," *World Development* 27, no. 9: 1715–33.

Biteye, M., "Announcing Digital Jobs Africa." The Rockefeller Foundation. Available at: http://www.rockefellerfoundation.org/blog/announcing-digital-jobs-africa (accessed October 17, 2013).

Biztech Africa, "ICT supports Ghana healthcare overhaul." biztechafrica.com, Available at: http://www.biztechafrica.com/article/ict-supports-ghana-healthcare-overhaul/7046/#.UpgkDsRUeSp (accessed November 27, 2013).

Bonsu, F. (2013), "National TB Prevalence Survey, Design and Implementation: Lessons from the Field." Available at: http://www.who.int/tb/advisory_bodies/impact_measurement_taskforce/meetings/accra2013_1_ghana_tbps_bonsu.pdf (accessed November 27, 2013).

Chacko, E. (2007), "From brain drain to brain gain: Reverse migration to Bangalore and Hyderabad, India's globalizing high tech cities," *Geojournal* 69: 131–40.

Chetty, L.R. (2012), "Challenges to regional integration and trade in Africa." thoughleader.co.za. Available at: http://www.thoughtleader.co.za/leeroy chetty/2012/06/12/challenges-to-regional-integration-and-trade-in-africa/ (accessed October 16, 2013).

United Nations Economic Commission on Africa (UNECA) (2004), "Assessing regional integration in Africa." ECA Policy Research Report. Addis Ababa: UNECA.

——— (2005), *Economic report on Africa 2005: Meeting the challenges of unemployment and poverty in Africa*. Addis Ababa: UNECA.

The Economist. "Is it a Phone, is it a Bank?" Available at: http://www.economist.com/news/finance-and-economics/21574520-safaricom-widens-its-banking-services-payments-savings-and-loans-it (accessed October 12, 2013).

——— "Telecoms in Ethiopia out of reach: The government expands the mobile-phone network but tightens its grip." Available at: http://www.economist.com/news/middle-east-and-africa/21584037-government-expands-mobile-phone-network-tightens-its-grip-out-reach (accessed October 15, 2013).

Ekine, S. (2010), *SMS Uprising: Mobile Activism in Africa*. Cape Town: Pambazuka Press.

Eksteen, S., Pretorius, E. and Breetzke, G. (2012), "South Africa: Teaching geography with GIS across diverse technological contexts." In A. Milson, A. Demirci and J.J. Kerski (eds), *International perspectives on teaching and learning with GIS in Secondary Schools*. Dordrecht: Springer, 225–32.

European Patent Office and United Nations Environment Programme. "Patents and clean energy technologies in Africa." Available at: http://documents.epo.org/projects/babylon/eponet.nsf/0/f87537c7cbb85344c1257b24005e7119/$FILE/patents_clean_energy_technologies_in_Africa_en.pdf (accessed November 22, 2013).

Fishbein, R. (2001), "Rural infrastructure in Africa: Policy directions." World Bank Africa Region Working Paper Series No. 18. Washington, D.C.: World Bank. Available at: http://www.worldbank.org/afr/wps/wp18.pdf (accessed October 16, 2013).

Global Centre for ICT in Parliament. "Legislative acts on ICT—Cybercrime." Available at: http://www.ictparliament.org/legislationlibrary/Cybercrime (accessed November 22, 2013).

Grady, H. "Global youth economic opportunities." Paper presented at Making Cents International's 2013 Global Youth Economic Opportunities Conference, Washington, D.C., September 10–12, 2013. Available at: http://www.rockefellerfoundation.org/blog/global-youth-economic-opportunities (accessed October 14, 2013).

Ighobor, K. "Africa's youth: a 'ticking time bomb' or an opportunity?" Available at: http://www.un.org/africarenewal/magazine/may-2013/africa%E2%80%99s-youth-%E2%80%9Cticking-time-bomb%E2%80%9D-or-opportunity#sthash.mj2178ff.dpuf (accessed October 18, 2013).

International Telecommunication Union. Measuring the Information Society 2012. Available at: http://www.itu.int/ITU-D/ict/publications/idi/index.html (accessed October 17, 2013).

——— Measuring the Information Society 2013. Available at: http://www.itu.int/en/ITU-D/Statistics/Pages/publications/mis2013.aspx (accessed October 17, 2013).

Internet World Stats. "Internet users, population and Facebook statistics for Africa 2012 Q2." Available at: http://www.internetworldstats.com/stats1.htm (accessed November 22, 2013).

Juma, C. and Lee, Y-C. (2005), *Innovation: Applying knowledge in development. UN Millennium Project, Task Force on Science, Technology, and Innovation*. London: Earthscan. Available at: http://www.unmillenniumproject.org/documents/Science-complete.pdf (accessed November 22, 2013).

Kalan, J. (2013), "African youth hungry for connectivity." Africa Renewal. Available at: http://www.un.org/africarenewal/magazine/may-2013/

african-youth-hungry-connectivity#sthash.PhaSoLUg.JFLMvq6o.dpuf (accessed October 16, 2013).

Karikari, I.B., Stillwell, J.C.H. and Carver, S. (2003), "Land administration and GIS: The case of Ghana," *Progress in Development Studies* 3, no. 3: 223–42.

Kharouni, L. (2013), "Africa: A New Safe Harbor for Cybercriminals?" Trend Micro Incorporated Research Paper. Available at: http://www.trendmicro.com/cloud-content/us/pdfs/security-intelligence/white-papers/wp-africa.pdf (accessed November 22, 2013).

Kitetu, C.W. (2008), "Gender, Science and Technology: Perspectives from Africa." CODESRIA Gender Series 6. Dakar: Council for the Development of Social Science Research in Africa. Available at: http://codesria.org/IMG/pdf/1prelim-gender.pdf (accessed November 22, 2013).

Kritzinger, E. and von Solms, S.H. (2013), "Cyber security for home users: A new way of protection through awareness enforcement," *Computer & Security* 29: 840–47.

Kyem, P. (2012), "Is ICT the panacea to sub-Saharan Africa's development problems? Rethinking Africa's contentious engagement with the global information society," *Progress in Development Studies* 12, no. 2–3: 231–44.

Kyem P. and LeMaire, P.K. (2006), "Transforming recent gains in the digital divide into digital opportunities: Africa and the boom in mobile phone subscription," *The Electronic Journal on Information Systems in Developing Countries* 28, no. 5: 1–16.

Lubua, E. and Maharaj, M. (2012), "ICT policy & e-Transparency in Tanzania." In *IST-Africa 2012 Conference Proceedings*, P. Cunningham and M. Cunningham (eds), IIMC International Information Management Corporation.

——— "State information protection laws and e-Transparency." International Conference on ICT for Africa, February 20–23, 2013, Harare, Zimbabwe. Available at: http://www.ictforafrica.org/attachments/section/4/ict4africa2013_submission_4.pdf (accessed October 16, 2013).

Luk, R., Zaharia, M., Ho, M., Levine, B. and Aoki, P.M. (2009), "ICTD for healthcare in Ghana: Two parallel case studies." Proceedings of the Third International Conference on Information and Communication Technologies and Development. Piscataway, NJ: IEEE Press, 118–28.

Macharia, K. "Kenyans Being Conned Through Hacked Facebook Accounts." allafrica.com. Available at: http://allafrica.com/stories/201311271472.html?viewall=1 (accessed November 28, 2013).

Mambara, J.L. (2007), "COMESA Customs Union: An Assessment of Progress and Challenges for Eastern and Southern Africa's Poor." Trade and Development Studies Centre. Harare, Zimbabwe. Available at: http://www.tradescentre.org.zw/index.php?option=com_docman&task=doc_download&gid=30&Itemid=21 (accessed October 17, 2013).

Maruping, M. (2005), "Challenges for regional integration in Sub-Saharan Africa: Macroeconomic convergence and monetary coordination." In *Africa in the World Economy—The National, Regional and International Challenges*. The Hague: Fondad, 129–55.

Matthews, A. (2003), *Regional integration and food security in developing countries*. Rome: FAO.

Microsoft Security Intelligence Report. "Running Unprotected: Measuring the Benefits of Real-Time Security Software." Microsoft Security Intelligence Report, Volume 14, July–December 2012. Available at: http://www.microsoft.com/security/sir/archive/default.aspx (accessed November 22, 2013).

Mistry, P. (2000), "Africa's record of regional economic integration," *African Affairs* 99: 553–73.

Mugabe, J.O. (2011), "Science, technology and innovation in Africa's regional integration: From rhetoric to practice." ACODE Policy Research Series, No. 44, Kampala, Uganda.

NEPAD (2006), "Africa's Science and Technology Consolidated Plan of Action." Pretoria: NEPAD Office of Science and Technology. Available at: http://www.nepad.org/system/files/ast_cpa_2007.pdf (accessed October 18, 2013).

Nganga, G. (2013), "Research boosted by multi-million dollar projects," *University World News* 15 November, Issue No: 296.

Nye, J. (2004), *Power in the global information age: From realism to globalization*. London: Routledge.

Onyach-Olaa, M. (2003), "The challenges of implementing decentralization: Recent experiences in Uganda," *Public Administration and Development* 23: 105–13.

Oppong, J.R. (2010), "Transport, communication and information technologies in Sub-Saharan Africa." In *Geography of Sub-Saharan Africa*, edited by S.A. Attoh, 243–64. New York: Prentice Hall.

Oppong, J.R. and Ofori-Amoah, B. (2012), "Ghana: Prospects for secondary school GIS education in developing country." In A. Milson, A. Demirci and J.J. Kerski (eds), *International Perspectives on Teaching and Learning with GIS*. Dordrecht: Springer, 115–23.

Parr, C. "Africa's mobile phone e-learning transformation." timeshighereducation.co.uk. Available at: http://www.timeshighereducation.co.uk/features/africas-mobile-phone-e-learning-transformation/2007120.fullarticle (accessed October 16, 2013).

Prensky, M. (2001), "Digital Natives, Digital Immigrants Part 1," *On the Horizon* 9, no. 5: 1–6.

——— (2001), "Digital Natives, Digital Immigrants Part 2: Do They Really Think Differently?" *On the Horizon* 9, no. 6: 1–6.

Purewal, S.J. "Hackers steal $6.7 million in cyber bank robbery." pcworld.com Available at: http://www.pcworld.com/article/248340/hackers_steal_6_7_million_in_cyber_bank_robbery.html (accessed November 22, 2013).

Qobo, M. (2007), "The challenges of regional integration in Africa in the context of globalization and the prospects for a United States of Africa." ISS Paper 145. Pretoria: Institute for Security Studies. Available at: http://www.isn.ethz.ch/Digital-Library/Publications/Detail/?ots591=0c54e3b3–1e9c-be1e-2c24-a6a8c7060233&lng=en&id=98933 (accessed October 16, 2013).

Tafirenyika, M. "Information technology super-charging Rwanda's economy." un.org/africarenewal. Available at: http://www.un.org/africarenewal/magazine/april-2011/information-technology-super-charging-rwandas-economy#sthash.yldUc6Mr.dpuf (accessed October 16, 2013).

Tamarkin, E. "Cybercrime: A complex problem requiring a multifaceted response." Institute for Security Studies Brief 51, February 2014. Available at: http://www.issafrica.org/uploads/PolBrief51Feb14.pdf (accessed May 17, 2014).

Troup, S. "Identifying digital opportunities for African youth." Available at: http://www.rockefellerfoundation.org/blog/identifying-digital-opportunities (accessed October 16, 2013).

UNESCO and African Union. "Science, Technology & Innovation Policy Initiative." Available at: http://www.unesco.org/new/fileadmin/MULTIMEDIA/HQ/SC/pdf/sc_sti_initiative_africa_en.pdf (accessed October 18, 2013).

United Nations Economic Commission for Africa (2010), "A technological resurgence? Africa in the global flows of technology." UNECA Series on Technology Transfer for Africa's Development. New York, Geneva: United Nations.

United Nations Statistics Division. "National accounts estimates of main aggregates: Per capita GDP at current prices—US dollars." Available at: http://data.un.org/Data.aspx?d=SNAAMA&f=grID%3A101%3BcurrID%3AUSD%3BpcFlag%3A1 (accessed February 23, 2014).

U.S. Department of Labor (2007), "Third Annual Report–Office of the Ombudsman Energy Employees Occupational Illness Compensation Program, Part E." Available at: http://www.dol.gov/EEOMBD/2007annualreport/ (accessed October 18, 2013).

——— FY 2010 Annual Performance Report. Available at: http://www.dol.gov/dol/budget/2012/PDF/CBJ-2012-V1–01.pdf (accessed October 18, 2013).

Van Niekerk, B., Pillay, K. and Maharaj, M. (2011), "Analyzing the role of ICTs in the Tunisian and Egyptian unrest," *International Journal of Communication* 5: 1406–16.

Viotti, E.B. (2002), "National learning systems: A new approach on technological change in late industrializing economies and evidences from the cases of Brazil and South Korea," *Technological Forecasting and Social Change* 69, no. 7: 653–80.

Vital Wave Consulting. eTransform Africa: Health sector study. Palo Alto: Vital Wave Consulting, 2012. Available at: http://siteresources.worldbank.org/EXTINFORMATIONANDCOMMUNICATIONANDTECHNOLOGIES/Resources/282822-1346223280837/Health_Fullreport.pdf (accessed November 27, 2013).

The White House, Office of the Press Secretary,. "FACT SHEET: Power Africa." Available at: http://www.whitehouse.gov/the-press-office/2013/06/30/fact-sheet-power-africa (accessed October 17, 2013).

The World Bank. "World development indicators: GDP (current US$)." Available at: http://data.worldbank.org/indicator/NY.GDP.MKTP.CD?display=default (accessed October 16, 2013).

——— "World development indicators: Mobile cellular subscriptions (per 100 people)." Available at: http://data.worldbank.org/indicator/IT.CEL.SETS.P2/countries?display=default (accessed October 16, 2013).

The World Bank and the International Finance Corporation. "Doing business—Getting electricity." Available at: http://www.doingbusiness.org/data/exploretopics/getting-electricity (accessed October 16, 2013).

Wright, J., Dawson, M.E., Jr. and Omar, M. (2012), "Cyber security and mobile threats: the need for antivirus applications for smart phones," *Journal of information Systems and Technology Planning* 5 (14): 40–60.

Yonazi, E., Kelly, T. Halewood, N. and Blackman, C. (eds), eTransform Africa: The Transformational Use of Information and Communication Technologies in Africa. The World Bank and the African Development Bank with the African Union, 2012. Available at: http://siteresources.worldbank.org/EXTINFORMATIONANDCOMMUNICATIONANDTECHNOLOGIES/Resources/282822-1346223280837/MainReport.pdf (accessed October 17, 2013).

Chapter 9

Regional Value Chains and Productivity Enhancement in Africa

William G. Moseley

Introduction

Value chains, or the linkages from raw materials to finished products,[1] have become a central focus of economic development activities in recent years. While the value chain approach is not a novel idea, it is being emphasized anew in development scholarship and practice (Bair 2005). To date, initiatives to facilitate value chain development have occurred largely within the borders of nation states, although it is increasingly understood that some value chains may make more sense at the regional scale. In fact, many of the world's most profitable value chains are international in scope due to globalization. Unfortunately, African states' participation in regional value chains has been limited thus far. A lack of economic cooperation and production across African borders may be linked in part to historical and political factors that exacerbate cross-border tensions. Other factors limiting economic cooperation and integration—especially within Africa's regional economic communities (RECs)—are more economic and cultural in nature, including poor infrastructure, linguistic barriers, weak regulatory environments, and poor border administration, each of which can increase transaction costs.

The goal of this chapter is to advance our understanding of the current state of African value chains, vertical integration,[2] production across borders,

1 This shorthand definition will be elaborated upon in the next section of the chapter.

2 Vertical integration is the degree to which a firm owns its upstream suppliers and its downstream buyers. Contrary to horizontal integration, which is a consolidation of many firms that handle the same part of the production process, vertical integration is typified by one firm engaged in different parts of production (for example, growing raw materials, manufacturing, transporting, marketing, and/or retailing). There are three varieties: backward (upstream) vertical integration, forward (downstream) vertical

and regional integration. The chapter explores the role of regionalism in value chain development and examines ways to expand its most valuable aspects. In so doing, the chapter tackles a number of interrelated questions:

- How does regional integration impact local productive capacity and intra-Africa value chain development?
- What types of opportunities exist for regional value chain development?
- Who are the actors involved, and what are their roles in value chain development?
- What are the concerns related to value chains and regional integration, and how might these be mitigated?
- What factors facilitate vertical specialization among specific economies with known complementarities?

The chapter draws lessons from best and worst practices in Africa aimed at building capacities for regional value chain development. It also explores what kinds of policies and capacity building initiatives would be most effective for allowing Africa to exploit cross-border value chain opportunities (at various scales) for economic development and improved livelihoods.

The overarching thesis of this chapter is that building more robust value chains in Africa is critical for transforming raw materials into finished products, encouraging industrialization, and moving African economies beyond their peripheral position. Regional value chains may further develop this capacity by leveraging complementarities among different African countries and fostering knowledge creation and skill enhancement within the region. That said, not all value chains are equal. Those value chains with Africa-based transformation and value added activities ought to be encouraged over those that simply reinforce peripheral commodity production.

---

integration, and balanced (both upstream and downstream) vertical integration (Knox and Marston 2003).

Review of Theoretical and Applied Literature on Regional Integration and Value Chains

The Value Chain Framework and Development in Africa

Value chains have become a central focus of development thinking in the past few years (Perez-Aleman 2008). According to Hellin and Meijer (2006, p. 4), "A value chain can be defined as the full range of activities which are required to bring a product or service from conception, through the different phases of production (involving a combination of physical transformation and the input of various producer services), delivery to final customers, and final disposal after use."

Within the African aid context, the global value chain approach is a key element in, for example, agricultural development that then leads to even broader forms of industrial development (Toenniessen et al. 2008). Continuing with the agriculture example, the Alliance for a Green Revolution in Africa (AGRA) uses value chains to a certain end and sees these as the sequence of activities focused on the transformation of a crop from the farm to national levels. At the farm level, the value chain framework promotes the "upgrading" of agricultural production and food security by integrating farmers into new input and output markets in order to increase production, sales, and income. At the national level, the value chain approach seeks to transform the structure of national economies by promoting investments in agroprocessing to add value to products previously exported as unfinished goods. Figure 9.1 depicts these different steps for the AGRA project from inputs, to farming, processing, distribution and trading. The value chain approach is a popular development tool because it focuses on the actors, activities, and barriers in the upgrading of productive activities at multiple scales.

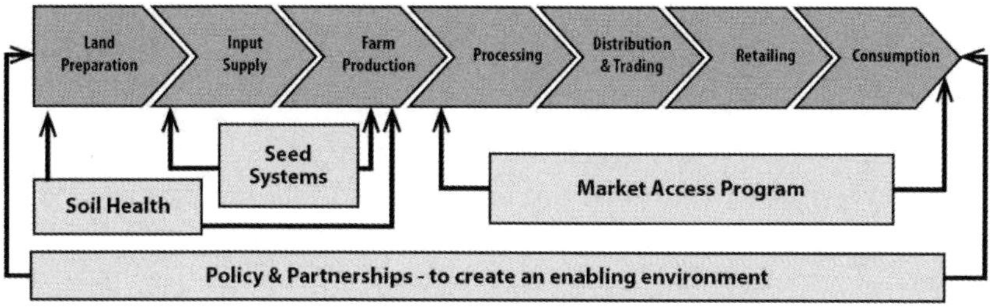

Figure 9.1 Alliance for a Green Revolution in Africa's (AGRA) value chain approach for agricultural products

Source: Toenniessen (2008). Used with permission.

Views on Value Chains

The value chain literature is dominated by economists and business management specialists but bears a strong resemblance to more interdisciplinary social science scholarship on commodity chains as well as other relevant economic geography literature on economic interdependence and agglomeration effects. Economists and geographers in the "new economic geography" tradition also have written about how poor infrastructure, linguistic barriers, weak regulatory environments, and poor border administration increase transaction costs between countries in Africa (Hausmann 2001; World Bank 2009).

As Bair (2005, p. 153) has noted, there was "an important but generally unacknowledged break between the original world-systems inspired tradition of commodity chain research and two subsequent chain approaches, the global commodity chain and global value chain frameworks." The economistic global value chain approach is increasingly focused on the meso and micro scales, Bair argues, and closer attention must be paid to "larger institutional and structural environments in which commodity chains are embedded" (2005, p. 153) because of concerns about uneven development. In other words, the economistic global value chain literature views globalization as largely positive, framing those not integrated into the global economy as disadvantaged. As such, in the case of agriculture, subsistence production is a problem and efforts must be made to incorporate disarticulated producers into the global system.

In contrast, the world systems theory inspired commodity chain approach sees these very same articulations as potentially problematic. For example, numerous scholars have used commodity chain analysis to describe how consumption in the global North has led to environmental degradation and poverty in Africa or other areas of the global South (Hartwick 1998; Tucker 2002; Bassett 2008). The rub in much of this analysis is that African producers have limited agency in their engagement with these chains, whereas firms based in the global North hold disproportionate sway (Mather 2004; Hughes and Reimer 2004). The question is how African producers and actors enhance their power vis á vis these chains.

One possible way for African producers to garner greater control within global value chains would be to encourage more upgrading of products on the continent. Daviron and Ponte (2005) describe how, with the exception of sub-Saharan Africa, manufactured goods have risen steadily during the past 25 years as a share of exports from developing countries.[3]

3 Unfortunately, Daviron and Ponte (2005) also show that this increase in export share of manufactured goods has been accompanied by a fall in the price of labor-intensive manufactures. In other words, the price of these manufactures seems to be

How does a country or region engage in upgrading (or further transformation, processing and/or value-added activities) and get higher returns? One solution may be to think about upgrading in multiple ways. Humphrey and Schmitz (2002) discuss four types of upgrading. The first way is functional upgrading—for example, adding new transformation functions that require more skilled labor inputs (as with turning cotton into textiles). The second type is process upgrading, or more efficient transformation through reorganization of production activities. The third way is product upgrading, which means moving into more sophisticated products that fetch a higher value. Finally, the fourth type is intersectoral upgrading, or applying competencies acquired in one function to another. Gibbon and Ponte (2005) suggest that there is a fifth type: upgrading at larger scales and the leveraging of market position. At this point in African development, policymakers are concerned mostly with the first and third types (functional and product upgrading), because many value added and transformation steps are simply non-existent in African countries at this juncture. The second, fourth and fifth types are still valid but are most applicable to existing value chains.

The value chain concept also has interesting, and seemingly contradictory, connections to an older literature on import substitution. That said, while this connection is somewhat missing in Anglophone scholarship, it is alive and well in the Francophone African policy literature pertaining to the "filière approach." Raikes et al. (2000, p. 390) suggest that the value chain approach may be improved by insights gained in filière work, especially in terms of enhancing "historical coverage and depth, enlarging the analysis to agricultural commodities, better handling of regulation issues, and including quality convention issues in analyzing commodity chain structure and restructuring."

While traditional import substitution industries often struggled because of small markets in many African countries, the potential for regional scale import substitution was not seriously considered in the first decades following African independence. During the first wave of dependency theory-inspired import substitution, Prebisch (1959) argued that tropical countries would be forever stuck as producers of primary products (and therefore fail to develop) unless they took proactive steps to change the nature of their economies in relation to those of others. The idea behind import substitution was that manufactured goods needed to be produced at home rather than imported from the core countries.

The import substitution policy was quite popular until the late 1970s, when the so-called "third world debt crisis" struck. This crisis involved a number of developing countries, including several in Africa, that were on the verge of defaulting on loans owed to creditors (mainly public creditors in the case

behaving like that of commodities. Kaplinsky (1993) argues that the commodification of labor intensive manufactures has led to growth only in low-wage, menial employment.

of Africa). The crisis was brought on largely by government involvement with increasingly inefficient, state-run enterprises and the energy crisis of the 1970s, when high oil prices were a challenge for many African oil importers. In response to the debt crisis, public lenders imposed a new neoliberal economic order in the 1980s–2000s that stressed small government, free trade, export orientation, and the privatization of state-run enterprises. Furthermore, the neoliberal era brought a decisive end to two decades of experimentation with import substitution in the African context.

Critics of neoliberalism suggested that this was a return to the economic policies of the colonial era. Furthermore, there was a concern that there had been a selective reading of history in order to make the case that import substitution was overly problematic and that a narrow focus on comparative advantage and commodity exports was the cure (Carmody 1998). With the newly industrialized countries (NICs) of the Asia-Pacific Rim being held up as the new development models, the storytellers conveniently ignored the active role that the state had played in initially protecting and nurturing what would become their major export industries. More recently, some economists have begun to argue that import substitution should be revisited in some cases as an economic policy (Brutton 1998; Amsden 2003). Scaling up and reinventing import substation at the regional scale within RECs would be another way to renew exploration of the viability of this approach. Rather than, for example, importing textiles or consumer goods from non-African sources, might not there be a way to produce these more competitively at the regional scale for internal regional markets?

Regional Integration and Value Chains

Regional economic integration[4] typically focuses on removing barriers to free trade and increasing the movement of people, labor, goods, and capital across national borders. It may also involve strategic investments in economic development initiatives that benefit multiple national stakeholders (Ndulu 2006).

Regional economic integration and cooperation may facilitate some types of upgrading and value chain formation. While national planners likely prefer to pursue upgrading and value chain formation within their own borders, this may not be possible for many goods in a significant number of African countries. It is important to recall that of the 48 African countries (continental

4 This is not elaborated upon to a great extent because it is discussed at length in other solicited papers.

countries plus Madagascar),[5] only 11 have populations of 25 million or more, and only 14 are estimated to have gross domestic products of US$50 billion or more. As such, roughly two-thirds of African nations are dealing with relatively small internal markets, making the traditional import substitution model (focused on upgrading of production for national markets) inherently limited. Because of constraints on demand within domestic markets, African upgrading is often focused on a handful of products with significant export potential. Unfortunately, a complicating factor for export-oriented upgrading is the relatively high number of landlocked countries in Africa—a third, or 16 of 48 countries. In the absence of efficient border crossings, being landlocked typically makes it difficult to cheaply move heavier products to port for export.

Due to small market size and high transit costs for many African countries, regional economic integration may be especially useful for reducing the expense of transborder transactions, fostering vertical integration, building agglomeration economies, increasing the size of internal markets, ensuring coordination, and sharing knowledge as well as R&D functions. New economic geographers have written extensively about the high costs of international border crossings in Africa (Faye et al. 2004; Arvis et al. 2007). Figure 9.2 depicts transit costs and times along selected major highway routes in West Africa. While some of these costs are accrued at roadside checkpoints within countries (which wouldn't necessarily be allayed by regional integration), a high proportion do occur at and around international border crossings. For example, according to Lamport (2013), international border crossing times for West Africa range from 4.5 hours at Kodjoviakope (a checkpoint on the Togo side at the southern Togo–Benin border) to 45 hours at Hillakondji checkpoint on the Benin side of that same border crossing. Minimizing the time and cost of international border crossings is critical for building regional value chains.

Regional integration may also foster agglomeration effects, which are the cost advantages that accrue to individual firms because of their location within a cluster. Examples of this might be easy access to ancillary services (repair shops, legal services), proximity to suppliers and buyers, and shared use of transportation infrastructure. As these savings are not due to a firm's own organization or methods of production, economists often think about these effects as a particular type of positive externality.

Related to agglomeration effects is the notion of localization economies. Here you have clustering of firms in one particular industry (as opposed to the more generic clustering with agglomeration effects) because they mutually benefit from positive externalities. There may be a shared pool of labor with special skills, specialized technical schools, research institutes, and so forth

5 While there are 55 African states recognized by the African Union and/or United Nations, here we focus on the 47 continental countries plus Madagascar.

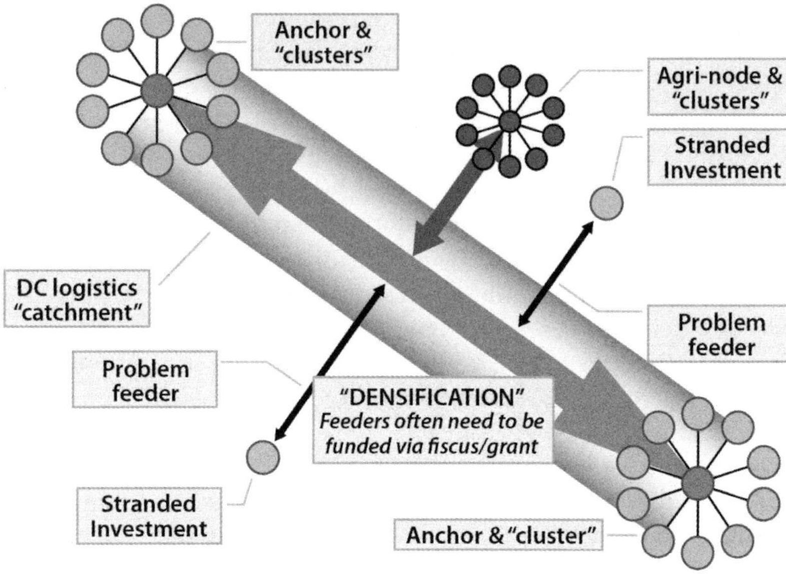

Figure 9.2 Idealized development corridor configuration

Source: Thomas (2009). Available at: http://www.fdi.net/documents/WorldBank/databases/africa_infrastructure/Thomas_SDI_paper_lowres.pdf. Used with permission.

(Knox and Marston 2003). The clustering of financial services in Johannesburg might be an example of a localization or agglomeration economy. There is a localization economy associated with diamond cutting in Antwerp in the Netherlands, an industry that Botswana is now trying to bring, at least partially, to Gaborone (more on this later in the chapter).

A key question with regional integration, and with some degree of specialization between countries, is who will do what? In other words, how does one rationally integrate different national players into a single value chain? One potential model for thinking about economic integration, regional value chains, and complementarity is the "flying geese paradigm" developed by Japanese economist Kaname Akamatsu, who in 1962 argued for regional economic integration between different types of economies. Written from the perspective of Japan in the 1960s, Akamatsu's thesis argued that Asian nations would catch up with the West by forming an Asian regional block within which the poorest countries produced the commodities that were subsequently transformed in the more advanced countries (or regional value chains). The metaphor was a flock of geese in V-formation, with Japan in the lead, then the second tier of NICs (South Korea, Taiwan, Singapore, and Hong Kong), followed by the lesser developed countries in the region. In other words, Akamatsu was essentially arguing for an acceptance of regional dualism as a way to break out of international dualism, or international core-periphery relationships.

One can certainly imagine such complementary economies in the African context. Countries with different factor endowments might include industrial South Africa and its neighbors, or food rich Mali and more agro-processor Côte d'Ivoire. Furthermore, the type of vertical integration (one firm engaged in different parts of production, such as growing raw materials, manufacturing, transporting, marketing, and/or retailing), already exists within some sectors in this region. For example, South African food retailers have spread across southern Africa (Economist 2013), including in their sourcing of supplies. South African capital has also moved into neighboring states to develop tourism opportunities (Rogerson 2011), with South African tour operators and hotel chains increasingly work across borders.

Exploring Opportunities for Regional Value Chains

In the face of high border crossing charges and tariffs, African countries (unfortunately) often find it cheaper to import goods from non-African origins rather than their neighbors, and/or export raw materials to non-African destinations(rather than adjacent states) for transformation. This section explores a few examples where regional value chains could make a real difference for economic development.

Example of Internally Oriented Regional Value Chain Opportunity

In recent decades, traders in coastal West African cities have often found it preferable to import rice rather than source it from their own hinterlands or neighboring states because of limited support for local producers, low international tariff barriers, poor milling quality and expensive internal transport costs. The structural adjustment era decimated support (in terms of extension and research) for rice production across West Africa. Declining import tariffs, combined with cheap rice from abroad, further facilitated dependence on imports (Carney 2008; Moseley et al. 2010). The growing reliance on imports was also exacerbated by slightly different factors in specific countries. Côte d'Ivoire, for example, suffered from low milling quality after large industrial mills were shut down following neoliberal reforms (Becker and Yoboué 2009). In contrast, The Gambia was plagued by poor roads that separated producers up country from the milling facility and major markets in Banjul (Carney 2008).

Over-dependence by urbanites on non-African rice supplies became a huge problem during the 2007–2008 global food crisis, when rice prices doubled (Seck 2008). The reality is that West African rice producers could supply these urban populations. The combination of a long history of rice production (African rice was originally domesticated in the region), shared research (such as ongoing work at the West Africa Rice Research Institute) and milling infrastructure, improved transportation networks, and more efficient border crossings could make the region more self-sufficient in rice production. While rice should not be emphasized at the expense of other food crops—especially orphan crops[6] needed for diverse agro-ecosystems that are more resilient in the face of climate change (Mortimore and Adams 2001)—there is an argument to be made for replacing non-edible cash crops with food crops, such as rice, that may be traded regionally. With a robust market for rice in West Africa (driven largely by a burgeoning urban population that prefers rice (Moseley 2011), the returns on this market may be better than on those for conventional cash crops. Such a shift might also add some stability to regional food markets and reduce the outflow of cash for food purchases.

Example of Externally Oriented Regional Value Chain Opportunity

Another example (or a missed regional value chain opportunity) related to high border transaction costs, lack of coordination, and missing shared investment is Ghana and Côte d'Ivoire's exportation of raw cacao rather than shared regional chocolate production (Ryan 2011). Côte d'Ivoire and Ghana are the top two cacao producers in the world and jointly account for 70 percent of global production. Yet West African cacao producers have been unable to leverage this dominance for a higher return on their crops. In fact, the typical cacao farmer sees only approximately 4 percent of the price consumers pay for a chocolate bar in the store. As such, the disconnect between the consumers of this luxury item and the poverty of those who produce its main ingredient, cacao (from the pods of cacao trees) is rather startling. Given that this crop originally hails from Latin America, and has virtually no place in West African cuisine, it might be tempting to abandon it altogether as a cash crop. Yet, West African farmers remain competitive in this arena because cacao is actually cheaper to produce on small farms, as the plants require a lot of individual attention. Ryan (2011) concludes that fair trade efforts to garner a higher return for West African farmers have been largely been unsuccessful. Rather, government and regional cooperation could play a critical role in developing chocolate production.

A regional value chain built around these two cacao producing powerhouses could retain a significantly larger proportion of profits in the region and create new employment opportunities. A shared chocolate production facility and

6 Neglected or underutilized crops that are important for subsistence, yet largely overlooked by the international research community, governments, and development actors.

related transportation arteries would most logically be located in the southern border area between the two countries. Differences in colonial language traditions (French and English) would clearly be an obstacle to be overcome.

Another regional value chain that exhibits huge potential is cattle and related products in the Horn of Africa and East Africa, including the countries of Tanzania, Kenya, Uganda, Somalia, and Ethiopia. Unlike the previous two examples, this regional value chain could supply both internal and external (mainly Middle Eastern) markets. The majority of cattle in the region are delivered on the hoof. The possibilities for upgrading in terms of meat products and hides are enormous. The largest internal regional market is likely Nairobi, and tremendous export potential exists for nearby Middle Eastern markets (European Union 2009).

By way of conclusion to this section, the examples reviewed suggest that regional coordination may allow different neighboring African countries to specialize and trade, with the overall goal of a higher level of regional import substitution or regional self-sufficiency. This was the essential idea of the flying geese paradigm, as well. Regional value chains may also figure into such a broader policy vision, with the added benefit that some types of production could be spread across multiple countries, making these key value chains shared rather than objects of competition. UNECA (2012, p. 64) arrived at a somewhat similar conclusion, noting: "the coordination of agricultural value chains on a regional scale is necessary for a balanced development of the sector, not only for exchanging best practices and sharing the results of research, but also in order for each member country to focus on the products in which they have a comparative advantage."

Key Actors in African Regional Value Chain Development

In early 2008, the Ministers responsible for Trade, Mining and Industry at the African Union (AU) began considering a new industrialization strategy based on development corridors, subsequently known as "A Plan of Action for Acceleration of Industrialization" (Jourdan 2008). The corridor approach was seen as a way to better link countries and create regional supply chains. The belief was that improved regional infrastructure and logistics would consolidate supply chains, enhance access to inputs at lower cost, and improve delivery of products to consumers. Furthermore, according to Thomas (2009, p. 1), this group "tapped into a rising tide of interest among African regional organizations, donors and other development professionals in the concept of Development Corridors (DCs) and Spatial Development Initiatives (or SDIs)."

The corridor approach has been linked explicitly to Asian experiences inspired by the flying geese paradigm discussed earlier. The Zambia–Malawi–Mozambique Growth Triangle "is a cross-border development initiative that was designed by replicating some of the perceived methods of the Asian Growth Areas, which aim to promote regional integration and thereby 'fast-track' development in a region" (Slocum-Bradley 2008, p. 92).

The development corridor idea was also rooted in a belief that Africa's comparative advantage lay in resource production and the upgrading of these commodities (Thomas 2009). Cross-continental development corridors would pave the way for resource-based regional value chains by overcoming infrastructure constraints. Furthermore, it was argued that these corridors would allow for the reinvestment of profits into human resource development and R&D, with the outcome being "resource-industrial clusters" (Thomas 2009).

Figure 9.2 depicts a hypothetical or idealized development corridor. In this transnational space, typically spanning two to three countries, one could imagine shared transportation infrastructure and R&D facilities. Such a space could also foster the agglomeration effects discussed earlier in this chapter.

There are currently 20 such corridors in Africa. The United Nations Conference on Trade and Development (UNCTAD) is recommending that African countries and RECs transform traditional transport corridors into development corridors. "Developmental regionalism encompasses cooperation among countries in a broader range of areas than just trade and trade facilitation. It should include investment, research and development crafting policies aimed at accelerating regional industrial development and regional infrastructure provision, such as building better road networks and railways" (UNCTAD press release, July 11, 2013). Transforming traditional transport corridors into development corridors may make sense in many instances because it leverages existing investments. That said, existing corridors may not always line up well with development opportunities.

Africa's RECs are now becoming increasingly engaged with development corridors and regional value chains. The eight RECs recognized by the AU, which form the "pillars" of the African Economic Community, are moving toward implementing the Abuja Treaty on freer intra-African trade at different speeds. The East African Community (EAC), the most advanced community, launched its common market in 2010. The Common Market for Eastern and Southern Africa (COMESA) initiated its Customs union in June 2009. The Southern African Development Community (SADC) and the Economic Community of West African States (ECOWAS) have made progress in building their free trade areas (FTAs) and plan to start Customs unions in 2013[7] and 2015, respectively. The Economic Community of Central African States (ECCAS) began its FTA in 2004 but is facing huge challenges in its practical application. The Arab Maghreb Union (AMU), the Economic Community of Sahel-Saharan States (CEN-SAD), and the Intergovernmental Authority on Development (IGAD) are moving slowly and are still in the early stages of cooperation among their member states (UNECA 2013).

Private sector firms are also central actors in regional value chains; players are as diverse as supermarkets, mining firms, agro-dealers and agro-processors, and many are engaged in working across African national boundaries. One example of a private firm operating at the regional scale is AAR Health (based in Nairobi, Kenya). Modern health-care facilities are scant in many areas of the region, and medical insurance is even more rare. This Nairobi-based private health-care company, which serves more than 140,000 members in East and Central Africa, operates in Kenya, Tanzania, Uganda and Rwanda. The company started in 1984 as a medical evacuation specialist for expatriates but eventually expanded to provide general healthcare coverage to individual and corporate clients at a range of income levels. AAR Health now employs more than 1,000 people and has revenue of US$21 million a year. According to the company's general manager, it hopes to expand further by focusing on patients who traditionally can't afford health care (Delevingne 2008). Given that insurance companies need large pools of clients in order to spread risk, it makes sense that such a company would operate regionally rather than nationally.

Another type of actor that is rarely discussed in the literature on value chains is the union, be it for laborers or farmers. Such organizations are important components of African civil society and can play key roles in mitigating some of the most egregious downsides of regional integration or development corridors. Unions often play critical roles in leveling the playing field across borders in terms of wages and producer prices. Strong producer unions can also advocate for African value chains on the international stage. A good example of this is when West African cotton farmer unions from Benin, Côte d'Ivoire, Niger, Mali, and Burkina Faso successfully joined forces with other cotton producers in Latin America and Asia to bring suit against the United States in the WTO over illegal cotton subsidies (Ledermann and Moseley 2008).

7 The latest reports suggest that the details of the SADC customs union are still being negotiated. See AllAfrica.com. 2013. "Tanzania: SADC to Deliberate On Customs Union." August 17. Available at: http://allafrica.com/stories/201308190027.html (accessed 24 Feb. 2014).

Challenges for Regional Economic Integration and Regional Value Chains

What are challenges for regional value chains? The objective in this section is to explore concerns related to regional value chains in hopes of mitigating potential downsides.

First, it is important to understand that increasing free trade between African nations, increasing foreign direct investment (FDI) by one African nation in another, and regional value chains, while somewhat related, are not the same thing. Clearly, growing free trade between African nations has not been without its consequences. For example, the import-substituting industries of Zimbabwe went into sharp decline after the end of South African minority rule and increasing trade in the region (Carmody 1998). More recently, aggressively expanding South African supermarket chains (and FDI) have put pressure on local retailers, leading to the thinning out of competition in some instances (Economist 2013). In theory, regional value chains would more explicitly involve players from multiple countries and thus avoid the worst of such problems.

Second, the regional value chain phenomenon is not without its critics, whose objections range from concerns focused on loss of choice related to consolidation, to deep seated mistrust of foreign investors (even if they are fellow Africans), to fears that regional value chains are just another form of neoliberal export orientation that perpetuate and deepen inequities.

For example, as large South African food retailers displace local chains and small independent outlets, some worry about the impact on diets (more processed foods) and the decline of credit options previously offered by small shops (Gomez and Ricketts 2013; Moseley et al. 2013). Schroeder (2012, p. 1) has described enclaves of South African investors in Tanzania (many whom are involved in the ecotourism industry) who have generated resentment because of their neocolonial attitudes: "the South Africans who followed their investments to Tanzania were not ANC stalwarts; these were instead the hated Boers or makaburu, a group of whites whose experience of being white and whose historical relationship with African blacks were profoundly and ineluctably shaped by apartheid."

Söderbaum and Taylor (2008b, p. 42) are concerned that regional value chains, as manifested in spatial development initiatives, reinforce power inequities. They note: "the SDI model … is explicitly connected to perceptions held at the elite level that, in an era marked by globalization, various types of regionalization are a crucial means by which states may come together and tap into this process in order to maximize their pulling power vis-à-vis international capital. It also reflects the dominance of certain ideas regarding how best to pursue economic development. Problematically, however, the SDI program is largely silent about endogenous development potential as well as about deep structural inequalities."

Third, the development corridor idea and spatial development initiatives are also not without their critics. To date, both have tended to promote export-oriented regional value chains. If two or more African nations can collaborate across borders in upgrading primary products and thereby increase the value added opportunities captured by Africans, then these initiatives seem well and good. The problem is that zones "where differences in factor endowments are exploited to promote external trade and direct investment for the mutual benefit of the participating countries" (Slocum-Bradley 2008, p. 92) often verge on exploitation. As such, arrangements that promote a fair exchange (such as the involvement of labor unions, as discussed earlier) seem critical.

Some of the ideas behind regional development corridors are consistent with the findings of the 2013 Africa Capacity Indicators Report on "Capacity Development for Natural Resources Management," such as the need to diversify African economies away from an overdependence on resource extraction and commodity production. That said, the risk of becoming overly dependent on resource-based production and industry is not widely acknowledged in corridor development plans.

It should be clear that regional value chains are a double-edged sword that may reinforce or deepen existing inequities or open up new possibilities for Africa to further develop internal markets and gain leverage in international trade. The import of critiques is that those promoting value chains and regional integration learn from them by considering the strengths and weaknesses of these approaches. We need not necessarily throw the baby out with the bathwater, but this input can contribute to positive changes in future initiatives.

Conclusions and the Way Forward

Regional value chains hold the potential to drive sustainable growth in income and employment in sub-Saharan Africa. Key to unlocking this potential is implementation of the kinds of policies likely to be most effective in achieving this goal. To succeed, those policies should be supported by capacity building initiatives that will allow African nations to expand cross-border value chains (at various scales) for economic development and improved livelihoods.

It makes sense to pool resources to engage in regionally relevant research and development. Throughout much of Francophone West Africa in the post-colonial period, the *Compagnie Française pour le Développement des Fibres Textiles* (CFDT), or French Textile Development Company, established vertically integrated supply chains for cotton production and transformation. While much about this system could be criticized (including the limited proportion of profits returned to farmers), one of its great strengths was regionally specific R&D for seeds and cropping systems (Bassett 2001).

Regional level R&D also applies to some aspects of tertiary education. For example, Botswana, Lesotho, and Swaziland historically shared some university functions. While much of this collaboration has been abandoned, especially as Botswana has grown wealthier and developed its own facilities, the benefits of collaboration and specialization should not be lost. Not all African countries, for example, can afford to develop their own medical schools. In fact, even relatively wealthy Botswana has struggled to do this. Developing complementary university facilities (for example, an engineering school in one country and a medical school in another) with reciprocity agreements would make a lot of sense.

Establishment of one-stop border posts. One of the main tools used for trade facilitation is the one-stop border post (OSBP). The concept is used to minimize delays at cross-border points on major transport corridors in a region (often caused by poor facilities, manual processes, lengthy and non-integrated procedures, and poor traffic flow). Under the OSBP concept, all traffic stops once in each direction of travel, facilitating faster movement of persons and goods and allowing border control officers from the two states involved to conduct joint inspections. The concept was first used at the Chirundu crossing between Zambia and Zimbabwe and was judged successful. It has now been widely adopted in various RECs, including COMESA, EAC, ECCAS, ECOWAS, and SADC (UNECA 2013).

Transformation of agricultural products is often more economical at the regional scale. Several African cities (among others, Nairobi, Johannesburg, Abidjan and Lagos) have served as regional hubs for transformation of agricultural products. While such industries may be unsustainable at the national scale (particularly in smaller African countries), regional markets make such industries more viable.

There are hopeful examples of agroprocessing at the national and regional scale that may be used to inspire other similar efforts. For example, at the national scale, the dairy industry in Kenya is also growing fast, and there would seem to be huge opportunities to cater to a more regional market (Scholten and Basu 2013). In fact, the pace of change in developing processed milk and cheese products has been referred to as a "white revolution" wherein producers are coming together in regional cooperatives to collect, pasteurize, package, and distribute milk.

In another example, a banana value chain has been developed in Kampala, Uganda. With support from the European Centre for Development Policy Management (ECDPM), bananas are being sourced from smallholders and then processed to obtain fresh, vacuum-sealed, peeled banana packages. Improved technology and support services are also made available to small farmers. The value chain contributes to better, safer, and longer storage of the number one staple in Uganda. The value added packaging also increases revenue, and now the group has started sourcing additional bananas from Kenya. While the approach is still handicapped by difficulties moving bananas across borders, the progress made to date is impressive (Rampa 2013). More broadly, the project hints at future prospects for value chain development.

In sum, the overarching conclusion of this chapter is that building more robust value chains in Africa is critical for transforming raw materials into finished products, encouraging industrialization, and moving African economies beyond their peripheral position. Regional value chains may further develop this capacity by leveraging complementarities between different African countries and fostering knowledge creation and skill enhancement within the region. That said, not all value chains are equal. Those value chains with Africa-based transformation and value added activities ought to be encouraged over those that simply reinforce peripheral commodity production.

References

African Capacity Building Foundation (ACBF) (2013), "Structured Transformation and Natural Resources Management in Africa." In *Africa Capacity Indicators Report*. Harare: ACBF, 147–62.

Akamatsu, K. (1962), "A historical pattern of economic growth in developing countries," *Journal of Developing Economies* 1, no. 1: 3–25.

Arvis, J., Raballand, G. and Marteau, J. (2007), "The Cost of Being Landlocked: Logistics Costs and Supply Chain Reliability." World Bank Policy Research Working Paper No. 4258. Washington, D.C.: World Bank.

Bair, J. (2005), "Global Capitalism and Commodity Chains: Looking Back, Going Forward," *Competition & Change* 9, no. 2: 153–80.

Bassett, T.J. (2001), *The Peasant Cotton Revolution in West Africa. Côte d'Ivoire, 1880–1995*. London: Cambridge University Press.

——— (2008), "Producing poverty: power relations and price formation in the cotton commodity chains of West Africa." In W.G. Moseley and L.C. Gray (eds), *Hanging by a Thread: Cotton, Poverty and Globalization in Africa*. Athens: Ohio University Press, 35–64.

Becker, L. and Yoboué, N. (2009), "Rice Producer-Processor Networks in Côte d'Ivoire," *Geographical Review* 99, no. 2: 164–85.

Carmody, P. (1998), "Constructing alternatives to structural adjustment in Africa," *Review of African Political Economy* 25, no. 75: 25–46.

Carney, J. (2008), "The Bitter Harvest of Gambian Rice Policies," *Globalizations* 5, no. 2: 129–42.

Daviron, B. and Ponte, S. (2005), *The Coffee Paradox: Global Markets, Commodity Trade and the Elusive Promise of Development*. New York: Zed Books.

Delevingne, L. (2008), "Africa's Best Small Companies," *Bloomberg Businessweek*, November 12.

The Economist. "Supermarkets in Africa: The grocers' great trek." economist.com. September 2013. Available at: http://www.economist.com/news/business/21586551-sluggish-home-market-pushing-south-africas-big-retail-chains-northward-grocers-great (accessed October 20, 2013).

European Union. "An Integrated Regional Value Chains Approach to Agricultural Development in Africa." *Economic Report on Africa 2009: Developing African Agriculture Through Regional Value Chains*, 143–82.

Faye, M., McArthura, J., Sachs, J. and Snow, T. (2004), "The Challenges Facing Landlocked Developing Countries." *Journal of Human Development* 5, no. 1: 31–68.

Gibbon, P. and Ponte, S. (2005), *Trading Down: Africa, Value Chains and the Global Economy*. Philadelphia: Temple University Press.

Gomez, M. and Ricketts, K. (2013), "Food value chain transformations in developing countries: Selected hypotheses on nutritional implications," *Food Policy* 42: 139–50.

Hartwick, E. (1998), "Geographies of consumption: a commodity chain approach," *Environment and Planning D: Society and Space* 16: 423–37.

Hausmann, R. (2001), "Prisoners of Geography," *Foreign Policy* January/February: 45–53.

Hellin, J. and Meijer, M. "Guidelines for value chain analysis." Available at: http://www.fao.org/fileadmin/templates/esa/LISFAME/Documents/Ecuador/value_chain_methodology_EN.pdf (accessed October 14, 2013).

Hughes, A. and Reimer, S. (eds) (2004), *Geographies of Commodity Chains*. New York: Routledge.

Humphrey, J. and Schmitz, H. (2002), "Developing Country Firms in the World Economy: Governance and Upgrading in Global value Chains," *INEF Report 61*. Institut für Entwicklung und Frieden der Gerhard-Mercator-Universität Duisburg.

Jourdan, P. (2008), "Plan of Action for African Acceleration of Industrialization—Promoting Resource-Based Industrialization: A Way Forward." Paper prepared for the African Union Commission, Addis Ababa, Ethiopia.

Kaplinsky, R. (1993), "Export Processing Zones in the Dominican Republic," *World Development* 21, no. 11: 1851–65.

Knox, P. and Marston, S. (2003), *Places and Regions in Global Context: Human Geography*, 2nd ed. Upper Saddle River, NJ: Pearson Education.

Lamport, J. (2013), "Corridor reports present detailed information on road governance." USAID. Available at: http://www.watradehub.com/competitive-environment/transport/corridor-reports-present-detailed-information-road-governance (accessed June 4, 2014).

Ledermann, S.T. and Moseley, W.G. (2008), "The World Trade Organization's Doha Round and Cotton: Continued Peripheral Status or a 'Historical Breakthrough' for African Farmers?" *African Geographical Review* 26: 37–58.

Mather, C. (2004), "Codes of conduct, retailer buying practices and farm labour in South Africa's wine and deciduous fruit export chains," *International Development Planning Review* 26, no. 4: 477–94.

Mortimore, M. and Adams, W. (2001), "Farmer adaptation, change and 'crisis' in the Sahel," *Global Environmental Change* 11, no. 1: 49–57.

Moseley, W.G. (2011), "Lessons from the 2008 Global Food Crisis: Agro-Food Dynamics in Mali," *Development in Practice* 21, no. 4–5: 604–12.

Moseley, W.G., Carney, J. and Becker, L. (2010), "Neoliberal Policy, Rural Livelihoods and Urban Food Security in West Africa: A Comparative Study of The Gambia, Côte d'Ivoire and Mali," *Proceedings of the National Academy of Sciences of the United States of America* 107, no. 13: 5774–9.

Moseley, W.G., Peyton, S. and Battersby, J. (2013), "The Real Solution to South Africa's Food Problem," *Aljazeera—English*. September 8, 2013. Available at: http://www.aljazeera.com/indepth/opinion/2013/09/20139483514342425.html (accessed October 18, 2013).

Ndulu, B.J. (2006), "Infrastructure, Regional Integration and Growth in Sub-Saharan Africa: Dealing with the disadvantages of Geography and Sovereign Fragmentation," *Journal of African Economies* 15, no. 2: 212–44.

Perez-Aleman, P. (2008), "Building Value at the Top and Bottom of the Global Supply Chain: MNC-NGO Partnerships and Sustainability," *California Management Review*, 51, no. 1: 24–49.

Raikes, P., Jensen, M.F. and Ponte, S. (2000), "Global commodity chain analysis and the French filière approach: comparison and critique," *Economy and Society* 29, no. 3: 390–417.

Rampa, F. (2013), "Bananas and bottlenecks: Piloting regional value chain cooperation for food security." European Centre for Development Policy Management, October 18. Available at: http://www.ecdpm-talkingpoints.org/bananas-and-bottlenecks-piloting-regional-value-chain-cooperation/ (accessed December 6, 2013).

Rogerson, C. and Visser, G. (2011), "African Tourism Geographies: Existing Paths and New Directions," *Tijdschrift voor economische en sociale geografie* 103, no. 3: 251–59.

Ryan, O. (2011), *Chocolate Nations: Living and Dying for Cocoa in West Africa.* New York: Zed.

Scholten, B. and Basu, P. (2013), "Linking Dairy Development to Africa's New Green Revolution." Paper presented at the Annual Meeting of the Association of American Geographers. Los Angeles, CA.

Schroeder, R. (2013), *Africa after Apartheid: South Africa, Race, and Nation in Tanzania.* Bloomington: Indiana University Press.

Seck, P.A. (2008), "Can rice crisis be turned into opportunity for Africa?" *Rural 21 The International Journal for Rural Development.*

Sisay, A. (2013), "UN wants new approach to Africa integration," *Africa Review*, July 12. Available at: http://www.africareview.com/News/UN-wants-new-approach-to-Africa-integration/-/979180/1913214/-/myxwg6/-/index.html (accessed October 20, 2013).

Slocum-Bradley, N. (2008), "The Zambia-Malawi-Mozambique Growth Triangle (ZMM-GT): Discursive Region-building in Africa and Consequences for Development." In F. Söderbaum and I. Taylor (eds), *Afro-Regions: The Dynamics of Cross-Border Micro-Regionalism in Africa.* Stockholm: Nordic Africa Institute, 90–102.

Söderbaum, F. and Taylor, I. (2008a), "Considering Micro-regionalism in Africa in the Twenty-first Century." In F. Söderbaum and I. Taylor (eds), *Afro-Regions: The Dynamics of Cross-Border Micro-Regionalism in Africa.* Stockholm: Nordic Africa Institute, 13–31.

——— (2008b), "Competing Region-building in the Maputo Development Corridor." In F. Söderbaum and I. Taylor (eds), *Afro-Regions: The Dynamics of Cross-Border Micro-Regionalism in Africa.* Stockholm: Nordic Africa Institute, 35–52.

Thomas, R. (2009), "Development Corridors and Spatial Development Initiatives in Africa." Multilateral Investment Guarantee Agency. World Bank Group. Available at: http://www.fdi.net/documents/WorldBank/databases/africa_infrastructure/Thomas_SDI_paper_lowres.pdf (accessed October 20, 2013).

Toenniessen, G., Adesina, A. and DeVries, J. (2008), "Building an Alliance for a Green Revolution in Africa," *Annals of the New York Academy of Sciences* 1136, no. 1: 233–42.

Tucker, R. (2004), "Environmentally Damaging Consumption: The Impact of American Markets on Tropical Ecosystems in the Twentieth Century." In T. Princen, M. Maniates, and K. Conca (eds), *Confronting Consumption.* Cambridge: MIT Press.

United Nations Economic Commission for Africa (UNECA). "Regional Integration: agricultural value chains to integrate and transform agriculture in West Africa." Niamey, Niger: Maison des Nations Unies, 2012.

——— "Assessment of progress on regional integration in Africa." Thirty-second meeting of the Committee of Experts, E/ECA/COE/32/3, AU/CAMEF/EXP/3(VIII). Abidjan, Côte d'Ivoire, March 21–24, 2013.

World Bank (2009), *World Development Report 2009: Reshaping Economic Geography.* Washington, D.C.: The World Bank.

Chapter 10

The Boko Haram Insurgency and the Changing Patterns of Regional Security Arrangements in Africa

Olawale Ismail

Introduction

Regional security and conflict management mechanisms dot Africa's security landscape in ways that suggest they are ritualized, indispensable, and prerequisite canons of peace and security. The Economic Community of West African States (ECOWAS), Inter-Governmental Authority on Development (IGAD), and Southern Africa Development Community (SADC) are essential to the African security discourse and policy making. Despite the convention of regions and regional security mechanisms in Africa as a separate (intermediate) level of analysis (Kelly 2007), there is neither a critical discourse of the orthodox approach nor adequate exploration of alternative perspectives. Moreover, critical issues abound in relation to their formalism (rhetoric, aspirations, and stated purposes) versus their reality (institutional setting, capacity for implementation, and impact) and their capacity to adapt and respond to emerging regional security challenges. There is a near consensus that the impact of regional security mechanisms is at best mixed (Omorogbe 2011; Obi 2009; Olonisakin 2004; Adebajo and Ismail 2004).

This chapter interrogates emerging patterns of regional security challenges and responses to the Boko Haram crisis in the Chad Basin to discern the conceptual and policy lessons and implications for regional security arrangements in Africa. The case study is unique for a variety of reasons; first, it encapsulates responses to a mutational variant of the new war thesis—transnational, cross-regional, protracted, irregular warfare linked to criminal networks and targets civilians. Second, the response thus far has been marked by the noticeable absence (at best low profile) of any of the orthodox regional security institutions. Third, the response mechanisms (cross-regional constellations) do not parallel any extant economic integration patterns. Against the background of the case study as an instance of armed insurgencies, the focus is on the "negative peace" component of regional security—the capacity to respond (prevent, manage, and resolve) to large scale armed conflict and violence within and across regions in Africa.

This chapter makes two central observations; first, given the patterns of emerging threats to regional security, ECOWAS (RECs) and by extension the AU are less well placed to provide or deliver regional security as envisaged in extant policy documents. As currently configured and capacitated, they are limited to legitimizing, coordinating and partnering in regional security interventions. There is a gulf between their declared aspirations and institutional operational capabilities, the changing nature of regional security challenges, and the limited or slow adaptability of RECs and AU to these. Second is the reality of an emergent modus operandi of and for regional security in Africa that involves different combinations of intra-, inter-, and extra-regional initiatives, partnerships, actors and interests. Regional security no longer equates to or parallels REC configuration as contained in AU's official policy assumptions. The definition and map of the "regional" in "regional security" is changing with emerging patterns pinpointing new boundaries, actors, and initiatives outside of conventional REC structures. Critically, extra-regional interests and actors are potentially playing game-changing roles in African regional security initiatives as defined by their funding, equipment support, and international legitimacy, for African regional security operations.

The Regional Security Conundrum in Africa

Post-Cold war Africa has witnessed a marked proliferation of regional security complexes: a set of units whose major process of securitization, de-securitization or both are interlinked such that their security problems cannot reasonably be analyzed or resolved apart from one another (Buzan and Waever 2003; Buzan 1991). There is hardly any African country or sub-region outside one or more regional security arrangements (Franke 2007; Mwagiru 2010). Indeed, regional security complexes and their operational mechanism, regional security orders—the range of instruments used to restrain and respond to violence in a defined geography (Lake 2009)—are the emerging drivers of political-economic integration in Africa.

Regional security policies and structures have a long history in post-independent Africa. They were part of the unstated rationale behind the establishment of the Organization of African Unity (OAU) and its anti-apartheid initiatives. Regional security in Africa operates at continental and sub-regional levels that are often confused or used interchangeably. There are three processes and phases in the evolution of regional security arrangements in Africa: first were continental-level initiatives kick-started by the creation of the OAU in 1963 and its stated interest defending sovereignty, territorial integrity, and independence (Article 1c), and the promotion of cooperation for defense and security (Article 2f) in Africa through provision for the Commission of Mediation, Conciliation and Arbitration (Article XIX of OAU Charter). Through the 1993 Cairo Declaration, the OAU created the Mechanism for Conflict Prevention, Management and Resolution (MCPMR) as a platform for preventing conflicts and undertaking peace-making and peacebuilding activities. The transformation of the OAU to AU in 2000 reaffirmed interest in regional security arrangements by its distinctive focus on regional (and collective) security arrangements as outlined under Articles 3(f) (promote peace, security, and stability), 4(d) (establishment of a common defense and security policy for Africa) and 4(e) (peaceful resolution of conflict among member states) of the AU Constitutive Act.

The second process was the creation of regional economic communities (RECs) from the 1970s, which institutionalized regional security initiatives in Africa as peace and security were identified as requisites for economic integration and development. The 1980 Lagos Plan of Action reaffirmed regional security thinking in Africa, and several RECs initiated policies to enhance regional security arrangements—for example, the Economic Community of West African States (ECOWAS) signed a non-aggression treaty in 1978 and a mutual defense pact in 1981. The onset of "new wars" in the 1990s elevated regional security arrangements among RECs, parallel to the emergence of the security-development nexus in global policy agenda.

The third process and phase was the integration of continental and sub-regional initiatives through the establishment of APSA. This emerged from the 2002 Peace and Security Council Protocol, which replaced the MCPMR with the African Peace and Security Council (PSC) alongside the creation of a Continental Early Warning System (CEWS), the African Peace Fund and the African Standby force (ASF) as a rapid response peace mission force made up of five regional brigades. The regional brigades include those of the Arab Maghreb Union (AMU), ECOWAS, IGAD, ECCAS and the SADC. This further legitimized existing (or provided a basis for the development of new) regional security policies and structures by RECs. In addition, it reaffirmed the configuration of regional security arrangements alongside REC processes.

The evolution and proliferation of regional security mechanisms in Africa is driven by at least five factors.

First is their formalization in extant international legal instruments, including the United Nations Charter Articles 52 and 53 and Chapter VIII, relating to regional organizations' role in pacific settlement and peace enforcement. These were reinforced by successive policy documents, such as the 1992 Agenda for Peace and the 2008 Report of the UN Secretary General on UN-AU cooperation on peace and security, which affirmed the importance of regional security mechanisms. African Union and its predecessor OAU reinforced regional arrangements through the 1980 Lagos Plan of Action, the 2002 AU Constitutive Act, 2004 Protocol Establishing the Peace and Security Council (Article 16), and the central roles given to regional security mechanisms (as units) in the establishment of the African Standby Force and Continental Early Warning Systems (Friedrich-Ebert-Stiftung 2011).

Second are the shifts in Africa's geo-strategic calculus, triggered by the brief loss of global geo-strategic value in the immediate post-Cold war era and the concomitant outbreak of Kaldors's (2006) "New Wars" in Liberia, Sierra Leone, Somalia and Democratic Republic of Congo that necessitated intra-African responses. Against the backdrop of a new wave of Pan-Africanism and African Renaissance, the enforced regional security experiments of the 1990s have been institutionalized and consolidated into multiple regional security mechanisms as ideological manifestations of "African solutions to African problems."

Third, regional security mechanisms have emerged in the context of heightened globalization and the trans-nationality (interconnectedness) of security threats leading to "new security assemblages" within which state power is reconfigured (Abrahamsen and Williams 2011; Tavares 2008).

Fourth is the external dimension, linked to Africa's geo-strategic re-emergence (new scramble for African resources) and the willingness of international partners to support and fund intra-African regional security mechanisms given the strategic and tactical advantages such regional arrangements have in conflict management (in terms of, for example, local leadership and knowledge of and proximity to context) (Van Hoeymissen 2011; Frazier and Stewart-Ingersoll 2010; Tavares 2009; Stein 2003) and the UN's increasing delegation of responses to peace and security issues to African institutions.

Fifth is the emergence of security issues, including joint trainings, and peacekeeping as the major driver of Africa's international relations (Ismail and Skons 2014). Security assistance and cooperation are increasingly the entry point, as much as the headline item in the bilateral and multilateral relations of most Africa countries in their intra- and extra-African relations.

The growth in regional security mechanisms has hardly escaped scholarly attention. Extant studies pinpoint their critical shortcomings, including gaps between stated purposes and aspirations (formalism) versus reality (institutions and capacity for implementation) (Obi 2009; Olonisakin 2004); little or no grounding in shared norms, especially those connected to good governance and human security (Weldesellassie 2011; Hammerstad 2005; Aning 2004); intra-regional tensions, cleavages, and even armed confrontation (Siradag 2012; Healy 2011); and duplication, poor internal funding base and donor dependence (Reno 2012). There is a consensus that existing regional security mechanisms are effective only in patches, such as ECOWAS in peacekeeping and norm development; IGAD in conflict mediation and early warning systems; and SADC in conflict mediation in Zimbabwe. Virtually all existing regional security mechanisms are marked by ongoing failure in promoting peacebuilding, post-conflict reconstruction, effective control against small arms and light weapons proliferation, and divergence of security policies, institutions, and practices (Omorogbe 2011; Adibe 2003). In fact, in a number of cases, especially in the AMU and ECCAS regions, efforts to make regional brigades (units of ASF) fully operational remain stalled. Despite the rhetoric of adopting norms, policy documents, and pronouncements committing to human security, the core of orthodox regional security institutions and mechanisms operate to protect regime security (Ismail 2011). Accordingly, extant studies proffer a number of prescriptions, including greater participation of civil society, greater confidence building measures among member states, increased political will and commitment, and building of synergies (Jaye, Garuba and Amadi 2011). However, these prescriptions are untested, sometimes abstract, and do not reflect the emerging dynamic in the nature, dimensions, and severity of regional security challenges.

Understanding the Boko Haram Insurgency

The dynamic of Nigeria's (and Lake Chad Basin area) peace and security landscape changed with the emergence of the *Jama'atu Ahlis Sunna Lidda'awati wal-Jihad* (People Committed to the Propagation of the Prophet's Teachings and Jihad) movement, popularly called Boko Haram, and its insurgency from 2009. The April 2014 abduction of over 200 school girls in Chibok town (Borno state, northeastern Nigeria) and the international media (the "#Bringbackourgirls" campaign) and diplomatic concern and policy attention it generated climaxed the internationalization of the Boko Haram insurgency, as well as exposed Nigeria and its mis-management of the insurgency (BBC April 21, 2014).

Boko Haram is a salafi-jihadi group that espouses messianic revivalism of Islamic religion and cultural practices (sharia). When translated literally, it means Western education (Boko) is forbidden (haram); however, the group's ideology transcends this to mean the rejection of western culture and civilization, of which education is a vehicle for its transfer. Agbiboa (2013, p. 9) quotes the late founder of the group (Mohammed Yusuf) as saying, "Western-styled education is mixed with issues that run contrary to our belief in Islam" and "our land was an Islamic state before the colonial masters turned it to a *Kafir* (infidel) land. The current system is contrary to true Islamic belief." Similarly, Minteh and Perry (2013, p. 12) cites the group's spokesperson clarification that "Boko Haram does not in any way mean Western education is a sin … [It] actually means western civilization is forbidden. The difference is that while the first gives the impression that we are opposed to formal education coming from the West … which is not true … the second affirms our belief in the supremacy of

Islamic culture, for culture is broader, it includes education but not determined by western education."

Boko Haram, similar to other ethno-political militias in post-1999 Nigeria, emerged against the backdrop of deepening poverty, socioeconomic deprivations, corruption, poor governance, police brutality and governance failures at different levels (Niworu 2013; Rogers 2012). The northern half of Nigeria, including the northeast corner (Boko Haram's base), is the poorest in the country: a 2010 assessment by the National Bureau of Statistics reported the national poverty rate was 60.9 percent, but it was 77.7 percent for the northwest and 76.3 percent for northeast, compared with 59 percent for the Southwest (BBC February 13, 2012). The World Bank also notes that economic growth and opportunities were not equally shared by different parts of the country; growth was fastest in southern and middle agro climatic zones, with much slower growth in northern states. This resulted in the largest number of poor people in northern regions (World Bank 1996).

Contemporary estimates (up to 2013) indicate that the Boko Haram insurgency caused more than 3,500 casualties, considerable extra-judicial killings by security agencies, and several thousand refugees and internally displaced persons since 2009 (Agbiboa 2013; IRIN January 20, 2012). It has also led to the imposition of curfews and a state of emergency that has paralyzed socioeconomic activities in affected areas (*Vanguard*, August 22, 2012); over 10,000 widows (*Punch*, August 12, 2013); diversion of state resources from social expenditure to security; destruction of social infrastructures, especially schools, including 209 schools in Yobe and 800 classrooms in Borno (Punch March 7, 2013; Leadership August 12, 2013); and stoking of inter- and intra-religious and inter-ethnic tensions and attacks in Nigeria (U.S. House of Representatives, September 13, 2013).

The Boko Haram insurgency is best understood in three phases. Phase one involved the evolution of the group; there are contrasting accounts regarding the movement's historical roots before 2002. However, there is some loose consensus that the group was an offshoot of the Nigerian Taliban Movement, and the top leadership of the group were adherents of the Ibn Taymiyyah Sect; the group relocated (undertook Hijra) from mainstream Maiduguri city (capital of Borno state) to the remote location of Kanema, Yobe state in 2002 to establish its own community, which was governed in accordance with strict Islamic law and culture (Sharia) (Adesoji 2010). The evolution of the group in the post-2002 period is documented in burgeoning research on the subject matter; disagreements with neighboring communities over fishing rights in 2003 led to violent clashes with locals and the police that snowballed into large scale police action in 2004 that displaced the group from its Kanema base.

Phase two laid the conditions and triggers for contemporary insurgency. It involved Boko Haram's regrouping in Maiduguri in 2004 and establishing a new base (Ibn Taymiyyah Masjid around the railway area, north of Maiduguri); expansion in the membership base of the group; contacts, cooperation and financial support from sociopolitical elites; and growth in the popularity and visibility of the group and especially its leader (Mohammed Yusuf). These developments were instrumental to creating the contemporary dynamic. Between 2005 and 2009, there were series of armed clashes and built-up tensions between the group's members and local police and between movement leadership and political elites in Borno. The massacre of more than a dozen police officers in July 2009 triggered a large-scale security operation in three northeastern states of Borno, Yobe, and Bauchi (the movement's strongest bases). Mohammed Yusuf was executed by security forces alongside his in-laws and, according to estimates, more than 1,000 Boko Haram members (Bamidele 2012).

Phase three encapsulates the contemporary dynamic; the movement's remnants regrouped in neighboring states and are reported to have established links with *salafi-jihadi* groups (Movement for Oneness and Jihad in West Africa, MUJAO; and Al Qaeda in Islamic Mahgreb, AQIM) and to have engaged in trainings in jihadi camps in northern Mali and Mauritania (Onapejo, Uzodike and Whetto 2012). From September 2010, Boko Haram restarted violent attacks to mark the onset of current insurgency; the targets of attacks have included the Nigerian Police headquarters, United Nations country office, police and military facilities, prisons, mosques and churches, banks, schools, government offices, telecommunication masts, markets and local communities (*The Sun*, September 13, 2012). The forms of attacks have included targeted killings and assassinations, bombings, kidnapping and armed robbery. Since late 2013, Boko Haram attacks have concentrated on staging surprise attacks on military facilities; suicide bombings (of civilian amenities such as markets and motor parks); multiple attacks against remote local communities; and most importantly, school girls (Chibok girls) and women from schools, markets communities and other public places (*The Guardian*, June 24, 2014).

The nature of weapons used and sophistication of attacks by Boko Haram has increased, evolving from the use of bows and arrows, dane guns, and old AK-47s to sophisticated AK-47s, rocket propelled grenades (RPGs), anti-aircraft guns, mortars and shoulder-held surface to air missiles, suicide bombings and improvised explosive devices (IEDs) (Walker 2012). Also, while Boko Haram attacks are still strongest in the northeast corner (Borno, Yobe, Adamawa, and Bauchi), they have also spread to areas in the central region of Nigeria (Niger, Kano, Kaduna, and Jos). Boko Haram has also splintered, with new factions such as the Jama'atul Ansarul Muslimina Fi Biladis Sudan (JAMBS), a more extremist faction with stronger ties to Al-Qaeda (*Punch*, February 19, 2013). Finally, the insurgency has transcended Nigeria to become a regional security challenge, drawing in neighboring countries (Cameroon, Niger and Chad); recruiting members from and using regional countries (Niger, Chad, Cameroon,

Mali, and Mauritania) as operational and training bases and safe havens; and qualitatively linking to other insurgencies in the Sahel (border areas in northern Mali, Mauritania and Algeria) (Onapajo, Uzodike, and Whetho 2012; U.S. State Department 2012).

The Boko Haram crises embody elements of continuity, changes, and paradoxes in Nigeria's security history; its violent attacks continued the pattern of ethno-political and ethno-religious groups bearing arms and attacking civilians, security agencies and rival groups across Nigeria. Historically, the composition, evolution and dynamic of the insurgency and government's counter-insurgency operations parallel those of the Maitatsine uprisings of the 1980s.[1] Similarly, Boko Haram appears to represent the northern equivalent of ethno-religious and ethno-political militias and their violence (as with the Odua People's Congress in the southwest, Movement for the Actualization of the Sovereign State of Biafra in the southeast, Movement for the Emancipation of Niger Delta in the south, and Tiv, Tarok, and Jukun militias in the north-central region) that have left their mark on Nigeria in the post-military era. Boko Haram, however, departs from other sub-national armed groups on account of its ability to integrate itself and its local agenda with regional and international armed groups and issues. Given the global context of the American-led war on terror, the religious (political Islam) dimensions of the Boko Haram insurgencies assume greater strategic visibility and significance. Unlike other sub-national insurgencies, the Boko Haram crisis has impacts on national, regional and international security and has attracted regional and global attention. Finally, the nature of response to the crisis is remarkably different: responses have transcended the Nigerian state to involve neighboring countries, regional allies and international partners.

Responding to Boko Haram: Ad-hoc Regionalism over Institutional Regionalism

Despite the regional dimensions and impacts of Boko Haram insurgency, it remains primarily a Nigerian security menace, and responses to it are located in and led by Nigeria. Paralleling it alongside the three phases of Boko Haram insurgency, Nigeria's responses have evolved from police action (phase one) to limited police-army security operation (phase two) and large scale joint security

1 The Maitatsine sect was a radical Islamic group founded by Mohammed Marwa, a native of Marwa, a border community with Cameroon. The sect was involved in a series of armed clashes with Nigerian security agencies between 1980 and 1985 in key northern cities of Kano, Gombe, Maiduguri, Bauchi, and Yola, with an estimated over 5,000 killed. See Falola (1998).

operations involving the army, air force, police, navy, state security service, and Ministry of Defence (phase three).

The contemporary response is largely a military-led and militarized approach. In September 2011, Nigeria formed a multi-agency task force, the Joint Task Force (JTF) to foster inter-agency cooperation, intelligence sharing and operational synergy. This was against the first declaration of emergency rule in selected local government areas in Borno, Niger, Plateau and Yobe. The JTF, which included more than 30,000 security personnel, was deployed to enforce emergency rule. A second, more substantive state of emergency was declared across three northeastern states (Borno, Adamawa, and Yobe) in May 2013, with 8,000 more combat troops and military hardware (fighter jets, attack helicopters, armored personnel carriers) deployed (*Daily Trust*, May 16, 2013; BBC News May 15, 2013). This was a tacit acknowledgement of the failure of previous limited emergency rule and security operations, as much as recognition of the growing spread and intensity of Boko Haram attacks. Nigeria has taken steps to improve intelligence training, counter-terrorism capabilities and intelligence infrastructures over the past three years. In November 2012, Nigeria announced plans to establish (and requested American support for) an intelligence fusion center to improve intelligence gathering, coordination and sharing across security agencies (U.S. State Department 2012). The United States, Britain, and France have confirmed their interest in and actual provision of intelligence assistance to Nigeria, especially in the area of training, acquisition of intelligence equipment and use of satellite imaging technologies to identify the Boko Haram base, track the group's movements, and plan security operations (*Punch*, February 4, 2013).

The deployment of JTF forces has generally involved mounting roadblocks, house-to-house searches, shootouts with and arrests of suspected and real Boko Haram fighters, suspension of mobile telephone services, and reports of widespread human rights abuses and extra-judicial killings (Aghedo and Osumah 2012). As part of improving security at border areas, JTF operations have also included the deportation of over 19,000 alleged foreigners (The Sun May 17, 2013). In August 2013, Nigeria announced the establishment of a new infantry unit (Seventh Army Division) based in Maiduguri that replaced the JTF and would become a specialist counter-terrorism unit (*Vanguard*, August 19, 2013).

In 2011, local vigilante groups comprising youth in areas affected by the Boko Haram insurgency formed a self-styled civilian JTF. This was reported to be ostensibly independent of government support, but it works alongside the military JTF by conducting searches and interrogating suspected members of Boko Haram who are either handed over to the military JTF or killed in extra-judicial circumstances. In other instances, members and communities with civilian JTF were targeted by Boko Haram fighters, and armed clashes continue to take place between the group's members and civilian JTF members (*The Sun*, July 29, 2013).

The external dimension of the military-led response was the (trans) formation of a Multinational Joint Task Force (MJTF) comprising security forces from Nigeria, Chad, Niger, and Cameroon (Alli 2012). The MJTF was originally established in 1998 to stem the tide of cross-border banditry, smuggling and criminality in Nigeria, Chad, and Niger. It was transformed into a counter-insurgency mechanism around 2010 following the resurgence of Boko Haram and the transborder nature of its operations (Alli 2012). Three developments led to the incorporation of Cameroon into the MJTF: bilateral security negotiations and agreements between Nigeria and Cameroon; kidnappings of foreign (French) nationals by Boko Haram affiliated groups (JAMBS) inside Cameroonian territory, and membership in the group by Cameroonians.

The MJTF represents a loose yet structured form of military-security cooperation and joint security operations among the participating countries. It is rooted in the peculiarities of the Boko Haram insurgency, namely, the multinational composition of its membership and transborder impact of its activities. Nigeria shares borders with Niger, Chad and Cameroon along its northeast corridor, which included strong Boko Haram bases in Borno, Yobe, and Adamawa states. Maiduguri in Borno state is perhaps the strongest base of and encapsulates the transborder and regional aspects of the insurgency. In Damasak, in the north of Maiduguri, Nigeria shares land borders with Niger (Diffa town); in northeast Maiduguri, Baga (Nigeria) and Jilbe (Chad); and Banki in southeast Maiduguri, is a common border town for Nigeria and Cameroon (*Sunday Trust*, October 23, 2011). Historically, the border areas have been poorly policed: centers of illicit trade (trafficking of people, arms, narcotics and contraband), with complex network of routes, pathways and forests and mountainous terrains (*Punch*, May 21, 2013). They are also areas with considerable government neglect marked by absence of meaningful socioeconomic infrastructure and official (government) presence.

The MJTF was legitimized and internationalized as a security cooperation mechanism and a form of regional security response arrangement by the May 2014 Paris Summit on Boko Haram involving Boko-Haram affected countries in the Lake Chad Basin (Nigeria, Cameroon, Benin, Niger and Chad), and international partners (France, United Kingdom, United States, and European Union) (BBC May 17, 2014). The summit provided international legitimacy for subsisting bilateral cooperation under the MJTF and called for strengthened intelligence sharing through a dedicated intelligence sharing pool, development of a Lake Chad Basin regional counter-terrorism strategy, and coordinated border management and surveillance systems, especially bilateral border patrols. International partners pledged coordinated technical support, training programs, and assistance in border management, mobilization of financial resources for addressing underlying socioeconomic development challenges, and support for international sanctions against Boko Haram and its affiliates through the United Nations system (*Sahara Reporters*, May 17, 2014).

The MJTF also emerged against the background of Nigeria's importance as a regional hegemon and its security interest. It involves joint security operations with contingents conducting security activities simultaneously along their border areas at designated times and locations. This strategy is meant to encircle Boko Haram fighters by cutting off escape routes from the rear (the other side of the border). There are also joint surveillance operations and co-sharing of intelligence (*Xinhua*, December 12, 2011). Within Nigeria and across its borders, MJTF operations have targeted disrupting operational camps of Boko Haram cells, denying insurgents safe havens, cutting off supply routes, and tracking cross-border movements. Moreover, there have been reported cases of joint responses to distress calls from local communities by MTJF forces (*This Day*, April 23, 2013). Despite the multinational nature of the MJTF, the initiative is clearly led by Nigeria, which oversees the central coordination of security operations, heads the MTF command structure and controls deployment of military hardware, including attack helicopters, fighter jets and APCs (*Punch*, September 25, 2013; *Vanguard*, April 24, 2013).

At the political level, the Nigerian government responded in two main ways. First was the passage of a counter-terrorism law (the Terrorism Protection Bill), which clearly defined the scope of terrorist actions, punitive measures against terrorism, and government policy response tools and instruments. Some arrested Boko Haram members have been put to judicial trial in the context of the new anti-terror law (*Punch*, May 7, 2013). Second is an attempt at exploring a negotiated settlement through dialogue with Boko Haram. This came against the backdrop of public criticisms and the failure of military responses to curb Boko Haram attacks. The government instituted an amnesty committee on Boko Haram in April 2013, ostensibly to make contact with and explore dialogue with group members and work out modalities for granting them amnesty as part of a negotiated settlement with the insurgency (*Vanguard*, April 5, 2013). This is in addition to formal and informal contacts with traditional rulers and native authorities in northern Nigeria and the appointment of a northerner as the national security adviser, all intended to solicit northern perspectives and enhanced visibility in counter-Boko operations. There have been three or more declarations of ceasefires by self-proclaimed representatives of Boko Haram or its factions at the prompting of behind the scenes negotiations with government officials. In all cases, the ceasefires have been smokescreens for further attacks by Boko Haram. It is unclear to what extent the government truly believes in negotiation and dialogue as a solution to the insurgency, and the history of Nigeria's previous responses to Boko Haram (in phases one and two) points to a preference for a military solution.

At the humanitarian level, there have been occasional provisions of relief materials for victims (families and communities) of Boko Haram attacks; however, these tokens have been largely symbolic in nature, rather than part of a coherent policy and counter-terrorist strategy. Worse still, there has been little or no effort to address the socioeconomic conditions underlying the insurgency or those offshoots of it.

Assessing the Status Quo: Interrogating the Role of ECOWAS

Boko Haram's main theaters of operation fall within ECOWAS region (Nigeria, Niger and Mali); however, it crisscrosses Cameroon and Chad, members of ECCAS. Interestingly, Nigeria, Niger, Chad and Cameroon are all members of the Lake Chad Basin Commission. ECOWAS's role thus far has been limited to providing diplomatic and political support (through releases of communiqués and press statements) for Nigeria and Nigerian-led MJTF counter-insurgency operations. In most cases, ECOWAS's declarations of support have followed damaging Boko Haram attacks; in the wake of the August 2011 and January 2012 attacks on the UN compound in Abuja and in Kano that claimed over 200 deaths, the ECOWAS Commission released a statement condemning the attacks and affirming support to Nigeria *(National Mirror*, January 26, 2012). The ECOWAS Parliament released a similar statement following the attacks in February 2012 (*Punch*, February 14, 2012).

ECOWAS's most recent engagement with the Boko Haram insurgency included two special summits of ECOWAS leaders in Accra. First, an extra-ordinary session was convened against the background of the Chibok abductions, rising book Haram attacks and other regional security challenges in the Lake Chad Basin area, northern Mali and Guinea Bissau. The meeting welcomed (endorsed) Nigeria's response to the insurgency, including the MJTF and resolutions of the Paris Summit. More importantly, the summit called for the establishment of a partnership with Central African States, and the Lake Chad Basin Commission in coordinating counter-terrorism effort and socioeconomic development programmes. It also called for the implementation of the draft ECOWAS Counter Terrorism Strategy, ECOWAS Sahel Strategy and the United Nations Integrated Strategy for the Sahel (ECOWAS May 30, 2014). A second regular summit followed in July 2014 which reiterated the resolutions from the May 2014 Summit and expressed continued concerns about the non-release of Chibok girls and Boko Haram attacks, and the growing menace of terrorism amongst member-states (ECOWAS, July 10, 2014).

It is instructive to note that the MJTF and bilateral security initiatives related to counter-Boko Haram operations have taken place without recourse to any extant regional security arrangement or mechanisms (Ismail 2013).

Also, following attacks against churches and Christians in June 2012, at the 41st Ordinary Summit of ECOWAS in Yamoussoukro, Côte d'Ivoire expressed solidarity and solicited support and cooperation with Nigeria's counter-terrorism efforts (Pana Press, July 2, 2012). It remains a puzzle that despite the clear regional dimension of the crisis and the possibility of triggering or adapting aspects of ECOWAS's protocol on mechanisms for conflict prevention, management, and resolution as well as its conflict prevention framework, ECOWAS continues to "wait at the fringes, without any direction and mechanism to deal with the Boko Haram insurgency."[2] Moreover, the ECOWAS Counter Terrorism Strategy and Sahel Strategy alluded to in the May 2014 Summit communique were neither finalized (nor publicly accessible), nor operational as at the time of writing (July 2014).

Overall, the government's counter-insurgency operation has recorded mixed progress; it appears to have reduced the scope and number of high value (strategic) attacks by Boko Haram; the insurgency's targets have been relocated from urban to rural areas and from government and international structures to local and private infrastructures. However, the prospect of sustainable peacebuilding remains gloomy for a variety of reasons. First is the absence of a comprehensive strategy that combines military strategy with socioeconomic intervention to address the grievances that underlie the crisis and the humanitarian fallouts of counter-insurgency operations (U.S. State Department 2012; Bamidele 2012). Second, the MJTF operations, similar to the 2009 clashes with Boko Haram, continue to be trailed by allegations of brutality, rape, and extra-judicial killings, thereby reducing the scope of effectiveness and exacerbating the crisis (Solomon 2012; Walker 2012). Third, the MJTF appears to lack the capacity for cutting edge intelligence to track and execute targeted attacks against Boko Haram fighters (as underlined by the resolutions from the May 2014 Paris Summit); MJTF operations continue to incur considerable civilian casualties. Fourth, the MJTF, especially the Nigerian component, continues to suffer operational lapses such as constant inter-agency rivalry, poor operational planning, ambiguous rules of engagement and command/control structures and inability to align military objectives with political strategies.

Finally, the Nigeria government continues to politicize the Boko Haram insurgency, especially seeking to derive political advantage from it through a series of official propaganda and denial of the true scale of the crises. For instance, the ruling political party (People's Democratic Party) continues to tag opposition political parties and social critics as Boko Haram sponsors and sympathizers; and in the wake of the Chibok abductions, the government failed to acknowledge the incident or act for nearly a month on the pretext that no

2 Media interview by Kwesi Aning, Director of Research, Kofi Anan International Peacekeeping Training Centre, Ghana, Ghanaweb, January 25, 2012.

abduction took place and that it was a political ploy by opposition groups to bring down the PDP government.

Assessing Conceptual and Policy Implications

Conceptual

The Boko Haram crisis and response patterns illustrate a rapidly changing security landscape in Africa that has conceptual implications for the way regional security in Africa is understood. First, the crisis clearly indicates that regional security does not parallel RECs and AU's policy definitions and assumptions. The assumed nexus between regional economic integration constellations and regional security in terms of the scope, boundaries, processes, and actors involved in regional security initiatives is empirically weakened. The process of regional economic cooperation and integration rarely follows the logic of emerging regional security needs and activities.

Second (and a corollary) is that emergent regional security crises and responses are redefining the boundaries and assumptions about the "regional." On the one hand, the scope of the regional is being redefined by new alliances, arrangements and partnerships. On the other, it is perhaps apt to consider notions of intra-, inter-, and trans-regional security in light of emergent insurgencies and counter-insurgencies crisscrossing conventional regional borders in greater depth.

Third, critically, conventional assumptions as contained in extant policy documents and treaties about the drivers and motivations for regional security initiatives by states in Africa are changing. Emerging patterns pinpoint the limitations of regional solidarity, membership in RECs, ratification of regional security protocols, and formation of regional security complexes or communities. Conversely, the pattern of emerging responses to regional security threats signal the centrality of national security interests, direct impacts from and proximity to sources of regional security threats as most relevant to regional security decisions, roles, and participation by African states. While the centrality of national security interests in states' behavior and policies is generally a recurrent feature of the post-Westphalian state system, it appears to have intensified or be intensifying in regional security thinking and initiatives in Africa. As such, orthodox regional security is splintering: regional security is, effectively, the security needs and activities of states under the direct impacted of or in close proximity to sources of regional security threats.

Fourth, the Boko Haram crisis points to a fusion of the two assumptions about the nature and sources of regional security threats. Throughout the existence of the OAU, threats to regional security in Africa were largely assumed or constructed around the "external" (actors, events and processes outside of a region and state). The AU in the post-Cold War era skews the definition and assumption of threats to regional security on the internal (actors, events and processes inside regions and states). The emphasis on the external and internal by the OAU and AU, respectively, reflects their historical milieu and the dominant forms of crises therein. However, the Boko Haram insurgency underline the duality of threats; the simultaneity of internal and external actors, events, processes and interests in breaches of regional security.

Policy

This chapter identifies four broad policy implications of the Boko Haram insurgency and responses to it. First, the reality of an ad hoc coalition and military cooperation by affected countries points to or raise the need for policy changes and amendments that transcend extant policy prescriptions of regional standby forces under the APSA-ASF framework to acknowledge other flexible forms of responses. The ad hoc approach to peace missions appears to embody important strategic advantages, such as faster reaction and deployment time, reduced bureaucracy and increased cost effectiveness (as the emphasis is on cooperation and joint operations, rather than elaborate institutional building). It is driven by informed self-interest (national security concerns) rather than short-lived considerations of political and regional solidarity. In essence, there is a need for greater flexibility and multiple forms and formats for undertaking peace missions to be officially acknowledged and integrated into existing ASF-based system.

Second, the Boko Haram crisis signposts of intra-, inter-, and extra-regional responses to regional security threats raise two important policy issues: governance dilemmas (transparency, accountability and oversight) and, inter-operability among RECs, and between RECs and other stakeholders (neighboring Africa states and extra-Africa actors) outside their membership. Extant AU and REC policy documents are extremely thin on the interoperability of regional security arrangements (protocols, response mechanisms, coordination and so forth) of two or more RECs. The only existing mechanism for potential inter-REC operability is in the context of the APSA, yet this contains assumptions of regional security operations on the basis of orthodox REC and ASF configuration. Moreover, there is as yet no policy guidance or framework for aligning ad hoc regional security by states affected by particular crises with existing REC regional security arrangements. Overall, the Boko Haram crisis pinpoints important policy and practical concerns (and gaps) about regulation and coordination among RECs, the interoperability of existing regional security arrangements, the possibility of joint regional security initiatives, and the scope for including third parties (extra-regional and extra-African actors) in regional security initiatives.

Third, the Boko Haram crisis and the involvement of international partners underline the game-changing interests and roles of extra-regional (extra-African) actors in emerging responses to regional security threats in Africa. This raises policy issues, specifically the need for a framework and principles to guide and regulate the terms of engagement with major international powers in regional security arrangements. Given the shortage of force enablers and multipliers, combined with limited capacity for intelligence-led and robust peace missions among a majority of African countries, there is a growing pattern of direct involvement and force projection by extra-African powers (France and the United States) in African regional security arrangements. A policy framework and guiding principles of extra-regional involvement in African regional security arrangements is required to ensure that African countries and RECs retain the strategic initiative and adapt such extra-African involvement to the needs of African countries and citizens over the long term.

Fourth, the Boko Haram crisis also underscores concerns about commitments to, and efficacy of, existing capacities for mediation and political settlement in regional security arrangement. Admittedly, the ECOWAS and AU include mediation and dialogue in their security architectures; however, there are critical practical policy concerns and needs (shortages) with regard to the number of skilled and experienced African mediators and negotiators relative to the scale of crises, institutional experiences and reflections (lessons learned), and operational capacity for non-violent responses to and resolution of regional security crises. It is instructive that the military component of the ECOWAS and AU security architectures (APSA) consistently attract the most financial and institutional attention, compared with mediation systems. The non-violent mechanisms of the ECOWAS remain underfunded, understaffed and underdeveloped relative to military response mechanisms to security crises.

Conversely, the response to the Boko Haram insurgency exposes increasing militarization in the form of military solutions to security issues and responses to complex insurgencies in Africa. This appears to underline the increasing internationalization of African security issues and responses to security challenges without critical reflections on the capacity, impact and outcomes of such approaches. There is a sense that the limited capacity, commitment to and failure of political settlement approaches—the preference for military solutions—serves the strategic interest of ruling elites and major powers rather than being suited to African realities. Military approaches, as in the case of Boko Haram and other insurgencies (northern Mali, northern Uganda and South Sudan), can achieve security stabilization only over the short term, as opposed to long-term sustainable peace. As such, the recourse to military solutions has meant that there are few or no available blueprints for post-counter insurgency peacebuilding. Even where there are existing peacebuilding policies and protocols (as with ECOWAS), questions mark remain regarding the likelihood of their becoming operational. This is particularly important given the strong religious foundations of emerging threats to regional security and the challenges and failures of post-insurgency peace building in the context of military interventions in religion-related conflicts globally (e.g. Afghanistan, Iraq, Pakistan, Lebanon, etc.).

Conclusion

This chapter examined the Boko Haram crisis and the responses to it. It observed that the crises signaled a mixture of continuities, changes, and mutations in the nature of insurgencies in Africa. The Boko Haram insurgency is rooted in local causes, notably multiple governance failures, in-country horizontal inequalities (the "Northern Phenomenon"), subsisting trends in border communities (linked to poor policing and activities of criminal networks), the increasing tendency to resort to the instrumentality of ethno-religious identities to mobilize for armed violence, and the fusion of local, national, regional, and international dynamics to create a "meta narrative" by insurgent groups. The impacts of the insurgency include the targeting of civilians (casualties, internally displaced persons, and refugees) and civilian infrastructures; disruption of socioeconomic infrastructures and processes, thereby worsening poverty levels; direct threats to or disruption of the established political order (democratic governance); regional spillovers; and the increasing internationalization of the crises (increasing involvement of major extra-African powers). The responses to the crisis are marked by limited use and failure of the mediation and political settlement approach and preference for military solutions; a tendency to resort to ad-hoc military and security cooperation and joint operations by the affected countries, rather than the use of subsisting regional security structures and resources; the reduction of the role of ECOWAS to provide political support and some level of coordination, as opposed to mobilizing existing regional security resources and making them operational; and the decisive role of regional and extra-regional actors in legitimizing responses, especially military action.

The conceptual implications of the foregoing include the emerging disconnect between REC configurations and regional security arrangements and responses; new patterns of crises and responses redefining the "regional" in the form of new alliances, arrangements and partnerships within, across and outside of conventional REC boundaries; the centrality of close proximity to and direct impacts from crises as key drivers of states' practical involvement in regional security activities in Africa (as opposed to membership of RECs, signatories of protocols and regional solidarity); and the duality of regional security threats through the fusion of internal and external sources.

The policy implications include the need for policy acknowledgement and integration of emerging patterns of ad hoc responses to regional security crises into extant security architectures (APSA-ASF); gaps around the interoperability of regional security instruments between two or more RECs and in resolving practical issues in making relationships among the AU, RECs and other stakeholders operational; and governance issues (accountability, transparency, and regulation) of emerging intra-, inter- and extra-regional roles in regional security arrangements, especially the need for a guiding framework and principles for extra-regional actors. Finally, there are gaps in the commitment to, usage of, and effectiveness of mediation and political settlement approaches to regional security, with institutional capacity-building efforts and finances overly committed to militarized responses.

As the Boko Haram crisis indicates, ECOWAS (and perhaps other RECs and the AU) is less able deliver regional security as envisaged in extant policy documents, in relation to emerging patterns of security threats. As currently configured and capacitated, ECOWAS is suitable to legitimizing and coordinating regional security interventions. There is a gulf between their declared aspirations and institutional operational capabilities, the changing nature of regional security challenges, and limitations in the ability to adapt to a changing landscape. Moreover, there is an emergent modus operandi of and for regional security in Africa that involves different combinations of intra-, inter- and extra-regional initiatives, partnerships, actors, and interests. Critically, extra-regional interests and actors are potentially playing game-changing roles in African regional security initiatives as defined by their funding, equipment support, international legitimacy, and robust force projection in African regional security operations.

References

Abrahamsen, R. and Williams, C. (2011), *Security Beyond the State*. United Kingdom and New York: Cambridge University Press.

Adebajo, A. and Ismail, R. (eds) (2004), *West Africa's Security Challenges. Building Peace in a Troubled Region*. Boulder and London: Lynne Rienner.

Adesoji, A. (2010), "The Boko Haram Uprising and Islamic Revivalism in Nigeria," *Africa Spectrum* 45, no. 2: 95–108.

Adibe, C. (2003), "Do Regional Organizations Matter? Comparing the Conflict Management Mechanisms in West Africa and the Great Lakes Region." In J. Boulden (ed), *Dealing with Conflict in Africa—The UN and Regional Organizations*. Basingstoke: Palgrave Macmillan, 21–40.

Agbiboa, D. (2013), "No retreat, No surrender: understanding the religious terrorism of Boko Haram," *African Study Monograph* 34, no. 2: 65–84.

Aghedo, I. and Osumah, O. (2012), "The Boko Haram Uprising: how should Nigeria respond?" *Third World Quarterly* 33, no. 5: 853–69.

Alli, W. *Role of Nigeria in Regional Security*. Abuja: Friedrich-Ebert-Stiftung Regional Office, 2012.

Aning, E. (2004), "Investing in peace and security in Africa: the case of ECOWAS," *Conflict, Security and Development* 4, no. 3: 533–42.

Bamidele, O. (2012), "Boko Haram catastrophic terrorism: an albatross to national peace, security and sustainable development in Nigeria," *Journal of Sustainable Development in Africa* 14, no. 1: 32–44.

BBC News. "Chibok abductions in Nigeria: more than 230 seized." BBC.co.uk. April 21, 2014. Available at: http://www.bbc.co.uk/news/world-africa-27101714 (accessed July 15, 2014).

———. "African leaders declare 'war' on Nigeria Boko Haram." BBC.co.uk. May 17, 2013. Available at: http://www.bbc.co.uk/news/world-africa-27451966 (accessed July 17, 2014).

———. "Nigeria declares massive military campaign on borders." BBC.co.uk. May 15, 2013. Available at: http://www.bbc.co.uk/news/world-africa-22544056 (accessed October 1, 2013).

———. "Nigerians living in poverty rises to nearly 61%." BBC.co.uk. February 13, 2012. Available at: http://www.bbc.co.uk/news/world-africa-17015873 (accessed October 1, 2013).

Buzan, B. (1991), *People, States and Fear*, 2nd ed. Boulder Colorado: Lynne Rienner.

Buzan, B. and Waever, O. (2003), *Regions and Power—The Structure of International Security*. Cambridge: Cambridge University Press.

Daily Trust. "Troops move to border towns." allafrica.com. May 16, 2013. Available at: http://allafrica.com/stories/201305160071.html (accessed October 1, 2013).

ECOWAS. "Final Communique: Forty-Fifth Ordinary Session of the Authority of ECOWAS Heads of State and Government." ECOWAS, Accra No. 134/2013, July 10, 2014. Available at: http://news.ecowas.int/ (accessed July 17, 2014).

———. "Final Communique: Extra-ordinary Session of the Authority of ECOWAS Heads of State and Government." ECOWAS, Accra No. 103/2013, May 30, 2014. Available at: http://news.ecowas.int/ (accessed July 17, 2014).

Falola, T. (1998), *Violence in Nigeria: The Crisis of Religious Politics and Secular Ideologies*. New York: University of Rochester.

Franke, B. (2007), "Competing Regionalisms in Africa and the Continent's Emerging Security Architecture," *African Studies Quarterly* 9, no. 3: 31–64.

Frazier, D. and Stewart-Ingersoll, R. (2010), "Regional powers and security: a framework for understanding order within regional security complexes," *European Journal of International Relations 16*: 731–50.

Friedrich-Ebert-Stiftung. (2011), "Overstretched and Overrated? Prospects of Regional Security Policy in Africa and its European Support." Report of International Conference by Friedrich-Ebert-Stiftung, Berlin, February 9–10.

Ghanaweb. "Boko Haram is a threat to ECOWAS sub-regional security." ghanaweb.com. Available at: http://www.ghanaweb.com/GhanaHomePage/NewsArchive/artikel.php?ID=228518 (accessed October 5, 2013).

The Guardian. "Boko Haram abducts scores of women and girls in Northern Nigeria, says locals." Theguardian.com. June 24, 2014. Available at: http://www.theguardian.com/world/2014/jun/24/boko-haram-abducts-women-girls-north-nigeria-kidnap (accessed July 16, 2014).

Hammerstad, A. (2005), "Domestic threats, regional solutions? The challenge of security integration in Southern Africa," *Review of International Studies* 31: 69–87.

Healy, S. (2011), "Seeking peace and security in the Horn of Africa: the contribution of the Inter-Governmental Authority on Development," *International Affairs* 87, no. 1: 105–20.

IRIN (2012), "Timeline of Boko Haram and related violence in Nigeria," irinnews.org. January 20. Available at: http://www.irinnews.org/printreport.aspx?reportid=97527 (accessed October 2, 2013).

Ismail, O. (2013), "Radicalization and Violent Extremism in West Africa: The Implications for African and International Security," *Journal of Conflict, Security and Development* 14, no. 2: 209–30.

——— (2011), "ECOWAS and Human Security." In T. Jaye, D. Garuba and S. Amadi (eds), *ECOWAS and the Dynamics of Conflict and Peacebuilding*. Dakar: CODESRIA, 206–27.

Ismail, W. and Skons, E. (eds) (2014), *Security Activities of External Actors in Africa*. Sweden: SIPRI/Oxford University Press.

Jaye, T., Garuba, D. and Amadi, S. (eds) (2011), *ECOWAS and the Dynamics of Conflict and Peacebuilding*. Dakar: CODESRIA.

Kaldor, M. (2006), *New and Old Wars: Organized Violence in a Global Era*. United Kingdom: Polity Press.

Kelly, R. (2007), "Security Theory in New Regionalism," *International Studies Review* 19, no. 2: 197–229.

Lake, D. (2009), "Regional Hierarchy: authority and local international order," *Review of International Studies* 35: 35–58.

Leadership. "Borno to reconstruct 823 classrooms destroyed by Boko Haram." leadership.ng. August 12, 2013. Available at: http://leadership.ng/news/120813/borno-reconstruct-823-classrooms-destroyed-boko-haram (accessed October 2, 2013).

Minteh, B. and Perry, A. (2013), "Terrorism in West Africa: Boko Haram evolution, strategy and affiliations." Paper presented at Midwest Political Science Association 71st Annual Conference, April. Palmer House Hotel, Chicago.

Mwagiru, M. (2010), "Conflict Early Warning and Response Mechanisms: A review of sub-regional organizations in Africa," *Africa Review* 2, no. 2: 163–74.

National Mirror. "Boko Haram: ECOWAS condemns attacks, condoles FG." nationalmirroronline.net. January 26, 2012. Available at: http://nationalmirroronline.net/index.php/news/29869.html (accessed October 2, 2013).

Niworu, S. (2013), "Boko Haram Sect: Terrorists or a Manifestation of the Failed Nigerian State," *Journal of Politics and Law* 6, no. 2: 245–50.

Obi, C. (2009), "Economic Community of West African States on the Ground: Comparing Peacekeeping in Liberia, Sierra Leone, Guinea Bissau and Cote D'Ivoire." *African Security* 2, no. 3: 135.

Olonisakin, F. (2004), *African Peacekeeping at the Crossroads: An Assessment of the Continent's Evolving Peace and Security Architecture*. New York: United Nations Peacekeeping Best Practices.

——— (2000), "Conflict management in Africa: The role of the OAU and sub-regional organizations." In J. Cilliers and A. Hilding-Norberg (eds), *Building Stability in Africa: Challenges for the New Millennium*. ISS Monograph 46, February, 50–57.

Omorogbe, E. (2011), "Can the African Union Deliver Peace and Security?" *Journal of Conflict and Security Law* 16, no. 1: 35–62.

Onapejo, H., Uzodike, U. and Whetho, A. (2012), "Boko Haram terrorism in Nigeria: The International Dimension," *South African Journal of International Affairs* 19, no. 3: 337–57.

Pana Press. "ECOWAS seeks assistance for Nigeria in fight against Boko Haram." panapress.com. July 2, 2012. Available at: http://www.panapress.com/ECOWAS-seeks-assistance-for-Nigeria-in-fight-against-Boko-Haram---12–833890–100-lang2-index.html (accessed October 1, 2013).

Punch. "Military deploys more fighter jets in Borno, others." punchng.com. September 25, 2013. Available at: http://www.punchng.com/news/military-deploys-more-fighter-jets-in-borno-others/ (accessed September 28, 2013).

——— "Boko Haram has created 10,000 widows in Borno—NGO." punchng.com. August 12, 2013. Available at: http://www.punchng.com/news/boko haramaram-has-created-10000-widows-in-borno-ngo/ (accessed October 1, 2013).

——— "Insurgents regroup in Adamawa mountains." punchng.com. May 21, 2013. Available at: http://www.punchng.com/news/insurgents-regroup-in-adamawa-mountains/ (accessed September 18, 2013).

——— "Court orders secret trial for Kabiru Sokoto." punchng.com. May 7, 2013. http://www.punchng.com/news/court-orders-secret-trial-for-kabiru-sokoto/ (accessed September 30, 2013).

——— "Boko haram destroys 209 public schools in Yobe—Governor." punchng.com. Available at: http://www.punchng.com/news/boko-haram-destroys-209-public-schools-in-yobe-governor/ (accessed September 20, 2013).

——— "New terrorist group claims responsibility for Bauchi kidnapping." punchng.com. Available at: http://www.punchng.com/news/new-terrorist-group-claims-responsibility-for-bauchi-kidnapping/ (accessed October 1, 2013).

——— "Boko Haram: US assists Nigeria with intelligence." punchng.com. Available at: http://www.punchng.com/news/boko-haram-us-assists-nigeria-with-intelligence/ (accessed October 3, 2013).

——— "ECOWAS Parliament expresses concern over Boko Haram." punchng.com. Available at: http://www.punchng.com/news/africa/ecowas-parliament-expresses-concern-over-boko-haram/ (accessed September 24, 2013).

Reno, W. (2012), "The Regionalization of African Security," *Current History* 111: 745–60.

Rogers, P. (2012), "Nigeria: The Generic Context of the Boko Haram Violence." Oxford Research Group, *Monthly Global Security* briefing, April 1.

Sahara Reporters. "Paris Summit on Boko Haram: Resolutions." Saharareporters.com. Available at: http://saharareporters.com/2014/05/17/paris-summit-boko-haram-resolutions (accessed 16 July 2014).

Siradag, A. (2012), "African Regional and Sub-Regional Organizations' Security Policies: Challenges and Prospects," *Journal of Academic Inquiries* 7, no. 2: 231–55.

Solomon, H. (2012), "Counter terrorism in Nigeria," *The RUSI Journal* 157, no. 4: 6–11.

Stein, J. (2003), "Taboos and regional security regimes," *Journal of Strategic Studies* 26, no. 3: 6–18.

Sunday Trust. "Red Alert at Nigeria's borders." beegeagle.wordpress.com. Available at: http://beegeagle.wordpress.com/2011/10/23/red-alert-at-nigerias-borders/ (accessed December 2, 2013).

Tavares, R. (2009), "Regional clustering of peace and security," *Global Change, Peace and Security* 21, no. 2: 153–64.

——— (2008), "Understanding regional peace and security: a framework for analysis," *Contemporary Politics* 14, no. 2: 107–27.

The Sun. "Boko Haram kills 25 'civilian-JTF members in Borno." sunnewsonline.com. July 29, 2013. Available at: http://sunnewsonline.com/new/cover/

boko-haram-kills-25-civilian-jtf-members-in-borno/ (accessed October 7, 2013).

——— "FG deports 19,000 aliens over Boko Haram." sunnewsonline.com. May 17, 2013. Available at: http://sunnewsonline.com/new/cover/fg-deports-19000-aliens-over-boko-haram/ (accessed September 30, 2013).

——— "Attacks on telecoms masts." sunnewslonline.com. September 13, 2012. Available at: http://sunnewsonline.com/new/editorial/attacks-on-telecoms-masts/ (accessed October 1, 2013).

This Day. "191 Killed in Multinational Task Force, Boko Haram Clash." thisdaylive.com. April 23, 2013. Available at: http://www.thisdaylive.com/articles/191-killed-in-multinational-task-force-boko-haram-clash/145671/ (accessed October 10, 2013).

U.S. House of Representatives. "Boko Haram: Growing Threat to the US Homeland." *US House of Representatives Committee on Homeland Security*, September 13, 2013. Available at: http://homeland.house.gov/sites/homeland.house.gov/files/documents/09–13–13-Boko-Haram-Report.pdf (accessed December 3, 2013).

U.S. State Department. *Country Reports on Terrorism 2012*. Washington, D.C.: U.S. State Department, 2012. http://www.state.gov/j/ct/rls/crt/2012/ (accessed October 5, 2013).

Van Hoeymissen, S. (2011), "Regional Organizations in China's Security Strategy for Africa: The sense of supporting African solutions to African problems," *Journal of Current Chinese Affairs* 40, no. 4: 91–118.

Vanguard, "Boko Haram: new army division takes over from JTF." vanguardngr.com. August 19, 2013. Available at: http://www.vanguardngr.com/2013/08/boko-haram-new-army-division-takes-over-from-jtf/ (accessed October 1, 2013).

——— "Baga Massacre: its Nigeria, Chad, Niger operation—Army." vanguardngr.com. April 24, 2013. Available at: http://www.vanguardngr.com/2013/04/its-nigeria-chad-niger-operation-army/ (accessed October 1, 2013).

——— "Boko Haram: Jonathan sets up Amnesty Committee." vanguardngr.com. April 5, 2013. Available at: http://www.vanguardngr.com/2013/04/boko-haram-jonathan-sets-up-amnesty-committee/ (accessed September 30, 2013).

——— "Northern economy collapsing, Northern Govs cry out." vanguardngr.com. August 22, 2012. Available at: http://www.vanguardngr.com/2012/08/northern-economy-collapsing-northern-govs-cry-out/ (accessed October 2, 2013).

Walker, A. (2012), "What is Boko Haram?" United States Institute of Peace, *Special Report 308*, June.

Weldesellassie, K. (2011), "IGAD as an International Organization, Its Institutional Development and Shortcomings," *Journal of African Law* 55: 1–29.

World Bank (1996), "Nigeria: Poverty in the midst of plenty, the challenge of growth with inclusion: a World Bank poverty assessment." Washington, D.C.: World Bank. Available at: http://www-wds.worldbank.org/servlet/WDSContentServer/WDSP/IB/1996/05/31/000009265_3961029235646/Rendered/PDF/multi0page.pdf (accessed December 1, 2013).

Xinhua. "Three Nigerian soldiers of the multinational joint task force killed." beegeagle.wordpress.com. December 2, 2011. Available at: http://beegeagle.wordpress.com/2011/12/13/3-nigerian-soldiers-of-the-multinational-joint-task-forcelake-chad-frontier-killed/ (accessed October 1, 2013).

Afterword

"African Agency" to Maximize the Continent's Policy Choices after a Decade of the BRICS: Beyond Dependency?

Timothy M. Shaw

The first decade of the twenty-first century for the global political economy was that of the BRICS as well as of financial crises especially around the North Atlantic. Africa like much of the global South weathered the US and EU contractions better than most as the BRICS' demand for its natural resources, especially energy and minerals, boosted its economies. A decade of unprecedented growth, however uneven, has led the continent to be able to anticipate the establishment of a set of "developmental states," as advocated especially by the UN Economic Commission for Africa (UNECA 2011, 2013), to balance the continuation of several "fragile" or "failed" states (Brock, Holm, Sorensen and Stohl 2012).

This Afterword is informed by contemporary titles in the IPENR Series such as Lorenz-Carl and Rempe (2013) and Scholvin and Struver (2014) on Africa; Vivares (2014) on Latin America; and Fanta, Shaw and Tang (2013) on the global South. It responds to the projection and challenge of the 2013 *Human Development Report* from the UNDP (2013, pp. 1–2):

> The South has risen at an unprecedented speed and scale … By 2050, Brazil, China and India combined are projected to account for 40% of world output in purchasing power parity terms …
> The changing global political economy is creating unprecedented challenges and opportunities for continued progress in human development.

The formulation and articulation of an Africa Mining Vision (AMV) at the turn of the decade (www.africaminingvision.org) would have been inconceivable before the current period. Now the continent is better able to formulate its own responses to the proposed "post-2015" development agenda: it can contribute to the continuing development of "transnational" "global governance"

(Harman and Williams 2014; Weiss and Wilkinson 2014a, b) through multi-stakeholder coalitions like the Kimberley Process Certification Scheme (KPCS) and Extractive Industries Transparency Initiative (EITI). At least some African actors—non-state as well as state—can now claim a degree of agency rather than endure continuing dependency (Brown and Harman 2013): the prospect of policy-making rather than –taking (Gyimah-Brempong, Shaw and Samonis 2012).

Africa inherited its subordinate place in a ubiquitous North-South axis; it now needs to advance and benefit from an impending East-South turn (Pieterse 2011); hence Forums on China-Africa Cooperation (FOCAC) and Tokyo International Conferences on African Development (TICAD) as well as the EU-African Summit (April 2014)?

What is Emerging in Africa? What Prospects for Sustainable Developmental States?

Africa can claim its share of "emerging" economies/states/markets/companies … and societies (Pieterse 2011): how to maximize balance among these sectors rather than expensive, counter-productive imbalances? And as some developmental states, including South Africa as the continent's BRICS, may aspire to being regional powers: how to advance regional development without exponential inequalities? Similarly, the continent is experiencing growing "varieties" of corporations, middle classes, civil societies, technologies, etc.: how to advance development without growing inequalities and alienation? And modern logistics/supply chains require basic infrastructures (see Chapters 7 and 9 above) from internet to couriers and container routes; so a mix of MTN/Vodacom, DHL/UPS and Maersk/MSC begin to define their Africa. Finally, given climate change as well as global reordering, Africa will have to confront the growing food/land/water nexus which the emerging economies are advancing (Cheru and Modi 2013). Already the continent has advanced novel forms of regionalisms such as trans-frontier conservation areas (TFCA) (Ramutsindela 2011) or peace parks, from micro- (Chapter 4) through meso- to macro-levels. Such innovations for regional cooperation will become ever more imperative as land grabs, water wars, and new security threats proliferate (see Chapter 10).

Inequalities on the Continent: Burgeoning Middle Class but Exponential Youth Un-/Under-employment?

Africa can benefit from "new donors" and "innovative sources of finance" but these are less familiar than EU and OECD sources: from SWFs and new foundations to the Gulf States, Korea, Turkey, etc., as well as the BRICS. Its growing middle class is evident in traffic jams, new shopping malls, proliferating banks and hotels (see Chapter 6), increasingly tied together by South African franchises and logistics. And the new global middle classes constitute a growing proportion of global tourism, now worth US$3 trillion each year, some 3 percent of the global economy, to Africa as elsewhere. But they are increasingly susceptible to a variety of "non-communicable diseases" (NCDs) such as cancers, diabetes and heart conditions. And the next generation is not so included as Africa's demographic transition has been slower than other continents: middle Africa has not (yet?) experienced declining levels of fertility, so its population could be some 2.7 billion by 2050, up from 1.6 billion in 2030 and just one billion in 2010. Youth un- and under-employment is very likely to grow, risking alienation and fundamentalism; most work will be informal and precarious (see Chapter 5 above).

However, new technologies (see Chapter 8) allow for the discovery of new sources of oil and gas from South Sudan to northern Mozambique so new regions may arise around pipelines and other energy logistics/corridors (see Chapters 2 and 7) (Lorenz-Carl and Rempe 2013). And novel forms of "global" or "private" governance, from the Kimberley Process Certification Scheme (KPCS) and Extractive Industries Transparency Initiative (EITI) and onto the "conflict minerals" component (#1502) of the omnibus Dodd-Frank bill, will present challenges of compliance and reporting (Hanson, Kararach and Shaw 2012).

"New" Regionalisms: New Sources of Conflicts and Forms of Cooperation

At the turn of the century, Southern Africa (Saunders, Dzinesa and Nagar 2012; Scholvin 2014, 2015) was assumed to be the most advanced region on the continent just as the EU was at the global level (Telo 2013): but, no more (Vivares 2014)? On the continent, innovative regional directions are concentrated in concentric circles around eastern Africa from more meso to more macro (see Chapter 3): the five-member East African Community (EAC), and/or the eastern African energy region from South Sudan to northern Mozambique (Scholvin and Struver 2014) and/or the Tripartite Free Trade Area (T-FTA) from Cape to Cairo (Hartzenberg 2012). And in Europe, the eurozone crisis of the PIIGS has corroded that global model (Telo 2013).

The West African Commission on Drugs (WACD) (http://www.wacommissionondrugs.org) is a particularly interesting regional response animated by the Kofi Annan Foundation: a non-state yet well-connected and informed response to the burgeoning problem of global drug supply chains being rerouted through West Africa as the "war on drugs" limits established logistics through Central America and the Caribbean. The West African Commission also takes its cue from earlier high-level Latin American and global commissions which advocate decriminalizing the drugs industry, turning it into a public health issue.

But the mix of alienation, fundamentalisms and small arms is destabilizing the Sahel with its high population growth rates and vulnerability to climate change: from the earlier Lord's Resistance Army (LRA) out of northern Uganda and then Boko Haram in northern Nigeria to Mali and Central African Republic (CAR) along with Darfur, where borders are virtually non-existent.

Meanwhile, "border" conflicts around energy and water proliferate and intensify as the new dams on the Nile in Uganda (Bujagali) and Ethiopia (Renaissance) confront the Nile Basin Initiative (NBI); hence the imperative of preventive diplomacy by the International Conference on the Great Lakes Region (ICGLR) around conflict minerals or the Intergovernmental Authority on Development (IGAD) around the two Sudans' warring communities.

African agency can capture some distinctive connections such as Bono and Geldof as established rock stars and the Gates and Ibrahim Foundations: onto celebrity/network diplomacy among heterogeneous actors, such as the Enough Project in Congo? Africa's "soft power" assets include culture (e.g. Nollywood and African singers/writers), sports (Africans in Olympics/UEFA/FIFA), religious leaders, etc.

Whose Policy Choices?

But, how efficacious is African agency (Brown ad Harman 2013) for non-state as well as state actors, especially African non-governmental organizations and think tanks (ACBF 2014) plus emerging MNCs from the global South (e.g. Embraer, Lenovo, Mexico Mobil, Reliance, Tata, Vale), especially South Africa, (e.g. Absa, Game, Old Mutual, Nandos, SABMiller, Sasol, Shoprite, Stanbic) plus new donors/DFI/varieties of finance, etc.?

The range of state and non-state actors on the continent has grown exponentially over the last decade, including new donors and investors, now including land as well as energy and minerals. In addition, the roles of African diasporas and their remittances are increasingly recognized especially as they advance MDGs in education, health, habitat, etc. The continent has over 30 million in its intra- and extra-continental diasporas, remitting some US$40 million each year (see Chapter 6).

And as part of agency, the continent can begin to define its own Science and Technology (S&T) policies (see Chapter 8) including IT and GM while building its own research parks and EPZs, including China's Special Economic Zones, and Corridors around South Africa, like the Maputo Development Corridor (see Chapter 7). Its DNA is unique and under threat from IP rules and aggressive Multinational Corporations. But a mix of diasporas and environmental activists may yet preserve its diversity?

What Policy Assumptions/Analyses?

Finally, in addition to policy choices by non-state as well as state actors both on and off the continent, Africa presents challenges to academic assumptions and analyses: how to define and advance "developmental states," "African agency," "new partnerships," etc., around post-2015 (UNECA 2011, 2013)? The continent's policy landscape has changed over the last decade (Ayuk and Kabore 2013): onto a variety of new voices from business schools, concerned diasporas, social media, think tanks, etc. ... but also how to respond to homophobia and fundamentalisms, both Christian and Moslem?

References

African Capacity Building Foundation (2014), *Africa Capacity Report 2014: Capacity Imperatives for Regional Integration in Africa*. Harare, ACBF.

Ayuk, E.T. and Kabore, S.T. (eds) (2013), *Wealth through Integration: regional integration & poverty-reduction strategies in West Africa*. Heidelberg: Springer for IDRC.

Brock, L., Hans-Henrik, H., Sorensen, G. and Stohl, M. (2012), *Fragile States: Violence & the Failure of Intervention*. Cambridge: Polity.

Brown, W. and Sophie, H. (eds) (2013), *African Agency in International Politics*. Abingdon: Routledge.

Cheru, F and Modi, R. (eds) (2013), *Agricultural Development & Food Security in Africa: The Impact of Chinese, Indian & Brazilian Investments*. London: Zed.

Cornelissen, S., Cheru, F. and Shaw, T.M. (2012), *Africa and International Relations in the 21st Century*. London: Palgrave Macmillan.

Dunn, K. and Shaw, T.M. (eds) (2013), *Africa's Challenge to International Relations Theory*. London: Palgrave Macmillan. Second expanded Classic edition.

Fanta, E., Shaw, T.M. and Tang, V. (eds) (2013), *Comparative Regionalisms for Development in the 21st Century: Insights from the Global South*. Farnham: Ashgate.

Gyimah-Brempong, K., Shaw, T.M. and Simonis, V. (2012), "Is Bilateral Aid Responding to Good Governance in Africa?" Harare: ACBF. Occasional Paper #18.

Hanson, K.T., Kararach, G. and Shaw, T.M. (eds) (2012), *Rethinking Development Challenges for Public Policy: Insights from Contemporary Africa*. London: Palgrave Macmillan for ACBF.

Harman, S. and Williams, D. (eds) (2014), *Governing the World? Case Studies of Global Governance*. Abingdon: Routledge.

Hartzenberg, T. et al. (2012), *The Tripartite Free Trade Area: Towards a new African Integration Paradigm?* Stellenbosch: Tralac.

Lorenz-Carl, U. and Rempe, M. (eds) (2013), *Mapping Agency: Comparing Regionalisms in Africa*. Farnham: Ashgate.

Ramutsindela, M. (2011), "Transfrontier Conservation and the Spaces of Regionalisms" in Shaw, Grant and Cornelissen (eds), *Ashgate Research Companion to Regionalisms*. Farnham: Ashgate, 361–73.

Saunders, C., Dzinesa, G.A. and Nagar, D. (eds) (2012), *Region-Building in Southern Africa: Progress, Problems and Prospects*, London: Zed for CCR.

Scholvin, S. (2014), *The Geopolitics of Regional Power: Geography, Economics and Politics in Southern Africa*. Farnham: Ashgate.

Scholvin, S. (ed.) (2015), *A New Scramble for Africa? The Rush for Energy Resources Southwards of the Sahara*. Farnham: Ashgate.

Telo, M. (ed.) (2013) *Globalisation, Multilateralism, Europe: Towards a Better Global Governance?* Farnham: Ashgate.

UNDP (2013), *Human Development Report 2013: The Rise of the South*, New York, March.

UNECA (2011), *Economic Report on Africa 2011: Governing Development in Africa—the Role of the State in Economic Transformation*. Addis Ababa.

UNECA (2013), *Economic Report on Africa 2013: Making the Most of Africa's Commodities: Industrializing for Growth, Jobs and Economic Transformation*. Addis Ababa.

Vivares, E. (ed.) (2014), *Exploring the New South American Regionalism* (NSAR). Farnham: Ashgate.

Weiss, T.G. and Wilkinson, R. (2014a), "Global Governance to the Rescue: saving international relations?" *Global Governance* 20(1), January–March: 19–36.

Weiss, T.G. and Wilkinson, R. (eds) (2014b), *International Organization and Global Governance*. Abingdon: Routledge.

Index

THE INTERNATIONAL POLITICAL ECONOMY OF NEW REGIONALISMS SERIES

Other titles in the series

Converging Regions
Global Perspectives on Asia and the Middle East
Edited by Nele Lenze and Charlotte Schriwer

The Geopolitics of Regional Power
Geography, Economics and Politics in Southern Africa
Sören Scholvin

Terror and Insurgency in the Sahara-Sahel Region
Corruption, Contraband, Jihad and the Mali War of 2012–2013
Stephen A. Harmon

The BRICS and Beyond
The International Political Economy of the Emergence of a New World Order
Edited by Li Xing

European Union and New Regionalism
Competing Regionalism and Global Governance in a Post-Hegemonic Era
Edited by Mario Telò

Reconfiguring Global Climate Governance in North America
A Transregional Approach
Marcela López-Vallejo

Re-mapping the Americas
Trends in Region-making
Edited by W. Andy Knight, Julián Castro-Rea and Hamid Ghany

Exploring the New South American Regionalism (NSAR)
Edited by Ernesto Vivares

China's Diplomacy in Eastern and Southern Africa
Edited by Seifudein Adem

Regionalism and Regional Security in South Asia
The Role of SAARC
Zahid Shahab Ahmed

Comparative Regionalisms for Development in the 21st Century
Insights from the Global South
Edited by Emmanuel Fanta, Timothy M. Shaw and Vanessa T. Tang

Mapping Agency
Comparing Regionalisms in Africa
Edited by Ulrike Lorenz-Carl and Martin Rempe

The EU and the Eurozone Crisis
Policy Challenges and Strategic Choices
Edited by Finn Laursen

China-Africa Relations in an Era of Great Transformations
Edited by Li Xing with Abdulkadir Osman Farah

The European Union Neighbourhood
Challenges and Opportunities
Edited by Teresa Cierco

The New Democracy Wars
The Politics of North American Democracy Promotion in the Americas
Neil A. Burron

The European Union after Lisbon
Polity, Politics, Policy
Edited by Søren Dosenrode

Roads to Regionalism
Genesis, Design, and Effects of Regional Organizations
Edited by Tanja A. Börzel, Lukas Goltermann, Mathis Lohaus and Kai Striebinger

New Regionalism or No Regionalism?
Emerging Regionalism in the Black Sea Area
Edited by Ruxandra Ivan

Our North America
Social and Political Issues beyond NAFTA
Edited by Julián Castro-Rea

Community of Insecurity
SADC's Struggle for Peace and Security in Southern Africa
Laurie Nathan

Global and Regional Problems
Towards an Interdisciplinary Study
Edited by Pami Aalto, Vilho Harle and Sami Moisio

The Ashgate Research Companion to Regionalisms
Edited by Timothy M. Shaw, J. Andrew Grant and Scarlett Cornelissen

Asymmetric Trade Negotiations
Sanoussi Bilal, Philippe De Lombaerde and Diana Tussie

The Rise of the Networking Region
The Challenges of Regional Collaboration in a Globalized World
Edited by Harald Baldersheim, Are Vegard Haug and Morten Øgård

Shifting Geo-Economic Power of the Gulf Oil, Finance and Institutions
Edited by Matteo Legrenzi and Bessma Momani

Building Regions
The Regionalization of the World Order
Luk Van Langenhove

National Solutions to Trans-Border Problems?
The Governance of Security and Risk in a Post-NAFTA North America
Edited by Isidro Morales

The Euro in the 21st Century
Economic Crisis and Financial Uproar
María Lorca-Susino

Crafting an African Security Architecture
Addressing Regional Peace and Conflict in the 21st Century
Edited by Hany Besada

Comparative Regional Integration
Europe and Beyond
Edited by Finn Laursen

The Rise of China
and the Capitalist World Order
Edited by Li Xing

The EU and World Regionalism
The Makability of Regions
in the 21st Century
*Edited by Philippe De Lombaerde
and Michael Schulz*

The Role of the European Union in Asia
China and India as Strategic Partners
*Edited by Bart Gaens, Juha Jokela
and Eija Limnell*

China and the Global Politics
of Regionalization
Edited by Emilian Kavalski

Clash or Cooperation of Civilizations?
Overlapping Integration and Identities
Edited by Wolfgang Zank

New Perspectives on Globalization
and Antiglobalization: Prospects for a
New World Order?
Edited by Henry Veltmeyer

Governing Regional Integration for
Development: Monitoring Experiences,
Methods and Prospects
*Edited by Philippe De Lombaerde,
Antoni Estevadeordal and Kati Suominen*

Europe-Asia Interregional Relations
A Decade of ASEM
Edited by Bart Gaens

Cruising in the Global Economy
Profits, Pleasure and Work at Sea
Christine B.N. Chin

Beyond Regionalism?
Regional Cooperation, Regionalism and
Regionalization in the Middle East
*Edited by Cilja Harders
and Matteo Legrenzi*

The EU-Russian Energy Dialogue
Europe's Future Energy Security
Edited by Pami Aalto

Regionalism, Globalisation
and International Order
Europe and Southeast Asia
Jens-Uwe Wunderlich

EU Development Policy
and Poverty Reduction
Enhancing Effectiveness
Edited by Wil Hout

An East Asian Model for Latin
American Success
The New Path
Anil Hira

European Union and New Regionalism
Regional Actors and Global Governance
in a Post-Hegemonic Era
Second Edition
Edited by Mario Telò

Regional Integration and Poverty
*Edited by Dirk Willem te Velde
and the Overseas Development Institute*

Redefining the Pacific?
Regionalism Past, Present and Future
*Edited by Jenny Bryant-Tokalau
and Ian Frazer*

Latin America's Quest for Globalization
The Role of Spanish Firms
*Edited by Félix E. Martín
and Pablo Toral*

Exchange Rate Crises
in Developing Countries
The Political Role of the Banking Sector
Michael G. Hall

Globalization and Antiglobalization
Dynamics of Change in the
New World Order
Edited by Henry Veltmeyer

Twisting Arms and Flexing Muscles
Humanitarian Intervention and
Peacebuilding in Perspective
Edited by Natalie Mychajlyszyn
and Timothy M. Shaw

Asia Pacific and Human Rights
A Global Political Economy Perspective
Paul Close and David Askew

Demilitarisation and Peace-Building
in Southern Africa
Volume I – Concepts and Processes
Edited by Peter Batchelor
and Kees Kingma

Demilitarisation and Peace-Building
in Southern Africa
Volume II – National and
Regional Experiences
Edited by Peter Batchelor
and Kees Kingma

Persistent Permeability?
Regionalism, Localism, and Globalization
in the Middle East
Edited by Bassel F. Salloukh
and Rex Brynen

The New Political Economy of
United States-Caribbean Relations
The Apparel Industry and the
Politics of NAFTA Parity
Tony Heron

The Nordic Regions and the European Union
Edited by Søren Dosenrode
and Henrik Halkier